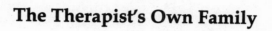

The Therapist's Own Family

THE THERAPIST'S OWN FAMILY
Toward the Differentiation of Self

Edited by

PETER TITELMAN, Ph.D.

Jason Aronson Inc.
Northvale, New Jersey
London

Library of Congress Cataloging-in-Publication Data

The Therapist's own family.

   Consists mostly of articles which appeared originally
in various sources.
   Includes bibliographies and index.
   1. Family psychotherapy. 2. Psychotherapists—
Family relationships. 3. Ego (Psychology) 4. Family—
Mental health. I. Titelman, Peter. [DNLM: 1. Family—
collected works. 2. Interpersonal Relations—
collected works. 3. Psychotherapy—collected works.
4. Self Concept—collected works. WM 420 T3985]
RC488.5.T477 1987   616.89'156   87-17128
ISBN 0-87668-921-7

Manufactured in the United States of America.

To my father, Leonard Titelman,
and in memory of my mother, Lory Titelman;
to my children, Sam and Claire;
and to the families of the contributors.

CREDITS

Chapter 2 is an amplified version of a paper presented at the Thirteenth Georgetown University Symposium on Family Psychotherapy, October 22, 1976.

Chapter 3 is a modified version of a paper appearing originally in *Georgetown Family Symposia, Vol. III (1975–1976): A Collection of Selected Papers,* edited by R. Sagan, pp. 234–245, Washington, D.C.: Georgetown University Family Center, 1978. Reprinted by permission.

Chapter 4 is a modified and amplified version of a paper appearing originally in *Compendium II: The Best of the Family: 1978–1983,* edited by E. Pendagast, pp. 293–295, New Rochelle, N.Y.: The Center for Family Learning, 1984. Reprinted by permission.

Chapter 5 is reprinted from *Second Pittsburgh Family Systems Symposium (1978): A Collection of Selected Papers,* edited by P. McCullough, J. Carolin, S. Rutenberg, and P. Titelman, pp. 116–132, Pittsburgh: The Family Institute of Pittsburgh, Western Psychiatric Institute and Clinic, University of Pittsburgh, 1978. Reprinted by permission.

Chapter 7 is an amplified version of a paper presented at the Pittsburgh Family Systems Symposium, The Family Institute of Pittsburgh, Western Psychiatric Institute and Clinic, University of Pittsburgh, 1983.

Chapter 8 is a modified version of a paper appearing originally in *Georgetown Family Symposia, Vol. II (1973–1974): A Collection of Selected Papers,* edited by P. Lorio and L. McClenathan, pp. 103–112, Washington, D.C.: Georgetown University Family Center, 1977. Reprinted by permission.

Chapter 9 is an amplified version of an article appearing originally in *Family Process*, Vol. 10, No. 3, pp. 345–359. Reprinted by permission.

Chapter 10 was presented at the Pittsburgh Family Systems Symposium, The Family Institute of Pittsburgh, Western Psychiatric Institute and Clinic, University of Pittsburgh, 1983. It was also presented at the Fifth International Congress of Family Therapy, June 1986, Jerusalem.

Chapter 11 originally appeared in *Georgetown Family Symposia, Vol. I (1971–1972): A Collection of Selected Papers*, edited by F. Andres and J. Lorio, pp. 152–169, Washington, D.C.: Georgetown University Family Center, 1972. Reprinted by permission.

Chapter 12 originally appeared in *Second Pittsburgh Family Systems Symposium (1978): A Collection of Selected Papers*, edited by P. McCullough, J. Carolin, S. Rutenberg, and P. Titelman, pp. 133–150, Pittsburgh: The Family Institute of Pittsburgh, Western Psychiatric Institute and Clinic, 1978. Reprinted by permission.

Chapter 13 originally appeared in *Pittsburgh Family Systems Symposia (1979–1980): A Collection of Selected Papers*, edited by P. McCullough and J. Carolin, pp. 140–149, Pittsburgh: Western Psychiatric Institute and Clinic, 1981. Reprinted by permission.

Chapter 15 is a modified version of a paper originally appearing in *Pittsburgh Family Systems Symposium (1977): A Collection of Selected Papers*, edited by P. McCullough, S. Rutenberg, and J. Carolin, pp. 75–91, Pittsburgh: Family Institute of Pittsburgh, Western Psychiatric Institute and Clinic, 1977. Reprinted by permission.

Chapter 16 is a modified and amplified version of a paper appearing in *Compendium II: The Best of the Family 1978–1983*, edited by E. Pendagast, pp. 299–302, New Rochelle, N.Y.: The Center for Family Learning, 1984. Reprinted by permission.

Chapter 17 is a modified and amplified version of a paper appearing originally in *Pittsburgh Family Systems Symposia (1979–1980): Collection of Papers*, edited by P. McCullough and J. Carolin, pp. 71–94, Pittsburgh: Western Psychiatric Institute and Clinic, 1981. Reprinted by permission.

CONTRIBUTORS

Ellen G. Benswanger, Ph.D.
Assistant Professor, Department of Psychiatry, and Director, Child and Youth Section, Office of Education and Regional Programming, Western Psychiatric Institute and Clinic, University of Pittsburgh.

Lorraine David, M.S.W. (pseudonym, 1930–1978)

Joseph M. DiCarlo, M.S.W.

Susan S. Edwards, A.C.S.W.
Private practice, Pittsburgh, Pennsylvania

Rabbi Edwin H. Friedman, D.D.
Private practice, Bethesda, Maryland

Susan W. Graefe, A.C.S.W.
Associate Director, The Family Institute of Rhode Island, East Greenwich, Rhode Island

C. Margaret Hall, Ph.D.
Associate Professor and Chair, Department of Sociology, Georgetown University, Washington, D.C.; limited private practice in family psychotherapy, Chevy Chase, Maryland

John J. Haverlick, C.S.W., A.C.S.W.
Co-founder of the Family Therapy Center of Poughkeepsie, Poughkeepsie, New York; Director of School Based Services, Astor Home for Children, Poughkeepsie, New York

Blanche E. Kaplan, C.S.W., A.C.S.W.
Private practice, Teaneck, New Jersey; Senior Faculty, Center for Family Learning, New Rochelle, New York; Adjunct Faculty, Hunter School of Social Work, Postgraduate Division of Gerontology, New York

Jack LaForte, Ph.D.
Co-Director, Family Living Consultants' Center for Family Studies, Northampton, Massachusetts; Family Therapy Consultant, Gandara Mental Health Center, Springfield, Massachusetts

James C. Maloni, Ph.D.
Clinical psychologist specializing in marriage and family therapy; private practice includes supervision, training, and consultation, Pittsburgh, Pennsylvania

Patricia Hanes Meyer, L.C.S.W.
Private practice in family therapy, including consultation and lecturing, Reston, Virginia

Glenn N. Scarbobo, M.S.W.
Vice-president, Diversified Services, Howard Community Hospital, Kokomo, Indiana

Stephanie St. John, M.S. (pseudonym)
Private practice

Peter Titelman, Ph.D.
Private practice, Northampton, Massachusetts; Co-Director, Family Living Consultants' Center for Family Studies, Northampton, Massachusetts; Director, Gateway/Worthington Health Association Family Therapy Program, Worthington, Massachusetts

Robert J. Valentine, M.A., M.Ed.
Faculty, Center for Family Learning, New Rochelle, New York; Priest of Roman Catholic Diocese of Bridgeport, Connecticut

ACKNOWLEDGMENTS

Jim Smith, M.S., and Jim Maloni, Ph.D., deserve special thanks for their thoughtful comments, criticism, and personal availability during the process of undertaking this project.

The colleagial presence of Sue Graefe, M.S.W., and Jack LaForte, Ph.D., was appreciated.

The thoughtful reflections of Pat Meyer, M.S.W., helped me clarify I-positions during the mid and later phases of organizing this book.

Encouragement, particularly during the early development of this book, was provided by my publisher, Jason Aronson, M.D.

Discussion with the contributing authors was stimulating, and their willingness to share their own family experiences was remarkably generous.

The unstinting care and patience of Judith Stark in typing the manuscript needs to be acknowledged.

The fine execution of the diagrams by Saundra Katz-Feinberg added significantly to the presentation of the book.

Finally, I would like to thank my wife, Claudia Titelman, Ph.D., for her patience and encouragement while this book was in process.

CONTENTS

Part I

The Context for Working with One's Own Family

Chapter 1

THE THERAPIST'S OWN FAMILY

Peter Titelman, Ph.D.

This book presents the work of several family therapists applying their versions of Bowen family systems theory toward self-differentiation in their own families. All therapists—whether dealing with families or individuals—are likely to function more effectively in their clinical work if they make the effort to become more responsible selves in relation to their own families.

Family therapists and their own families, like their clients and their families, are coping with the universal issue of the interplay of separateness and connectedness. Each has to deal with his or her own version of the same universal issues and forces: individuality and togetherness. Family therapists face toxic issues in their own families, just as the families seen in clinical practice struggle with them.

A central goal in learning Bowen family systems theory is to develop the ability to see the theory as it relates to self. The optimal training for a family therapist involves a balance and integration of three factors: (1) theoretical understanding of family systems theory; (2) exploration and work on the therapist's own family, and (3) supervised clinical work.

The family therapist's family of origin or extended family work, individually with a coach or with a group of fellow family therapists, is an ameliorative and fruitful provision in the midst of the emotionally charged work of doing family therapy. Working toward becoming a more responsible and differentiated individual in one's own family provides an avenue for lessening tendencies to become overinvolved with one's clinical families, and it helps the family therapist avoid emotional "burn-out," a common occupational hazard for psychotherapists.

Individually oriented psychotherapists, educators, and those in other health-related fields are also subject to toxic issues and conflicts in their own families. Enhanced functioning in their families can be an important factor in improving their personal and professional functioning. In this regard, participation individually or in a group setting in family of origin work may also be fruitful for them.

Responsibility and Being a Family Therapist

The goal of extended family work is helping family therapists become more responsible—more differentiated—in dealing with both clients and their own families. Becoming a well-trained, responsible family therapist involves an effort to "know thyself in the context of one's family." Motivation to be a family therapist often emerges from an individual's experience in his or her own family. Understanding and making efforts toward modification of the dysfunctional aspects of one's functioning in one's own family, in order not to project personal biases and unresolved difficulties onto the clinical families, is crucial. This reminds us of that ancient piece of advice for physicians, which may be paraphrased, "Family Therapist, heal thyself."

Defining self in one's family and in one's profession as family therapist is an interlocking process. The position the therapist plays in relation to the client family will be similar to the position that is played in the therapist's own family. Family therapists tend to be mediators, communicators, bridging family members, and overfunctioners in their families of origin. Although family therapists include all sibling positions, a high percentage (based on the author's experience) are of the overresponsible oldest type in comparison with other sibling positions and roles.

As is the case for most psychotherapists, family therapists, show a propensity to become overresponsible and emotionally overinvolved in relation to their clinical families. To the degree that the family therapist is overinvolved emotionally with clinical families, there may be a corollary underinvolvement with his/her own family. Working on understanding and modifying the position in one's own family is one way of working on the issue of being more responsible for self.

The projection of the family therapist's anxiety onto clients is often a covert process, used to relieve the anxiety of the therapist. This process resembles the method by which the therapist deals with anxiety as it has been passed down from previous generations to the current generation in his or her own family. One can achieve a calmer state in self by becoming clearer about how much anxiety is derived from self, how much from the clinical family, and how much as a reaction to a similar issue in one's own family.

The need to take care of the other is an expression of the undifferentiation of the therapist. The problem of overfunctioning and overresponsibility in clinical families is a type of fusion akin to that of the anxious mother, whose worry about her child allows her to be less anxious—at the expense of the child, who in turn feels more anxious.

By working on one's position in the family, the family therapist is more able to come to terms with anxiety. Anxiety and emotional blocks in the clinical work with families, including identification with certain sibling positions, specific types of triangles, and difficulties with particular content issues, can most often be traced back to unresolved processes in the family therapist's own family. When family therapists do not understand this risk, they may attempt to alter or modify emotional processes they have been avoiding in their own family. The result is inappropriate expectations and goals for the clinical families.

The Family Therapist's Own Family and Its Relationship to Being a Family Therapist

Bowen (1978b) was the first family therapist to share publicly his conception of the extended family as being integral to family theory and therapy in clinical practice, through applying it to his own family. This was as Promethean an achievement as Freud's self-analysis through the interpretation of his own dreams, more than sixty years before Bowen's work.

In Bowen's family systems theory, the paradigm of the family as a system must be understood firsthand, as well as theoretically. Bowen has constantly been concerned with clarifying the personal experience from which his theoretical hypotheses emerged. The more family systems therapists work on, and modify, their experience and position in their own families, the more they are likely to be able to comprehend the family as an emotional system. From this perspective, family therapists should work on relationships in their own family systems in order to function more effectively as coach or therapist.

Since Bowen described his own differentiating efforts in his family of origin, those who draw upon the Bowen family systems model have emphasized that the best way of "learning systems" is to attend to your own family as an emotional relationship system (Bowen 1978a,b,c, Carolin 1977, Kerr 1984). One learns about human systems and, specifically, the family as a multigenerational emotional system, by becoming more knowledgeable and objective about self and family. Family systems theory is learned, to a great extent, by personal appropriation. Lectures and readings can aid in learning the theory, but the ability to think in terms of systems depends primarily on emotional changes taking place on the part of the learner.

The Family Therapist's Own Family and Increasing Neutrality

All family theory and therapy is concerned with the issue of how the therapist becomes fused, triangled, or induced into the emotional systems of the client families. And, in turn, there is a general concern for how the therapist gets "unstuck" from the clinical families with whom he is engaged. Family of origin work is seen as a major means by which this "unclumping" process can be acccomplished in conjunction with learning the theory didactically and receiving clinical supervision.

The family therapist has two main, related problems in dealing with the fundamental issues of connectedness and separateness as they are confronted in clinical work. The first is overinvolvement—getting too caught up in the family's problem(s). The other is distancing, or backing away from the family's problem(s). When the therapist cannot maintain neutrality and gets caught up in the overlapping emotional processes of the clinical family and his own family, the therapist becomes either *oversympathetic* or *rejecting*. The therapist's own extended family work is a key way of working toward gaining a better level of neutrality. Neutrality is a position one seeks to achieve, but it is never fully accomplished.

Doing family therapy, carrying on own family work, and training to become a family therapist share similar fundamental dimensions. Each process involves learning to observe, comprehend, and relate to an emotional system without emotionally fusing or cutting-off from it.

The Family Therapist's Own Family and Training

Family therapists' efforts to understand, explore, and modify their position in the family of origin is analogous to the individual therapist's undergoing personal therapy or psychoanalysis. Individually oriented therapists, particularly those in the psychodynamic and existential orientations, have used personal therapy to grow as therapists and to deal with the issues of transference and countertransference. In order to understand better one's work with families, it is posited that having a fuller understanding of one's own family of origin—an understanding tempered by less reactivity and more objectivity—facilitates not only the personal growth of the family therapist but also contributes to one's becoming a better therapist.

Besides Bowen (1978a,b) there are other family therapists, including Framo (1979), Kramer (1985), and Satir (Nerin 1985), who believe that attention to the therapist's own family is an important component in the training and growth of the family therapist. Their approaches differ from Bowen's.

Among those who identify themselves with a Bowen family systems theory orientation, there is considerable variation in viewing the place of family of origin work on the part of the therapist in training. All hold that the goal of training is to increase the coach/therapist's level of objectivity/neutrality and capacity to understand and utilize theory. Some family systems therapists who utilize Bowen theory tend to focus more on teaching theory, using a variety of material from the natural sciences, as a means of helping the trainee to gain neutrality and an increased level of objectivity—viewing the human dance as being a part of the natural world. Others focus on the acquisition of clinical theory and practice, and the application of clinical theory to clinical research. Some family systems theorists put the priority in training on the extended family work of the therapist-in-training. The perspective of this author gives priority to the therapist's own family work, clinical theory, and clinical practice.

Other family therapy theories are more technique oriented in the training of family therapists, and do not include development of the therapist's self. This is in contrast to the Bowen family systems approach, in which the differentiation of self of the trainee is a central aspect of the training. Minuchin (1981) and Haley (1976) believe that the therapist's work on his own family is not relevant to becoming a successful family therapist. The Bowen family systems approach, however, utilizes the therapist's own family work to engender the capacity, during training, for lessening emotional reactivity toward clinical families and fostering greater objectivity and neutrality in relation to them. The training for structural and strategic family therapies utilizes live supervision with the supervisor and/or team as the device for engendering greater objectivity, lessening reactivity, increasing self-observation, and seeking detriangulation for the therapist-in-training.

Both Bowen family systems and structural and strategic approaches attempt to teach therapists-in-training not to get "sucked in," triangled, or seduced into covert alliances. All three approaches seek a balance—being connected with family without being emotionally fused or cut-off—but they accomplish this through different means. The use of live supervision or involvement in a team does not have the efficacy that family of origin work provides in the training of a family therapist. Those technique-oriented approaches rely on the capacity of the team or supervisor to get the trainee "unstuck" in relation to the clinical family; they do not foster differentiated functioning on the part of the trainee working directly with the family.

Misconceptions Regarding the Family Therapist's Own Family Efforts

Family of origin work should not be undertaken as a way to change one's family. Rather, it is something done for self. If a therapist, or client in family therapy, is undertaking family of origin work with the overt, or covert, agenda to help, save, or change his or her family, then the therapist is avoiding looking at the role self is playing. Probably such an effort is a continuation of the therapist's role as "helper" or "savior" within the family of origin.

Another misconception of extended family work is that it can be a technique separate from the understanding of theory. The use of family of origin work as an adjunctive tool can easily lead to distortion and be not only unproductive, but sometimes destructive. Family of origin work, from this perspective, is not meant to be viewed as a technique separate from the understanding of theory; and it should not be used as a simple adjunct technique in training or therapy, as is the case with family sculpting, role-playing, and the family reconstruction technique.

One important way to minimize the dangers of simplification and distortion of this approach is to utilize coaching when working on one's own position in the family. Just as the individual therapist is too emotionally involved to be objective enough to be his or her own therapist, likewise the family therapist needs a coach for guidance in a disciplined effort in embarking on and carrying out extended family work.

There is a danger that mental health professionals will hear and use material on the therapist's own family in an oversimplified and reductionist manner. A further concern is that family of origin work will be taken as a simple technique, without the benefit of adequate grounding in the context of family systems theory.

Differentiation of self is a long-range process. It is not something that can be accomplished by simply gathering family data in the form of a family diagram, or devising a task or two to do with one's family. Differentiation cannot be accomplished by making one presentation to a group of professionals as an adjunct training task, or through one or two visits home. It involves a lifetime commitment.

FAMILY SYSTEMS THEORY

The efforts in this volume to define self in relation to one's family of origin represent the contributors' application of their perspectives on Bowen's family systems theory, as originated and developed by Murray Bowen (1978c). This section provides a broad overview of the author's version of the theoretical base that undergirds the work of the family therapists whose contributions are presented herein. Selected references on Bowen-oriented family systems theory and therapy are given in Appendix A.

The Extended Family and the Context of Evolution

One can make an analogy between an individual's relation to the family and that of a grain of sand on the beach. The individual is an almost infinitesimal part of a far-reaching panorama that spans many generations, a tiny speck, the meaning of which only makes sense in the context of millions of others, and is almost indistinguishable. Yet, each person is also different, separate, and individual.

Understanding man and the family in the context of the natural world is an attempt on the part of Bowen (1978c) and other family systems theorists to find an adequate theoretical framework for understanding the process of continuity and change of individuals within families over multiple generations. A framework based on evolutionary biology appears to be a useful strategy to help the family therapist obtain a broader focus, to be a better observer and lower emotional reactivity in order to become more emotionally neutral. Using evolutionary theory in this way provides the family therapist with a broader theoretical context in the effort to become more objective, so as to avoid tendencies to fuse, merge, or clump with the families with whom one is working.

Bowen (1984) presented the following summary of evolution as a context in which to place man's capacity for objectivity in perspective, and to indicate that man as an emotional being is a part of the evolving world of nature. He stated that 400 million years ago the universe, according to some theories, started with a "big bang." Life appeared 350 million years later, and 200,000 years ago, man became a primitive thinking being. The Stone Age culture arose 20,000 years ago. Writing emerged 10,000 years ago, and 5,000 years ago, culture emerged.

A characteristic of all life is that it reproduces with tiny changes; it is evolutionary. In regard to one's position in a nuclear family, according to Bowen (1984b), an individual cannot make the timetable go much beyond 100 years. Using that period of time as a scale for the entire period that the universe has existed, it would be eighty-eight years before life appeared, only four hours ago that the human race emerged, and two hours ago that we learned to read and write. Culture would have developed only an hour ago. Columbus would have discovered American only eighteen minutes ago. And the length of a human life would be forty-five seconds. From the perspective of evolution, our ancestors are specks of cosmic dust.

A little bit of evidence can give a mock-up of the extended family. Bowen (1984) describes his exploration of the family as a multigenerational emotional system as being analogous to paleontology. Whereas Freud described his delving into the area of unconscious motivation, the depth of the psyche, as a form of archeology that explored the levels of consciousness and their meaning, Bowen seeks the meaning of emotional family patterns of behavior in the context of a paleontology-like exploration of multigenerations, going back even to our animal roots.

According to Bowen (1984), if one knew what went on in a nuclear family, with microscopic detail, one would know everything about the past generations. The past is visible in the present, and the past of the family can be reconstructed from the present. Conversely, given knowledge about the way a family operated and its patterns as manifested in the distant past, a reasonably accurate profile of how that family would evolve and appear in future generations could be drawn.

Bowen, in his work on his own family, went back fifteen generations, or 275 years. Beyond 75 years, Bowen states (1984), it is difficult to do genealogy. Therefore, it is important to know one's nuclear family in minute detail.

The patterns and variables that transmit themselves over multiple generations of extended family should be looked upon as being made up of biological, psychological, genetic, and immunological factors.

The Family as a Multigenerational Emotional System

The family viewed as a multigenerational emotional system means that the context to be considered is at least three generations, and preferably more. Figure 1-1 illustrates the conception of the family as being made up of the interlocking emotional fields of the nuclear and extended families.

The nuclear family—mother, father, and children—constitutes one emotional field. The father's family of origin—he, his siblings, and parents—constitutes another emotional field, and the mother's family of origin constitutes a third emotional field. The nuclear family and families of origin of both spouses/parents, and each of their respective extended family systems, constitute three interlocking emotional subsystems.

The nuclear and extended family systems are described as interlocking, because what occurs in one of the subsystems has an effect on the functioning of the other systems with which it is connected. And they are interlocking because the father/spouse of the nuclear family is also a son in his family of origin. Furthermore, he is a grandson/nephew/cousin in the extended family. The mother/spouse in the nuclear family is also a daughter in her family of origin and a granddaughter/niece/cousin in her extended family. And the children in the nuclear family are grandchildren and cousins in the paternal and maternal extended family systems.

The term *emotional* connotes that the family is a system that *automatically* responds to changes of connectedness–togetherness and separateness–individuality with and between the membership of the extended family.

The term *field* is used to describe the constant fluidity of movement, of emotional action and reaction, that occurs within and across the subsystems that constitute the family as a multigenerational system or unit. It is not merely the relationship between an individual and his or her parents that is essential; rather, the family of origin provides an emotional field of meaning that an individual is connected to, fused with, or cut-off from, which influences him and which he in turn influences (Titelman 1984).

The Family as an Emotional System/Unit and the Law of Compensation

The family is a system, insofar as change in one part is followed by compensatory change in other parts. The functioning of one part of a

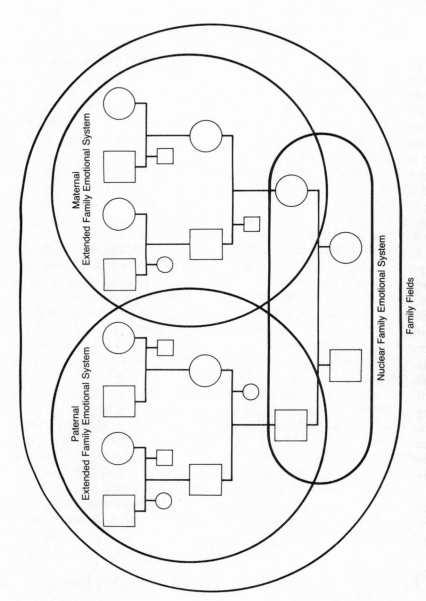

Figure 1–1. Multigenerational family emotional system.

family is dependent on the functioning of the extended families of which it is a part, and also on its subsystems.

There are innumerable ways in which the important function of compensatory balance illustrates how the family operates as a system. The overadequate–inadequate/overfunctioning–underfunctioning reciprocity is the way a dysfunctional but stable balance emerges to deal with undifferentiation in the presence of anxiety. It is manifested between spouses, in parent–child relationships, and between siblings. One form of compensatory balance in families is the overresponsible–underresponsible reciprocity. An example is provided by the typical marital dance that occurs when an eldest, responsible daughter and a youngest, dependent son unite. She will often play the role of "big mother" to his "little boy." And the more the wife overfunctions and is overresponsible, as programmed in her position growing up in her family of origin, the more the husband plays the irresponsible, underfunctioning position, as programmed in his growing up in his family.

Another example of compensatory balance in the marital relationship occurs when one spouse is the emotional overfunctioner and the other is the cognitive overfunctioner. In this situation a wife, for example, may express the feelings and emotions for both herself and her husband, and the more she becomes simply emotional and expresses emotionality, the less her husband expresses feeling. In turn, he may express more and more in terms of intellectualization. This leads to a polarized compensation, in which the wife is overly emotional and the husband is overly rational. A further instance of compensatory balance in the marital relationship is that of the pursuer and the distancer (Fogarty 1979). When the pursuer advances, the distancer goes farther away. The pursuer–distancer reciprocity can exist around any of a number of issues. The wife may be an emotional pursuer and the husband an emotional distancer. The husband may be the pursuer in the area of sexual closeness, with the wife being the distancer in that area.

A good example that illustrates the overadequate–inadequate reciprocity process in the nuclear family, between parents and a child, is Bowen's (1978c) description of the family with a schizophrenic member. In those families that Bowen observed during his research project on schizophrenia and the family at the National Institute of Mental Health, from 1954 to 1959, the following description was formulated: In these families, there was an overadequate mother, a dependent "baby," and a distant father. The projection process involved the mother's "projecting" her worries and anxieties onto the child. In this way, the mother functions better by ascribing certain aspects of self to the child—she then feels less of her own helplessness. What begins as a *feeling* in the mother becomes a *reality* in the child. Sometimes this projection occurs in relation to physical illness. In Bowen's (1978c) words, "the soma of one person reciprocates with the psyche of another person" (p. 59). In this intense *fusion* between mother and child, often there is an uncanny reading of the patient's mind. Anxiety in the mother is an automatic sign for the child/patient to help the mother by becoming her "baby." The patient acts "as if" the mother would die without his or her help, and if mother dies, the patient, too, would die. In this schizophrenic family process there is an overadequate mother, with a "helpless" patient and a peripherally attached father. This is an extreme example of compensatory functioning in the nuclear family. However, this process is at one end of a continuum of the emotional process that is found in all nuclear family emotional systems.

In the area of sibling overadequate–inadequate reciprocity, there are typically a number of roles, including "the good child" and "the bad child," or "black sheep," among other compensatory relationships between siblings. Besides these, there is the sibling profile, of the responsible eldest child of each sex and the less responsible, dependent, youngest child, of one or both sexes (all things being equal).

The Extended Family Is Like a Tree: An Analogy

The multigenerational extended family is like a tree: the nuclear family is built on, and depends upon, the connection to the extended family, as the smaller branches of a tree are supported by the larger branches, which in turn are supported by, and grow in relation to, the structure of the trunk, flare, taproot, and a multitude of smaller roots. The strength of the family depends upon the healthiness of its roots. If the roots are cut, the family will suffer.

Just as the basic issue for the individual in relation to the family is the balance between connectedness and separateness, individuality and togetherness, so too the survival of the tree is dependent on the ecological balance in terms of its pattern of closeness and distance with respect to other members of its species. Too much closeness to other trees will lead to smothering and overgrowth of the tree(s), a tangling of the roots, like fusion in the family, leading to a lack of space to grow. This process for the family eventually leads to extinction and death. The tree without sheltering contact or cross-fertilization in relation to other members of the species may not be able to reproduce. This would be analogous to the family member(s) emotionally cut off, lacking root support, nurturance, and structure from relations to the extended family in regard to the stresses emerging through the life cycle.

Connectedness and Separateness as the Primordial Dimensions of Human Existence

The broadest theoretical postulate of Bowen family systems theory is the conception of the family as a multigenerational emotional unit or system, made up of interlocking family fields: the nuclear family field and the two extended family fields. *Separateness/individuality* and *connectedness/togetherness* are conceived from this author's perspective as being primordial at biological, psychological, and sociological levels of human existence, in regard to influence on the family emotional fields. In Bowen family systems theory, individuality and connectedness are conceived of as two counterbalancing life forces. These forces are conceived of as having an emotional–instinctual base. In people, these forces are interrelated biological, psychological, and sociological dimensions. Togetherness refers to a person's need for emotional connectedness with others and intolerance of separateness. Individuality refers to the capacity to tolerate difference and to function as a separate being.

The primordial existential and structural issues of family life revolve around the dimensions of connectedness/togetherness and separateness/individuality. Family systems theory, as is the case for all theories of family therapy, puts these dimensions into a context in the domain of the self–other boundary within the family. In the broadest sense, boundaries in families are conceptualized here as the modes through which individual family members accomplish the following existential mandates: to maintain their individuality and connectedness in relation to the family's emotional oneness; provide means through which individuals separate feeling from thinking, and feelings from actions; provide the barrier that divides and connects roles of family members in regard to generation, division of labor, division of emotional function in the family, and maintenance of individual identity within the family in general.

The Concept of Differentiation of Self and Its Evolution

The existential domain of self–other *boundary* within the family is addressed in Bowen's family systems theory by the concept *differentiation of self.* This is central to Bowen's theoretical approach and operates at a variety of levels. Differentiation is a process that can never be fully actualized. It is not a product; it is an activity, not an outcome.

The differentiation level of an individual is determined by a complex interplay of the following variables, among others: (1) the differentiation level in the parents at the time the individual is born; (2) the sex of the individual, and how it fits into the family plan; (3) the individual's sibling position; (4) normality (or lack of it) in the individual's genetic composition; (5) the emotional climate in each of the parents and in their marriage before and after the individual's birth; (6) the quality of the relationship each of the parents had with *their* parental families; (7) the number of reality problems in the parents' lives in the period before and in the years after the individual's birth; (8) the parents' ability to cope with the emotional and reality problems of their time; (9) the differentiation level in each of one's parents, which was determined by the very same order of factors in the context into which they were born, and (10) the differentiation level of each grandparent, which was, in turn, determined by the same factors in their families of origin—this proceeded back in the same manner through the generations (Bowen 1978c). This is not to say that these are all the factors that determine level of differentiation. According to Bowen (1978c):

> . . . the biological, genetic, and emotional programming that goes into reproduction and birth is a remarkably stable process, but it is influenced to some degree by the fortunes, misfortunes, and fortuitous circumstances when things go wrong. All things being equal, you emerge with about the same basic level of differentiation your parents had. This is determined by the process before your birth and the situation during infancy and early childhood. This is then modified to some degree by the fortunes and misfortunes during later childhood and adolescence. All things equal, the basic level of differentiation is finally established about the time the young adult establishes self separately from his family of origin. I am talking about basic levels of differentiation that proceed through the generations as a stable process. [pp. 409–410]

Differentiation of self can be applied to characterization of the individual's level of emotional functioning, the functioning within the nuclear family, including the marital relationship and the parent–child relationships, and the relation of the individual to the family of origin. At the level of the individual, differentiation of self applies to the level of integration of self. This concept defines people according to the degree of differentiation or undifferentiation between emotionally reactive and cognitively goal-directed functioning. All individuals can be located on the continuum that constitutes this universal characteristic.

At the level of the nuclear family, differentiation of self, or its converse, undifferentiation of self, is described in terms of the way family members are emotionally stuck together. Bowen (1978c) initially utilized the term *undifferentiated family ego mass*. This concept describes the shifting patterns of the emotional process in the undifferentiated emotional oneness of the nuclear family. The intensity of an individual's involvement depends on his or her basic level of involvement in the nuclear family's emotional system. The number of family members involved is determined by the intensity of the emotional process and the functional state of individual relationships to the central amalgamated ego at the moment.

Bowen developed his concept of the undifferentiated family ego mass (a term he later changed to the *nuclear family emotional system*) from family research that focused on the entire nuclear family unit. In this concept, differentiation (or undifferentiation) of self denotes a continuum of modes through which family members express emotional oneness, and the ways this emotional "clumping," or "stuck-togetherness," operates as an underlying glue, no matter how much family members deny it or pretend to be autonomous with respect to each other.

When Bowen's clinical focus shifted to the marital couple, excluding the child-identified parent, differentiation of self began to be discussed in terms of the emotional attachment, or fusion, between spouses.

Finally, following a paper presented in 1967 describing his own efforts toward differentiating himself in his own family of origin, Bowen's (1978b) focus on differentiation of self, theoretically and clinically, became a concern with the degree of unresolved emotional attachment to one's family of origin.

The evolution and the broadening of the concept of differentiation of self, from the focus on the nuclear family emotional system to a focus on marital fusion, and then to the current focus on each spouse's unresolved attachment to his or her family of origin, involved several phases. Initially, the focus was on the concept of fusion/undifferentiation in the context of the nuclear family emotional system. A second phase emerged with the clarification of the concept of the emotional triangle; with this came a shift of focus, theoretically and clinically, toward the marital pair.

Triangles involve patterns that repeat over time, in which people come to have fixed roles in relation to each other. Predictably, there are two close sides and one side in conflict.

Triangles form, inevitably, when the stability of a two-person system is subject to anxiety in relation to nodal events, examples being marriage, loss of job, and transitions in the family life cycle. A typical instance is the addition of a first child, which alters a two-person marital system to a three-person nuclear family. The introduction of anxiety, acute or chronic, unbalances the forces of togetherness/fusion and individuality/separateness. The introduction of anxiety into a two-person system disrupts the calmness that allows a two-person system to be stable, with the persons able to deal directly with each other. Anxiety in interaction with the basic levels of differentiation of the selves of the twosome creates a situation in which the degree of undifferentiation, activated in the presence of anxiety, leads to the engagement of the most vulnerable other person to become a triangle. The function of the triangle is to control anxiety when the stability of a comfortable closeness/distance is threatened.

There are many variations of the triangles typically found in families. In the family characterized by *marital conflict*, the central triangles are frequently constituted by one spouse's being fused or linked with one of the following: an outsider (opposite or same sex), an object (such as a substance, e.g., alcohol or drugs), an ideology (such as women's liberation), an activity (such as work or a hobby), or an extended family member(s) (such as parents—the in-laws triangle). The other spouse is in the distant or outside position. In the family characterized by *dysfunction in one spouse*, involving an overfunctioning-underfunctioning reciprocity between the spouses, the central triangles consist of the dysfunctional spouse in the close position in relation to a symptom (physical, emotional, or social); the other spouse occupies the distant or outside position.

In families that characteristically utilize *projection to the child* (*child-focused* families), the central triangles include the following: *the symbiotic parent-child triangle,* with one parent and a child in an overly close relationship, with the other parent in the distant position; the *negative child triangle,* in which two parents are in a close position, and their conflict is covert—covered over at the expense of jointly directed hostility toward a child; the *favored child/disfavored child triangle,* in which one or both parents are in a close relationship with the favored child(ren), and the disfavored child(ren) occupies the outside position toward which negativity or conflict is directed, and the *parentified triangle*, in which a child overfunctions in relation to one or both parents, who are in dysfunctional position(s). In the last triangle, the child whose role is to serve as a parent for a parent can be either in a distant or fused position with the underfunctioning parent, depending upon how that parent's perception of his or her need for being taken care of by the parentified child is being met, and the way in which the parentified child perceives and feels about such a role. The other parent is in the close or distant position with the spouse, depending upon the positive or negative valence that exists between the underfunctioning parent and overfunctioning child, and the marital relationship pattern.

A further development in theory involves defining the concept of emotional cut-off. The concept of interlocking triangles was linked to the interlocking process of fusion and emotional cut-off, and this in turn led to a shift in the focus of the theory and therapy from the marital fusion to each spouse's unresolved attachment to family of origin.

The term *interlocking triangles* describes the phenomenon that emerges when, anxiety having overloaded the system, and the initial triangle is unable to stabilize the situation, others are triangled into the process, thus forming a series of interlocking triangles. Bowen (1978c) indicated that if the interlocking triangles cannot contain the anxiety within the family system, then the family triangles in people from outside the system, such as workers from social agencies, schools, and therapists. This maneuver may result in externalizing family conflict; for example, two outside agencies or workers come into conflict over the family, while the family gains a sense of calmness (Bowen 1978c, p. 374).

Central to Bowen's conception of triangles is that tension with ensuing triangulation moves downward from the top of a system, family, or other group, with those at the bottom—the least powerful, least mature individuals—becoming symptomatic, in conflict, and perhaps excommunicated or "fired" by the system. Since the extrusion of a triangled individual at the bottom of the system does not actually alter the presence of conflict higher up in the system, conflict will erupt in a subsequent twosome (Bowen 1978c, p. 374).

The concept of *emotional cut-off* refers to the phenomenon of emotional distancing, whether the cut-off takes the form of internal mechanisms or physical distancing (Bowen 1978c, p. 535). The more Bowen's focus shifted from observing and working directly with fusion in the nuclear family emotional system and fusion in the marital relationship toward a focus on an individual's unresolved attachment to his family of origin (notably his/her parents), the clearer it became that cut-off is as prevalent a form of dealing with undifferentiation in the presence of anxiety as are the various forms of fusion (symbiotic and hostile, among others). By continuing to understand in greater depth the impact of the multigenerational process, Bowen was able to see that emotional cut-off is the flip-side of fusion. Emotional fusion and emotional cut-off constitute an intertwined, multigenerational phenomenon.

Emotional cut-off is the extreme end of the separateness–connectedness continuum; at the other end is dysfunctional connectedness: fusion. And in between the extremes of cut-off and fusion are a myriad of forms and degrees of relational distance and closeness. Conflict and blame, finally leading to cut-off between two or more family members can often set the ground for subsequent cut-off between individuals, subgroups, or entire branches of families in succeeding generations.

Figure 1-2 illustrates the notion that an imbalance of separateness and connectedness—undifferentiation in the face of anxiety—evokes either fusion or cut-off, which in turn evokes, or is counterbalanced by, the opposite dimension. Family systems theory posits that to the degree that there is fusion in one or more relationships in a single generation, there is correlative emotional cut-off in one or more relationships in another generation.

Bowen asks the question, "What are you looking for in exploring extended family?" For Bowen (1984), "Marriage leads to cut-off from the families of origin. The biggest task is to get through and beyond cut-offs—two or three generations—to understand the struggles they

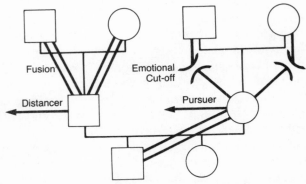

Figure 1–2. Multigenerational interlocking of fusion and emotional cut-off.

went through . . . everyone left tracks." The feeling world goes back three to five generations. Beyond the fifth generation, it is more of a factual world—it is easier to be objective when looking at generations further back.

The Function of the Coach in Family Systems Therapy

Individual psychotherapy locates emotional problems within the individual. Individual psychotherapy that is based on psychodynamic, existential, and humanistic theories focuses on intervention in the *therapeutic relationship* (whether that be understood in terms of transference, encounter, unconditional positive regard, or modeling, among other formulations). Such therapy attempts to modify one person's feelings, thoughts, and behavior; the focus is on but one generation, and the therapy works through the dyad of therapist and client. If there is a focus on the three-person relationship, it is indirect, and occurs in terms of the reexperiencing of the oedipal relationship in the therapeutic transference.

Family therapy of the structural, strategic, experiential varieties locates emotional problems within the family as a unit. The intervention is focused on units of three, the triangles within the nuclear family. This approach to therapy focuses on boundaries and interpersonal transactional patterns. It is always a *transgenerational* model, in that it involves parents (one generation) and children (a second generation). Family therapy traditionally involves a relationship to the whole family (nuclear).

In contrast to transgenerational, nuclear family-oriented family therapy, Bowen family systems therapy is multigenerational insofar as its focus is on a minimum of three generations: children (third generation), parents (second generation), and grandparents (first generation). Family systems therapy involves a coach seeking to have a neutral relationship with the family, whether meeting with an individual, couple, or larger groupings of the nuclear and/or extended family. Whereas transgenerational family therapy deals with triangles, family systems therapy deals with interlocking triangles.

Bowen (1978c) describes the role, function, and process of family systems therapy as coaching, rather than therapy. The coach attempts to stay outside of the family emotional process and seeks to maintain a research focus: the capacity to ask unending meaningful questions and to evoke from the client(s), be it the therapist in training or any client(s), willingness to take responsibility for making changes in their lives.

THE CHOICE OF THE TERM COACH AND ITS ANALOGICAL IMPLICATIONS

Like a football coach, the Bowen family systems coach is on the sidelines. Both serve as teachers/consultants who prepare the players/clients, but the player(s)/client(s) need to translate the learning into action on the playing field and the family turf. The coach for systems work diagrams the patterns or plays, the roles, strengths, weaknesses, and interdependencies, and helps devise a game plan or strategy, but the individual(s) in the family have to execute them. The coach provides a wide-angle view, without which the worker can get caught in the pits, watching one block or one pass receiver, thus missing the whole flow of interaction between the interlocking parts of the family. The coach reviews what worked and did not work with the family, and adjustments are made for the next contact with the family. The systems coach and the sports coach both teach the client family member(s) or team member(s) the theory, application, and long-term conditioning for how the sport or the family operates.

EVOLUTION OF BOWEN FAMILY SYSTEMS THERAPY

In family systems therapy, the primary goal is the *differentiation of self* of one or more members of a family—basic, or solid, rather than symptomatic change. The process involves helping one or more members of a family modify their position in one or more primary triangles, or primary interlocking triangles, coaching them in efforts to differentiate a self in relation to family of origin. The role of the coach is to remain in emotional contact with the family, without fusing with them. The coach attempts to stay detriangled and tries to help them stay on a self-determined course.

Initially, Bowen family systems therapy sought differentiation within the nuclear family, based on the concept of the *undifferentiated ego mass*. With Bowen's defining of the concept of the emotional triangle, however, the focus of his therapy shifted from seeking a modicum of differentiation within the nuclear family to a focus on the fusion in the marriage. In this approach, the therapist substitutes his or her self for the triangled child or other family member. The process is directed through the coach, rather than encouraging direct communication between spouses. The method involves each spouse's talking and listening to the other more objectively. The therapist questions one spouse while the other listens. Then the coach asks the other for a response. This method externalizes both intrafamilial and intrapsychic process; it helps one spouse hear what the other is feeling and thinking. Each learns about the other, and this helps create a boundary where undifferentiated fusion had been. The goal here is to reduce emotional reactivity. The basic principle is: ". . . the original two-person tension system will resolve itself automatically when contained within a three-person system, one of whom remains emotionally detached" (Bowen 1978c, pp. 174–5). Bowen's theory involves working with the top of the system: the two most important members, the spouses, rather than the triangled child.

A variation of working with the couple is working with the more motivated spouse. The coach teaches that individual about his or her place in triangles, and ways of detriangling. This is done in addition to coaching both spouses in regard to working on the relationships with members of each one's extended family.

Then the focus of coaching shifted to differentiation based on the concept of *interlocking triangles*. This involves a back-and-forth movement focusing now on the marital fusion and again on the spouses' unresolved attachment to their families of origin. The nodal event in the shift of focus on the marital couple to the extended family was Bowen's presentation, in 1967, of his own efforts to differentiate self from his family of origin (Bowen 1978b). It was a breakthrough in his work, and his presentation of that work changed the nature of coaching for the Georgetown group, so that they bypassed the marital fusion, the nuclear family, in favor of focusing on the extended family. The new focus became differentiation of self in relation to one's family of origin:

> The over-all conclusion from that is that *families in which the focus is on the differentiation of self in the families of origin automatically make as much or more progress in working out the relationship system with spouses and children as families seen in formal family therapy in which there is a principal focus on the interdependence in the marriage.* [Bowen 1978a, p. 545]

THE PROCESS OF DEFINING SELF IN ONE'S FAMILY OF ORIGIN

The work of defining self in relation to one's family of origin is based on understanding one's own position within the primary triangles in the family of origin. This effort is based on the circularly interlinked tasks of becoming a better observer and controlling one's own emotional re-activeness. The process utilizes a variety of means of gaining access to the family, including visits, letters, and phone calls, in order to clarify the relationship system. The effort is to develop, if possible, one-to-one relationships with all significant members of the extended family. This approach focuses on detriangling in the presence of emotional issues with two or more family members present (Bowen 1978a).

Although understanding one's place in the family is necessary, the actual work of modifying one's position is based on thoughtful action in the family system, rather than insight. Differentiation is based on taking an *action* stand; self is defined by the ability to take an I-position.

Bowen (1978b) has described a predictable three-phase reaction to an individual's efforts to be more differentiated in relation to his or her family of origin: (1) "You are wrong," or some version of that; (2) "Change back," which can be communicated in many different ways; and (3) "If you do not these are the consequences" (p. 495). If the differentiating one can stay nonreactive, change will eventually be accepted by the family. Maintaining relationship contact is essential to avoid emotional cut-offs.

MAIN FUNCTION OF THE COACH

The coach helps the worker assess and clarify the relationship between an individual and the nuclear and extended family. This includes help in tracking emotional trigger mechanisms and the assessment of planned versus reactive distance and togetherness.

A second function of the coach involves both staying detriangled from the individual and the family and helping the person detriangle from the family of origin through the following means: (1) systems questions; (2) I-positions; (3) humor; (4) reversals, and (5) being unpredictable.

The coach also functions in *demonstrating* differentiation by taking I-position stands during the course of therapy. The I-position is particularly useful early in therapy as an *operating principle* on the part of the coach in relation to the trainee or client. However, it is also of use throughout therapy. The more the coach can clearly define himself in relation to families, the easier it is for the individual client(s) to define themselves to each other.

A fourth coaching function involves *teaching the function of emotional systems:* When anxiety is high, teach through I-positions. When anxiety is at a medium level, teach through the use of parables or displacement material, that is, stories about how other families operate and make efforts to modify their life situation. When anxiety is at a low level, teaching directly about how family systems operate can be useful.

Another area of the coach's function has to do with helping the trainee or client *formulate tasks*. This is done through a variety of *modalities* of contact: phone calls, letter writing, and visits. Tasks are formulated for several *types* of contact: contact-for-contact, issue dealing, utilizing nodal events (Meyer 1976). The coach helps plan the *frequency and duration of contacts* with members of the family of origin: less/more contact, length of contact, and place or location of contact.

The coach provides support for continued differentiating efforts in the face of resistance of the family to the individual's beginning or changing efforts to be a more differentiated self.

In Chapter 2 of this book, "Patterns and Processes in a Therapist's Own Family Work: Knowledge Required for Excellence," Patricia Meyer describes the patterns and processes involved in the therapist's own family work.

THEMES FROM THE THERAPISTS' WORK IN RELATION TO THEIR OWN FAMILIES

Bowen's paper "Toward the Differentiation of Self in One's Own Family" was the historical watershed. Presented at a family therapy and research conference in 1967, it was initially published, anonymously, in 1972, at the insistence of the publisher, in a book edited by J. Framo, *Family Interaction.*

Since the first published paper dealing with the family therapist's own family, Friedman's "The Birthday Party: An Experiment in Obtaining Change in One's Own Extended Family," was in *Family Process* in 1971, the number of papers dealing with family therapists' work with their own families has been fewer than fifty. A list of significant papers on the family therapist's own family that are not included in this book is given in Appendix B.

Not unlike other individuals, family therapists usually start with a desire to change their own family. Gradually, there is a shift toward looking at the part self plays in one's family. Then, there is often a beginning acceptance of the members of one's family and less of a need to change or improve them. The focus changes more toward making an effort to work on changing self in relation to the family, and less on changing the other members. Finally, there often *are* changes in the family, both positive and negative, which seem to be a byproduct of the change the family therapist (or any individual working on maturation) is making for self.

The contributors to this volume took different routes toward doing family of origin work. The majority started while in a family therapy training program, but the routes to becoming active in doing family of origin work with their own families varied for these therapists. Some went directly into exploring their own family; others started with clinical work first, and still others started with the theory first and then got involved with family of origin work. A minority of the contributors to this volume were in marital or nuclear family systems therapy as steps preceding a focus on family of origin work. All of the contributors have been involved in systematic coaching in individual and/or group formats; and most received, in addition to formal coaching, informal coaching from family systems-oriented colleagues. Formal coaching ranged from one to three years, with most of the contributors seeking additional intermittent consultations.

All of the chapters are concerned with defining self in relation to the balance of separateness and connectedness. They all deal with fusion/cut-off issues. They deal with differentiation, the basic parental triangle, and multigenerational process.

The chapters on the family therapists' own families are clustered around the following themes: family life cycle, emotional cut-off, and the nodal events of illness and death. There is overlap in themes, in that most of the chapters deal with the patterns of fusion and/or emotional cut-off, family life cycle issues, and nodal events—including illness or death.

Part II, *Family Life Cycle: Leaving Home, Marriage, Children, and the Family of Origin in Later Life,* includes chapters highlighting family life cycle stages and issues. Part III, *Bridging Emotional Cut-Offs,* contains chapters dealing with strategies to explore emotional cut-offs, including the issue of emigration in the present and past generations as a factor in the presence of the phenomenon of emotional cut-off. Part IV, *Illness and Death,* includes chapters dealing with the impact of polio and cancer on those family therapists' efforts to become more differentiated. Finally, there are chapters on the issue of dealing with the impact of death in the family on self-differentiation efforts.

The contributors to this volume share a common foundation. They have each used their own versions of Bowen family systems theory in doing their own family of origin work. The contributors' involvement in the process of "own family work" ranges from seven to twenty-one years.

Family Life Cycle: Leaving Home, Marriage, Children, and the Family of Origin in Later Life

This part comprises seven chapters. There are two chapters, Glenn Scarboro's "The Delusion of Differentiation: Notations on Family Process" and Robert Valentine's "Freedom of Choice versus Honoring Commitment," that deal with the issues involved in the leaving-home stage of young adulthood.

Scarboro describes how he was fused and unseparated from his family before undertaking his family of origin work. In his words: "I was still overly involved with my mother and still significantly distant from and underinvolved with my father." By dealing more directly with the emotionally hot issues of homosexuality and money, Scarboro was made able to leave home and to worry less about these issues and his parents. He says, "In essence, a more reasonable balance between closeness and distance . . . has gradually been achieved." A more personal relationship with his father became a source of strength and nourishment. Scarboro's family of origin work exemplifies the idea that you have to "go home, to leave home."

For Valentine, religion was an emotion-laden issue in his family. His original choice to become a priest was in part related to his identification with his mother and her family, who were very religious, whereas his father's family were not. Valentine had always felt rejected by his maternal family until he became a priest. Part of becoming a priest involved a process of distancing, whereas part of the process of leaving the priesthood had to do with fusing with psychology and cutting-off from religion. He came to understand that reactively choosing to be a priest and reactively leaving the priesthood represented undifferentiation in relation to his family and peers. He eventually returned to the priesthood and continued to be a family therapist as well.

The family life cycle stage of marriage is the focus of St. John's "Becoming Real." She explores the interlocking process of how she had been in an overresponsible position both in relation to her spouse and in the interlocking triangle with her parents. Her effort was to become less overresponsible in her relationship with both husband and parents. In relation to her husband, she began "not doing for him," which had involved cleaning, writing letters to his family, among other functions. In relation to her mother, she began to ask her for advice, letting her mother *be* a mother and letting herself be a daughter. At the same time, she began to seek more contact with her father, and worked on her position in the interlocking of the nuclear and extended family emotional process.

One chapter focuses on children and how they interlock with the family of origin: Jack LaForte's "Efforts to Modify One's Position in Interlocking Triangles."

LaForte deals with interlocking triangles in his nuclear family and family of origin: mothers and sons in the togetherness position, with fathers in the distant position. He started with nuclear family issues, and then he moved to working on his relationship with his family of origin and the interlocking process. The initial focus of LaForte's work was on the nuclear family, with a specific goal of lowering the level of emotional reactivity between himself and his son. LaForte then describes three phases in his extended family work. The first phase involved thinking in terms of his own patterns being linked to his family of origin. In the second, he began to develop the specific focus of his extended family work.

LaForte diagrams the interlocking triangles that form in the emotional system during periods of tension. His strategy involved dealing, in an interwoven way, with the triangles of self, his mother, and his father and the triangle involving himself, his wife, and his son, and the interlocking nature of the relationship between the two triangles. In the third phase of LaForte's work, having gained some movement in relation to his son and lowering reactivity to him and to his mother, LaForte decided to focus more directly on his family of origin: self, mother, father, and sister. His goal was to have more of a one-to-one relationship with each member of his family of origin, especially his father and mother. He describes his efforts to move from a position of passive, distancing rebellious youngest to being a more responsible, active member in the family.

Three chapters, Susan Edwards' "Defining a Self After the Last Child Leaves Home," Blanche Kaplan's "Taking a Giant Step: First Moves Back into My Family," and Edwin Friedman's "The Birthday Party Revisited: Family Therapy and the Problem of Change," involve self-differentiation efforts in the family life cycle context of dealing with parents in later life.

The first, "Defining a Self After the Last Child Leaves Home," explores the author's differentiating efforts after her children had left home. Edwards had, at one point, tried to "fix up" her nuclear family before her children left home. She soon realized that the effort was a belated and futile one to modify unresolved issues involving emotional attachment issues between herself and her parents; she perceived that these issues were being replayed with her husband and her children. She abandoned the project and began to consider her relationship to her parents and her one sibling, an older sister. The result was a shift in focus away from her children and husband towards her parents, from whom she had merely physically separated. The focus was on modifying the triangle in which Edwards' sister was close to mother and Edwards was in the outside position. One significant point of the chapter is that when the author set out to define a self in relation to her parents, there was a beneficial "spin-off" to the nuclear family system, including the younger generation (it should be noted that spin-offs are not always beneficial).

Kaplan's chapter deals with the primary triangle, her relation to a distant father and a mildly distant mother. In exploring her father's family of origin she discovered that her father was emotionally cut-off as an adolescent. His mother and five younger brothers died in a concentration camp. A visit to her paternal uncle, in Europe, involving the experience of emotional closeness with him which she has not felt in relation to her father, helped to make her father more knowable.

The goal of Kaplan's work, as illustrated by six visits and the in-between intervals, involved her efforts to gain a greater sense of emotional connection with each of her parents, particularly her father, from whom she felt very distant. Since her parents were elderly, the motivation to connect with them before they died was strong. The central issue involved dealing with distance in relation to aged parents. Kaplan describes how a gain in closeness in relation to her family of origin made for less intensity and allergy in her marriage. Extended family work, differentiating a self, as Kaplan and many of the other contributors point out, takes one on a long, bumpy road with many emotional ups and downs and involves sustained motivation that far exceeds the excitement generated by a few visits home. It is a lifetime effort.

Friedman's "The Birthday Party Revisited: Family Therapy and the Problem of Change" adopts one aspect of Bowen's (1978b) reported work, as described in his paper, "On the Differentiation of Self," a focus on planned strategy, executed at a nodal event, a surprise seventieth birthday party for Friedman's mother. In the author's relatively tranquil family system a "tempest in a teapot" is created; there is an effort to devise an experimental situation, in the context of a significant event, during which one provides disequilibrating information and behavior in relation to the various members of one's family, thus providing an opportunity to modify one's standard operating position in relation to the family, in such a way that one can be more responsible for self and at the same time be a more responsible member of the family. This involves an effort to avoid occupying one's predictable position in the family's configuration of undifferentiation. Although the focus of Friedman's reports on his extended family work was on certain planned nodal events, he had spent a considerable period of time developing a carefully planned study to understand, map out, and relate with his family prior to the nodal events described. He had been doing extended family work under the guidance of a coach for two years prior to his putting on the birthday party for his mother. Friedman cites five varieties of technique used in his own family work: (1) being straightforwardly analytic; (2) telling stories (displacement material) about one of his clients; (3) performing verbal reversals; (4) performing behavioral reversals, and (5) playing the anti-therapist role in his family (stirring up trouble and not being helpful or responsible).

In reflecting upon his own continued family work and his coaching, over the past twenty years, he cites the following changes in his thinking: (1) "The primary purpose for all work in one's family of origin has to be for one's self, and it cannot be just in the service of self-differentiation—one has to get a kick out of it"; (2) "Families can come together again even after a generation of distance, and sometimes only after a generation has passed or has 'passed away' "; (3) To bridge that distance there must be a catalytic family member prepared to take advantage of catalytic moments; (4) Family of origin work is a life-time project, it cannot be ". . . given the priority of something to be accomplished in the near future"; (5) "The importance of nodal events, family reunions of any type, and rites of passage cannot be underestimated; (6) The effort put into family of origin work will enhance the development of the "leader," whether or not he or she is a therapist.

Bridging Emotional Cut-Offs

The next cluster of chapters is grouped under the rubric "Bridging Emotional Cut-Offs." The chapters are: Ellen Benswanger's "Strategies to Explore Cut-Offs," C. Margaret Hall's "Efforts to Differentiate a Self in My Family of Origin," Joseph DiCarlo's "A Voyage into an Italian Family," and James Maloni's "At Least Three Generations of Male

Distancing." These deal with the ubiquitous phenomenon of emotional cut-off as it is manifested in different ways, contexts, and in varying degrees. They describe strategies to explore emotional cut-offs, including the issue of emigration in the present and past generations as a factor in the presence of the phenomenon of emotional cut-off.

The context for emotional cut-off in Benswanger's situation was the remarriage of her father after his first wife's death. For Hall the context involves family nearing extinction and the issue of migration to the United States on her part. In DiCarlo's story, the emigration of his father was part of a cut-off process. The work of reconnecting with the paternal side of the extended family helped DiCarlo reconnect with his dead father. In Maloni's work, the issues of emigration and loss are central. He too can be seen as the bridging family member, attempting to bridge family cut-offs. His closeness to his mother and his distance from his father follow the pattern of male distancer and overresponsibility that emerged in the shadow of the relationship of the father's and grandfather's emotional cut-off. Issues of guilt, responsibility, and loyalty are significant to the multigenerational process. These chapters describe a phenomenon that is seen as characteristic of family therapists: being the "bridging" members of their families. The effort is to open up one-to-one communication between self and extended family members without participating in the long-standing process and structure of interlocking triangulation.

Benswanger's "Strategies to Explore Cut-Offs" describes the concept of emotional cut-off as originated and developed by Bowen. She describes the essential features. The three major foci around which cut-offs are identified are (1) social/emotional; (2) financial/material; and (3) functional. Important examples in each of the three areas are cited. Cut-offs involve the process of blaming, scapegoating, and projection of the "bad." According to Benswanger, when a single member or one side of the family is the focus of the cut-off, the "badness" in the family can be projected onto that person or branch. Subsequent efforts are directed to justifying the rejection and persuading others to participate.

Benswanger describes her efforts to rework the cut-off in her family of origin. She describes four distinct phases in the process of reconnecting: (1) a preparation phase; (2) a sequence of strategies designed to reinterpret the cut-off; (3) the actual implementation of the reconnection, and (4) the aftermath.

Hall's goal in working to define a clear "I" position within her family, described in "Efforts to Differentiate a Self in My Family of Origin," in a broad sense involved an imbalance in the direction of cut-off. She had left England, following getting married, and came to live in the United States. Six visits, and the ramifications from them, constitute the bulk of the family work she describes in her chapter. Prior to that series of visits, Hall had not returned to England for 9 years. Even though her presentation highlights activities and strategies based on "operational blueprints," specifically the utilization of de-triangling moves and reversals (taking the opposite position to what one would ordinarily do in order to disequilibrate the family system), her work was based on a thorough foundation of data gathering. Family systems theory guided Hall's hypotheses and was the ground for the interventions during the eighteen-month period of the extended family work she describes.

Hall characterizes her family as one of decreasing size—an "extincting" family—based on deaths and lessening births in the recent generations, rigidity of emotional patterns, and the presence of emotional cut-off.

Like the majority of family therapists who embark upon own family work, Hall was stimulated to engage in, and intensify her efforts, following significant nodal events in the family. In her case, the nodal events were at least eight deaths in a six-year period. Hall believes that a self can be more effectively differentiated in a family system at a time of slight unrest in that system.

Hall is clear in stating what all the contributors agree upon: work on differentiation of self depends on having an adequate knowledge of family systems concepts. She found that family members who are relatively cut off from the rest of the system provide more information than members comparatively "in" the system. Further, Hall found a marked similarity in the thought patterns of those "in" and "out" of the system (the definition of "in and "out" naturally comes from the position of the person doing the work; from a wider viewpoint, the ins and outs are reciprocal or complementary parts of the same system).

DiCarlo, describing his extended family work, focuses on two trips he took to Italy, one with his nuclear family and one with his mother. The purpose of the first trip to Italy was to gather information about his extended family. DiCarlo acknowledges that he also was seeking to reestablish ties between his mother and her two living sisters. The role of bridge builder was one he consciously took on, between siblings and their mother and between his mother and her siblings.

During the first trip to Italy, DiCarlo confirmed many emotional patterns. He found that the issues were no longer "black and white," and people were not divided into firm categories of good and bad, as they were in his mother's perceptions, partly formed by forty-six years of absence and one-sided and second-hand reports.

DiCarlo came to several conclusions based on his work: (1) his father distanced self from his family in migrating (that crystallized the process); (2) his mother distanced from her family when she left Italy to come to the United States, and (3) the author's role as bridge-builder emerged in relation to emotional distancing and feelings of guilt from not being able to meet his mother's expectations.

Maloni's chapter, "At Least Three Generations of Male Distancing," focuses on the phenomenon of emotional distancing and cut-off. He describes a dramatic phase of his work, which involved a trip to Italy with his father.

Maloni describes three generations of a closeness–distance problem. Paternal grandfather, father, and the author himself, physically or emotionally, were emotional distancers. Central to this process was the early death of fathers. The paternal grandfather migrated to the United States at the age of twenty, in order to provide better support for his mother and sister. About five years later he returned and married Maloni's grandmother, for which act he was disowned by the paternal great-grandmother; he had no contact with her for the remaining sixteen years of his life. The cut-off was still active sixty years later when Maloni's father attempted to contact, in Italy, a female cousin on the paternal side of the family.

One of the interesting points concerning intergenerational maturation was that Maloni's father developed an interest in reconnecting with his family in Italy after retiring, and this coincided with Maloni's rise in interest in his extended family triggered by a crisis in his nuclear family. Reconnecting with his own background on the part of his father, through his first visit to Italy (almost sixty years after emigrating), and reconnecting with his extended family background helped Maloni in his efforts to connect with his father. It is important to note, however, that three years of systematic work with his extended family (via formal coaching) preceded this trip to Italy.

Illness and Death

In the final section, the chapters are clustered around the themes of "Illness and Death." The chapters are Susan Graefe's "No Sympathy: A Response to a Physical Disability," Lorraine David's "The Use of Terminal Candor," John Haverlick's "A Son's Journey: Reflections After My Father's Death" and this author's "Reaction to Death in a Family." David and Haverlick deal with death before it happens, in order to negate or diminish the "emotional shock wave phenomenon." David, Haverlick, and Graefe bring out the value of using extended family as a support network. The latter two, and this author, all deal with the process whereby a "projected one" becomes one who focuses on others, going from "cared-for" to "caregiver." The inherent problem for the therapist in becoming a caregiver is overcoming the dysfunctional aspect whereby this role acts as a means of avoiding and managing anxiety that belongs to self, and self in relation to the therapist's own family. Another theme that emerges from this cluster of chapters is that severe illness and death represent maximal opportunities for working on differentiation of self.

Graefe's chapter, "No Sympathy: A Response to a Physical Disability" deals with the experience of having polio and the way in which her family handled that issue. Graefe writes about the programming in her family that brought about the shift from being a "receiver of care" to being a "caregiver," in the form of being a family therapist. She considers a major issue of being a therapist: the balance of doing for self versus doing for others. In her reaction to polio she was programmed to be so stoic and strong that she developed as an overresponsible child in relation to family, this pattern then continuing in her marital and nuclear family relationships. She also played that role in her development as a social worker. Graefe came to understand that she had become an overfunctioner to compensate for having polio. Her effort was to allow herself to be taken care of, instead of having to overfunction, be overresponsible, and overdoing.

Graefe took the risk of sharing with her parents and several friends and colleagues a videotape of a consultation with Bowen about the work she had been doing with her extended family during the previous ten years. She describes the potential dangers of this type of sharing. Family members, friends, and colleagues are often negatively reactive to the spoken and written perceptions of family events and interactions, becoming " . . . fused with any emotions expressed and thus be unable to view the material objectively. This can lead to overidentification with the writer and lack of separateness." However, Graefe's experience in sharing both the tape and the writing has been very positive. With her parents, it provided a new level of understanding, and it opened conversation about topics they had previously been unable to address.

In reflecting upon her experience in her family and choice of profession she found that her inclination to overfunction must not be allowed to deter her clients from reaching their maximum levels of functioning. On the other hand, Graefe believes that personal awareness of the potential of emotional shock wave patterns can, indeed, be helpful in encouraging clients to be more open and communicative at the time of loss or serious stress and to avoid harmful denial.

David's goal, as detailed in "The Use of Terminal Candor," was to deal openly with her impending death, from leukemia, in order not to be cut off from family and friends. David became determined to change position in her family, making an effort to modify being overly responsible, so that her death would not set off what Bowen has described as the "emotional shock wave" phenomenon. Moreover, David wanted to change family patterns of avoiding unpleasant topics, so that she could be more comfortable and less vulnerable during this stressful period.

When David went into remission, she began a schedule of visiting her parents and extended family members on a one-to-one basis. She engaged in a life-review with each of her parents. She worked to change her position of being the overfunctioning caretaker and protector, by asking her parents to come and be with her when she went to the hospital, even though they were elderly and her mother was prone to depression.

In relation to her children, David began to turn over more responsibility to her husband; this enabled her to stop overfunctioning and to allow the children to help her, instead of vice versa.

A fuller emotional sharing with her parents came about by sharing her work, articles, courses, and a taped interview that her son had done with her for a school class.

The following are some of the principles that emerged for David from her extended family work: (1) often it is more productive to start from the periphery; (2) one may reduce the level of anxiety by developing an open relationship network at the "outer edges" of the system, and (3) one becomes less reactive when one has access to information. David describes how working on open communication about her leukemia and impending death was beneficial for herself and her family. David wrote her paper in 1977. She died in the spring of 1978.

Haverlick, in his chapter "A Son's Journey: Reflection After My Father's Death" delineates a central nodal event in the life of his family, the death of his father from cancer. He describes a pattern common to many of the contributors—an effort to modify his position in the basic triangle, in which his position was closer to his mother and more distant from, and at times conflictual with, his father. The terminal illness of his father provided Haverlick a special opportunity to work on getting closer to his father. He sought to know his father better before he died, with the goal that this work would minimize emotional shock waves that might emerge from his father's death.

Haverlick addresses how reconnecting prior to a major loss can aid in minimizing the emotional after shocks following an important death in the family.

In addressing the phenomenon of emotional shock waves, Haverlick speaks of lack of openness and the degree of emotional dependence denied by the family as being two major factors that will influence future after shocks in the family. He hypothesizes that there will be more symptomatology following a death when there is less viable contact with the extended family. Haverlick describes increasing his support network after developing a more personal relationship with his father. The latter led to greater contact with his paternal extended family. The ramifications for Haverlick of undertaking the family of origin work included being able to be closer to his son and lessening of the emotional shock wave phenomenon in his family, at least until now.

In "Reaction to Death in a Family," this author describes how a focal point of the emotional family system involved a multigenerational projection process related to the issue of unresolved anxiety regarding the alleged suicide of his maternal grandfather and the depression of his father. This chapter describes an effort to modify the position in the basic triangle in which he found himself close to his mother, with his father in the outside position. He discovered that uncovering nodal events can help provide the key to understanding the multigenerational projection process.

Titelman posits the death of a key family member as being the most significant nodal event in a family system. Such a death represents a maximum opportunity to define self in one's family, by defining and taking I-positions. Titelman was the projected-upon one and the mediator in his family of origin. His position in the family altered from being the one who was most cared for to being a "caretaker," a family therapist.

Titelman concludes that it is a three-generation-plus process whereby a family creates a therapist to "cure" its problems. His hope was that family of origin work help him *not* to fulfill that mission.

Rather, developing a clearer, more solid self in relation to his family is the goal.

REFERENCES

Bowen, M. (1967). Toward the differentiation of self in one's own family. In *Family Interaction: A Dialogue Between Family Researchers and Family Therapists,* ed. J. L. Framo, pp. 111–173. New York: Springer-Verlag, 1972.

Bowen, M. (1978a). Toward the differentiation of self in one's own family. In *Family Therapy in Clinical Practice* pp. 529–547. New York: Jason Aronson.

Bowen, M. (1978b). On the differentiation of self. In *Family Therapy in Clinical Practice* pp. 467–528. New York: Jason Aronson.

Bowen, M. (1978c). *Family Therapy in Clinical Practice.* New York: Jason Aronson.

Bowen, M. (1984). The therapist's family of origin. Workshop for Family Living Consultants of the Pioneer Valley, Northampton, Mass., March.

Carolin, J. (1977). A beginning note on some implications of Bowen Family Systems Theory for educational thought. In *Pittsburgh Family Systems Symposia (1979–1980): A Collection of Selected Papers,* ed. P. McCullough and J. Carolin, pp. 134–139. Pittsburgh: The Family Institute of Pittsburgh, Western Psychiatric Institute and Clinic, University of Pittsburgh.

Fogarty, T. (1979). The distancer and the pursuer. *The Family* 7:11–16.

Framo, J. L. (1979). A personal viewpoint on training in marital and family therapy. *Professional Psychology* 10:868–875.

Friedman, E. (1971). The birthday party: An experiment in obtaining change in one's own extended family. *Family Process* 10:345–359.

Haley, J. (1976). *Problem-Solving Therapy: New Strategies for Effective Family Therapy.* New York: Jossey-Bass.

Kerr, M. (1984). Theoretical base for differentiation of self in one's family of origin. In *Family of Origin Applications in Clinical Supervision,* ed. C. E. Munson, pp. 3–36. New York: The Haworth Press.

Kramer, J. R. (1985). *Family Interfaces: Transgenerational Patterns.* New York: Brunner/Mazel.

Meyer, P. (1976). Patterns and processes in working with one's family. Paper presented at the 13th Georgetown University Symposium on Family Psychotherapy, Oct.

Minuchin, S. (1981). *Family Therapy Techniques.* Cambridge: Harvard University Press.

Nerin, W. F. (1985). *Family Reconstruction: Long Day's Journey into Light.* New York: W. W. Norton.

Titelman, P. (1984). A family systems assessment profile: A schema based on Bowen theory. *The Family* 11:71–80.

APPENDIX A
SELECTED REFERENCES ON FAMILY SYSTEMS THEORY AND THERAPY

The Best of The Family, 1973–1978. New Rochelle, N.Y.: The Center for Family Learning.
The Best of The Family 1978–1983. Ed. E. Pendagast. New Rochelle, N.Y.: The Center for Family Learning.
Bowen, M. (1978). *Family Therapy in Clinical Practice.* New York: Jason Aronson.
Bradt, J. (1980). *The Family Diagram: Method, Technique and Use in Family Therapy.* Washington, D.C.: Groome Center.
Carter, E., and McGoldrick, M. (1976). Family therapy with one person and the family therapist's own family. In *Family Therapy: Theory and Practice,* ed. P. Guerin, pp. 193–213. New York: Gardner.
Carter, E., and McGoldrick, M. (Eds.). (1980). *The Family Life Cycle: A Framework for Family Therapy.* New York: Gardner.
The Family, vols. 1–14. (1983). New Rochelle, N.Y.: The Center for Family Learning; and Washington, D.C.: The Family Center, Georgetown University Medical Center, Department of Psychiatry.
Friedman, E. H. (1985). *Generation to Generation: Family Process in Church and Synagogue.* New York: Guilford.
Georgetown Family Symposia: Systems Therapy. (1971). Ed. J. Bradt and C. Moynihan. Washington, D.C.: Georgetown University Family Center.
Georgetown Family Symposia, Vol. I (1971–1972). (1974). Ed. F. Andres and J. Lorio. Washington, D.C.: Dept. of Psychiatry, Georgetown University Medical Center.
Georgetown Family Symposia, Vol. II (1973–1974). (1977). Ed. J. Lorio and L. McClenathan. Washington, D.C.: Georgetown University Family Center.
Georgetown Family Symposia, Vol. III (1975–1976). (1978). Ed. R. Sagar. Washington, D.C.: Georgetown University Family Center.
Guerin, P. (Ed.). (1976). *Family Therapy: Theory and Practice.* New York: Gardner.
Guerin, P., Fay, L. F., Burden, S., and Kauggo, J. (1987). *Evaluation and Treatment of Marital Conflict.* New York: Basic.
Kerr, M. (1981). Family systems theory and therapy. In *Handbook of*

Family Therapy, ed. A. Gurman and D. Kniskern, pp. 226–264. New York: Brunner/Mazel.

Kerr, M. (1984). Theoretical base for differentiation of self in one's family of origin. In *Family of Origin Applications in Clinical Supervision*, ed. C. Munson, pp. 3–36. New York: The Haworth Press.

Kerr, M. (1985). Obstacles to differentiation of self. In *Casebook of Marital Therapy*, ed. A. Gurman, pp. 111–153. New York: The Guilford Press.

McGoldrick, M., and Gerson, R. (1985). *Genograms in Family Assessment*. New York: W. W. Norton.

Pittsburgh Family Systems Symposium (1977): A Collection of Selected Papers. Ed. P. McCullough, J. Carolin, and S. K. Rutenberg. Pittsburgh: The Family Institute of Pittsburgh, Western Psychiatric Institute and Clinic, University of Pittsburgh.

Second Pittsburgh Family Systems Symposium (1978): A Collection of Selected Papers. Ed. P. McCullough, J. Carolin, S. K. Rutenberg, and P. Titelman. Pittsburgh: The Family Institute of Pittsburgh, Western Psychiatric Institute and Clinic, University of Pittsburgh.

Pittsburgh Family Systems Symposia (1979–1980): A Collection of Selected Papers. Ed. P. McCullough and J. Carolin. *Pittsburgh: Western Psychiatric Institute and Clinic*.

Toman, W. (1969). *Family Constellation: Its Effects on Personality and Social Behavior*, 2nd ed. New York: Springer-Verlag.

APPENDIX B
SELECTED PAPERS ON THE FAMILY THERAPIST'S OWN FAMILY

Anonymous. (1973). A family therapist's own family. In *Georgetown Family Symposia, Vol. II (1973–1974)*, ed. J. Lorio and L. McClenathan, pp. 19–27. Washington, D.C.: Georgetown University Family Center.

Anonymous. (1979). The management of loss in the therapist's own family. In *The Best of The Family, 1973–1978*, ed. E. Pendagast, pp. 249–254. New Rochelle, N.Y.: Center for Family Learning.

Anonymous. (1984). In search of family. In *The Best of The Family, 1978–1983*, ed. E. Pendagast, pp. 269–273. New Rochelle, N.Y.: The Center for Family Learning.

Anonymous. (1984). My trip into separateness and connectedness. In *The Best of The Family, 1978–1983,* ed. E. Pendagast, pp. 274–278. New Rochelle, N.Y.: The Center for Family Learning.

Bowen, M. (1978). One the differentiation of self. In *Family Therapy in Clinical Practice,* ed. M. Bowen, pp. 467–528. New York: Jason Aronson, Inc.

Colon, F. (1973). In search of one's past: An identity trip. *Family Process* 12:429–438.

Erickson, W. (1979). Reconnecting: A therapist's own family. In *The Best of The Family, 1973–1978,* ed. E. Pendagast, pp. 206–208. New Rochelle, N.Y.: The Center for Family Learning.

Feikema, R. (1978). Birth: The addition of a new generation and its impact on a family system. In *Second Pittsburgh Family Systems Symposium (1978): A Collection of Selected Papers,* ed. P. McCullough et al., pp. 101–115. Pittsburgh: The Family Institute of Pittsburgh, Western Psychiatric Institute and Clinic, University of Pittsburgh.

Guerin, P., and Fogarty, T. (1972). The family therapist's own family. In *The Book of Family Therapy,* ed. A. Ferber, M. Mendelsohn, and A. Napier, pp. 445–457. New York: Jason Aronson.

Kuhn, J. (1977). Interlocking triangles: Church-family issues. In *Georgetown Family Symposia, Vol. II (1973–1974): A Collection of Selected Papers,* ed. J. Lorio and L. McClenathan, pp. 175–181. Washington, D.C.: Georgetown University Family Center.

Lampiris, B. (1978). Cut-offs and illness. In *Second Pittsburgh Family Systems Symposium (1978): A Collection of Selected Papers,* ed. P. McCullough, J. Carolin, S. K. Rutenberg, and P. Titelman, pp. 151–165. Pittsburgh: The Family Institute of Pittsburgh, Western Psychiatric Institute and Clinic, University of Pittsburgh.

Maloni, J. C. (1980). Adopted by the spouses: The burial of a biological family. In *Third Pittsburgh Family Systems Symposium (1979–1980): A Collection of Selected Papers,* ed. P. McCullough et al., pp. 150–157. Pittsburgh: The Family Institute of Pittsburgh, Western Psychiatric Institute and Clinic, University of Pittsburgh.

Paddack, C. (1974). The resurrection of the dead: A way of working on relationships in the extended family. In *Georgetown Family Symposia, Vol. I (1971–1972),* ed. F. Andres and J. Lorio, pp. 127–135. Washington, D.C.: Department of Psychiatry, Georgetown University Medical Center.

Rutenberg, S. (1977). On the loss of innocence: The search for my history. In *1977 Pittsburgh Family Systems Symposium: A Collection of Selected Papers,* ed. P. McCullough, J. Carolin, and S. Rutenberg, pp. 130–133. Pittsburgh: The Family Institute of Pittsburgh, Western Psychiatric Institute and Clinic, University of Pittsburgh.

Rutenberg, S. (1978). Impasse and repercussions after three years of extended family work. In *Pittsburgh Family Systems Symposia (1979–1980): A Collection of Selected Papers*, ed. P. McCullough and J. Carolin, pp. 105–111. Pittsburgh: The Family Institute of Pittsburgh, Western Psychiatric Institute and Clinic, University of Pittsburgh.

Salin, L. (1984). Breaking a hundred-year barrier. In *The Best of The Family, 1978–1983*, ed. E. Pendagast, pp. 279–286. New Rochelle, N.Y.: The Center for Family Learning.

Chapter 2

PATTERNS AND PROCESSES IN A THERAPIST'S OWN FAMILY WORK: KNOWLEDGE REQUIRED FOR EXCELLENCE

Patricia Hanes Meyer, L.C.S.W.

It is not possible for me to write a chapter concerning differentiation in the human species without first acknowledging the contribution made by Murray Bowen, M.D. for his discovery and description of this significant foundation of human functioning. What follows reflects the years of effort that have gone into attempting to understand Bowen family systems theory.

Although laws are now in effect in many states to define ethical behavior for the various disciplines in the mental health field, the focus in this chapter concerning ethical professionalism will be quite different.

There is no way for two human beings to relate to each other outside the context of subjectivity. How much subjectivity is present, will, indeed, vary depending on the maturity of the two individuals as well as chronic and acute anxiety present in the two lives; but however high or low in intensity, subjectivity will be present. It is for this reason that in this chapter, building knowledge about one's own extended family system and about self—so as to know as much as possible about the nature of one's own subjectivity—is seen as an issue of personal and professional ethics rather than an issue of preference in theoretical orientation. Regardless of the theoretical approach upon which a therapist bases clinical practice, subjectivity will be present to interfere with the therapeutic process unless the therapist has come to know his or her own subjectivity so well that it can be kept *out* of the individual's work.

Making a serious, broad study of extended family and its emotionality is, in fact, an act of respect for the automatic processes of transference and countertransference. There is no other means to assure self of

43

minimizing reactivity to the other than through understanding, as much as possible, the emotional family system, its impact on self, and the impact of self upon it. Only then can a therapist have the fullest sense of *who* he is and *what* his own extended emotional history has been, separate from the individual or family sitting in his office. Certainly analysis can help accomplish some degree of this learning, but outside of a vigorous study of the family system as well as the emotional system of self, it is not possible to understand thoroughly the context of self. Before discussion of defining of self and increasing responsibility of a therapist, we shall consider differentiation.

The experience of emerging out of one's own family is different from developing factual knowledge that provides an objective means to understand one's own family. In the theory developed by Bowen, such knowledge requires not only time devoted to remembered history and experiences but also a rigorous study of historical fact, including a serious effort to develop into a significant member of one's own family (Bowen 1978).

Differentiation, the cornerstone of Bowen's theory, describes the basis for all human behavior. It is a concept that describes the two pulls under which all individuals live, that of togetherness–sameness–belonging on the one hand and individuation–separateness–principle on the other. It does not separate "health" in one individual from "pathology" in another, but rather it attests to the common nature of man in living amidst these two powerful pulls. What separates one individual from another is the nature of balance of these two forces.

For the individual whose togetherness pulls outweigh those for individuation, life will prove difficult. This is so, because every dilemma and decision will be impacted by the automatic pull to seek approval and avoid disapproval from important others. Hence, the simplest task can become a strenuous effort to please, and the outcome unlikely to achieve it. Such an exquisite sensitivity to another's emotionality is complicated by the likelihood that in significant others with whom one surrounds oneself resides the same automatic pull for approval. In general, individuals seek out others whose emotionality is of a similar nature, geared to feelings and approval or to the self, its goals and principles.

For the individual whose pulls to be self outweigh those of belonging, the task of life, while no less complicated, will be less arduous. This is so because such an individual will "feel" the emotionality of important others while remaining focused on the objective facts, dilemmas, alternatives, and likely consequences of his/her actions. Approval would be pleasant, but, if the project or task at hand is to be completed with excellence, then the process of focus on objectivity will continue. Hence, the individual can stay on a factual course, with heightened reactivity and anxiety ever present unless the emotionality reaches such a pitch that its impact cannot be countered. Even then, the individual who focuses on fact rather than feeling as a guide has an advantage in that recovery from the feeling orientation will, in most cases, come when there is time to sort out factually what has occurred.

Many factors influence base-level differentiation—the level of balance between feeling and thought in any given individual. None is more powerful than the balance of the two in the individual's parents, for their level of maturity forms much of the fabric within which the individual's functional characteristics have developed. Another factor, specialness in the family, would have to be considered: has an individual emerged into a special position in the family, thereby receiving more than a predictable amount of the family's emotionality, either positive or negative (Bradt and Moynihan 1971)?

Nodal events and the frequently acute emotionality that is attached to them represent another (e.g., premature or at-risk birth, gender that carries added specialness for the family system, personal appearance similar to a significant family member). Certainly, genetic inheritance must be included, although it remains difficult as yet to know how much and in what ways it has an influence.

Because knowledge of differentiation in the human is critical to understanding behavior, excellence in therapy requires some degree of mastery of its conceptual principles. Once differentiation is reasonably well understood on an abstract level, building knowledge of it on an extended family level and within self becomes possible. It is then that there is the opportunity to minimize transference and countertransference and, thus, to permit the individual or family unit to proceed with the compelling task of discovering emotionality within self and within its extended system, rather than between the self and the nonrelated therapist. Only then can an individual know his or her own immaturity factually; without this, becoming more responsible for self and to other is not possible. The question, whether a therapist must undertake the difficult task of discovering the nature of human functioning, extended family functioning, and the functioning of self as a framework from which to increase the base level of functioning and responsibility actually does not bear discussion: the decision to enter the mental health field—specifically psychotherapy—compels the work and effort required.

This is not to say that once differentiation is known and has become a beacon in one's life, an excellent therapist has come to exist. Indeed, there is a body of knowledge concerning skill in every aspect of the therapy process that must be known, as well, if there is to be mastery in therapy (just as flying skill is as necessary to the pilot as is knowledge of aeronautics). Without the neutrality of maturity and understanding of human emotionality, technique stands by itself, a specific response to a specific dilemma. Without knowledge of the process of change that occurs throughout the course of therapy, there would be severe limitations on the amount of change that might come, beyond lowered anxiety, increased calmness, and increased capacity to think.

Mastery and excellence in the functioning of a therapist require a balance in the individual's knowledge of human functioning, functioning of self, and the therapeutic process. Establishing this balance requires vigorous, hard work at a time when immaturity is pulling one to get on with the "doing" and leave the "understanding" for later. This is so, in part, because in learning family systems theory the individual must begin to discover the nature and intensity of subjectivity within self in order to have the capacity to "see" it in the emotional systems in which he lives. Yet, without this knowledge of theory of human functioning, a therapist will remain limited in his or her ability to provide for another a process for change of self.

Like all concepts studied and learned by individuals, becoming a self in one's own family as a means to increase maturity and, thus, the capacity for excellence in therapy, has been misunderstood in a myriad of ways. Some individuals have thought the concept to mean genealogy, and have gathered enough facts to paper the walls of the courthouses in which they have gathered data. Yet, the focus may not have included as well the living family, those persons alive, and issues that remain potent for the extended system. On the other hand, there are those who consider work with family to mean social contact through events, reunions, and the like; little focus is placed on extended historical facts, nor on the difficult task of discovering and countering family process that promotes immaturity in the system and in self. Actually, work on self requires a good balance between gathering the facts of family history and a carefully built effort to know living family, with its past and current emotional issues, and to establish—issue-by-issue, person-by-person—a carefully defined position for self with respect to the issues and within the relationships that reflect the most responsible functioning of which that self is capable.

THE HUMAN EMOTIONAL SYSTEM

Understanding the human emotional system is necessary if an individual is to understand accurately one's own. Knowing as fully as possible the nature of human functioning provides a context for knowing the functioning of self. Such clarity acts, then, as a framework from which a therapist can know *what* he thinks about occurrences in the human system with whom he works, *how* the events can be understood, and *what* actions will yield what general outcomes.

The Distribution of Responsibility

Intergenerational connectedness can be seen in the distribution of responsibility between generations (Meyer 1980). Such distribution lies almost entirely with the parental generation when progeny are young. Although infants have the capability of signaling distress (being hungry, wet, tired, frightened) through infant cry, beyond this action there is dependency upon the parental generation to respond by meeting the requirements and wants of the moment. As the infant grows and develops new strength, ability, and understanding, there comes into being a capacity to master aspects of his or her own functioning. In a family unit that is functioning adequately, the parental unit will, in time, decrease functioning *for* the other as the other becomes capable of assuming new areas of responsibility for self. This transfer of responsibility is not always smooth, because parents may be unaware of new abilities to explore the world in their young. Like the infant, older children, too, have ways to signal their discomfort, and in time an adequately functioning parental unit will again decrease its responsibility in balance with the new mastery of the other.

Adolescence is the developmental time to begin preparation toward a significant decrease in dependency and the literal preparation to be responsible for all arenas of one's own life.

As an adolescent gains success in moving towards responsibility for self, his or her very success may trigger crises for the parenting unit, who may have handled their own emotional dependency through distancing mechanisms and, in particular, focus on parenting. The more significant the parenting process is to the emotional stability and well-being of the parent, the more reactivity can be expected when an adolescent moves away from dependency and towards self—the parent is left with a void.

Depending upon the level of maturity of the parent, several responses to experiencing an emotional void are possible. If the parent cannot decrease the personal distress, and anxiety remains high, the adolescent sits with a dilemma. If there is continued movement toward self-functioning, there will be an anxious mother with whom to reckon. If the adolescent sustains the effort but cannot master the dependency, conflict may become chronic between mother and child. If the adolescent cannot tolerate the anxious state of the mother and gives up the push for independence, the mother will become calmer and the adolescent will have given up a more mature level of self, perhaps forever. The fact is, no human is sufficiently mature to assume entirely the responsibility for his or her own life and sense of well-being. Rather, each older adolescent or young adult enters adulthood with some degree of unresolved attachment to the parenting generation, financially, functionally, or emotionally. This unresolved attachment will be reflected in the individual's life choices, nature of relationships, and symptoms that develop during his or her lifetime. Manifestations of the unresolved immaturity can be seen in every arena of life. Figure 2–1, showing the distribution of responsibility, follows.

One aspect of knowledge that must be understood is the nature of interconnectedness between and among our generations of families. Although the interconnectedness includes many levels, three will be

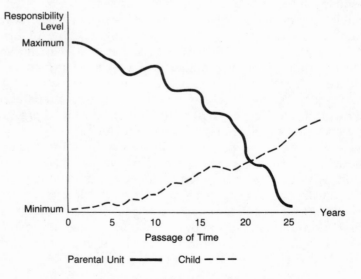

Figure 2–1. Distribution of responsibility.

discussed in this chapter: emotional, financial, and functional. At different periods in a family's life course, there may be connectedness in all three categories, in only two, or in simply one.

Emotional Interconnectedness

Emotional interconnectedness may be the most powerful force in families. Unlike the others, it is continually active, whether observable or not, within each generation, and with the generations that have preceded and those that follow. It has to do with the manner in which generations *act and react* to each other as inividuals pursue their life course. It is affected by the broad, extended system and impacting upon it at the same time. The interconnectedness can be seen, for instance, in the number of individuals whose lives reflect a likeness or oppositeness to the parental unit. In the broader picture, a family pattern can often be seen flip-flopping over and over in the system. For example, a parent in one generation may be overstrict and raise a child who, upon becoming a parent, is overpermissive with children. In the next generation there may be a child who, like the grandparent, is overly strict upon becoming a parent. This process of just-like versus opposite-to can be seen in every arena of human functioning (e.g., in the decision-making process of where one chooses to live, choice of work, choice of life style, involvement or lack thereof in politics, religion, choice in reproduction). The severity of the process is governed by the general level of maturity of the extended system and the individuals within it: the greater the level of maturity, the fewer the extreme choices to be seen. An individual will be neither just like nor opposite to important others. Rather, individuals within the system will chart their own course with some degree of freedom from *reacting* to the generations above. Indeed, every life decision is not connected to family of origin. However, life decisions in emotional arenas may predictably evoke the emotional themes that a family of origin has had about the issue. The more intensity that a family experienced about an issue (e.g., focus on money for a wealthy family who lost everything in the Depression), the greater will be the likelihood of influence on the individual from that historical crisis and the reactivity associated with it.

Financial Interconnectedness

Parent generations provide financial support for their children. Once those children become adolescents, variations occur in the manner in which the generations remain financially connected. Some adolescents split off from the parent generation, ending financial support forever. In such families, functional interconnectedness and active emotional contact will often end just as abruptly.

In other families, parents continue financial support for several years, while their young attempt to find a life direction. In yet other families, financial support continues to permit the pursuit of education or to provide seed money through a loan, for the purchase of a home or the starting of a new business. There are families in which the financial bond never ends. Parents may provide the financial base for the young adult's life style (of which they may not approve), or simply fund certain items for the other's life: insurance, child-birth costs, vacations, automobiles, and so forth. Parents may have to resupport their adult child at crisis points over many years, such as at the time of divorce. In such families, functional interconnectedness may continue indefinitely and active emotional contact can be expected to continue.

Financial interconnectedness also may be seen between adult children and aging parents. The onset of debilitation from aging in the parental generation may reactivate financial connectedness, now in the opposite direction as illness and physical care require outlays of money that aging parents may not have. It is now the younger generation that is the financial provider for the older generation.

Financial connectedness between generations may end abruptly and never reactivate; may continue in an informal, undefined way; continue in a formal, defined way; or never end at all. A family system in which there is individuation among its members will respond to other generations when there is a reality to which an individual can contribute. A family in which there is less maturity may respond on the basis that the other expects it or, without the contribution, would not survive at all.

Functional Interconnectedness

Functional interconnectedness for a parenting generation concerns all aspects of the life of the young. Once children are in the later years of childhood and enter adolescence, more and more of the responsibility for self can be absorbed by the younger generation. In late adolescence, functional connectedness may end abruptly and never reactivate as a result of a cut-off. Functional support may be provided into postadolescent years as the young adult attempts to start his or her own life course. It may be provided in response to events in the family, for example, when grandparents respond to the birth of a new family member by temporarily running the household for the young parents.

In evaluating the nature of connectedness between generations, the critical criteria will center on whether the response of one generation to another is due to dependency in another generation or to factual events that have impact upon individuals who maintain their own life responsibilities. Failure to understand interconnectedness of self and others would make it virtually impossible to sidestep the emotionality and reactivity that may be present in every therapy hour. It is not sufficient to know one's own emotionality. Instead, having the broadest framework of knowledge about human functioning *and* one's own extended family's functioning is required to keep subjectivity at a minimum, and thoughtfulness at a maximum, in therapy.

THE TASK OF A THERAPIST: BECOMING A SELF IN ONE'S OWN FAMILY

The therapist who begins a study of his or her own family may encounter several obstacles early on in the effort (Meyer 1976). There is often a significant lack of knowledge about the family. Further, one side of the family line, the maternal or paternal, may have been known while the other side remained unknown. History of the extended system may have have been known through numerous emotional myths regarding family members and the family history. There is often a lack of knowledge and/or understanding of the impact of events upon the larger system, and also of the connectedness that may exist between events and their emotional aftermath. At the same time, appreciation may be lacking for the degree to which the family emotional system may impact on an individual's functional characteristics, and of the impact of *those* characteristics on the larger emotional system.

There are two distinct categories of work which must be completed if self is to develop broad knowledge about one's own emotional fabric, out of which functional patterns have emerged. First, there is the gathering of factual data and second, the formation of person-to-person relationships made possible by knowing and resolving emotional issues and polarizations. Data that need to be gathered are both historical and emotional in nature.

Historical data are the type of material found in any genealogical search, the persons, places, dates, and circumstances of every family — the statistical and demographic facts. Focusing far wider, however, the evaluation also scans all the arenas of life–longevity, health history, work history, and nature, severity, and duration of life problems. The purely demographic facts can be obtained, on many levels, from cemetery, city and county, state, and national (military, census, immigration) records, which are stored at the National Archives and the Library of Congress Annex. There is often also history recorded and passed down from one generation to another—a fact often unknown to some in the family. Not infrequently, one hears someone proclaim early in therapy that no written or organized history exists, only later to discover historical records, ranging from a few typed sheets to printed volumes. This search also often leads to the discovery of living family members previously unknown. There is a tendency among those pursuing genealogical data as part of an effort to establish greater emotional solidness to underestimate the emotional impact and significance of discovering straight facts about one's historical origin.

Data on the emotional system of an extended family differ from demographic or genealogical data in several significant ways. There is the ever present obstacle of subjectivity, in self and in others, which acts as a barrier to hearing accurately and being neutral toward material that is being presented by another human who, too, is influenced by subjectivity.

Characteristics that are important to ascertain in assessing the emotional history of a family would include general functioning: achievements, the existence of major emotional problems, health, job history, relationships. All patterns and processes from generation to generation would be sought, with a look at the broad picture of facts rather than at an imbalance, a major achievement in work in the midst of personal turmoil and problems. First, however, the individual has to know his or her own subjectivity to be able to make accurate observations about emotional material and then, from a more neutral position, build person-to-person relationships with important others.

There are at least three different avenues for gaining knowledge about the emotionality of extended family and building significant relationships: making personal contact-for-contact with important others, utilizing the impact of nodal events, and issue dealing.

Contact-for-Contact

Perhaps the least understood process for many, the failure to establish contact-for-contact with a family member or section of a family system may account for a significant quantity of those efforts that fail. This is the case, because making contact and simply becoming knowledgeable about the facts in the lives of family members may provide the start of a relationship that becomes personal in nature and thus be a foundation upon which learning and dealing with emotional issues becomes possible. In fact, it is not uncommon for emotional issues to be brought forth naturally by the other once a personal relationship has developed. Discussion of highly charged emotional material between two connected family members is quite different from the presentation of emotional material between two members who have never previously spoken about anything personal.

Many who begin an effort to become a self in family of origin do so after years of minimal interest in family, or even demonstrated disinterest. To launch into contact with family from a distant position in one's system about emotional issues for which there is significant emotionality, without first establishing contact that reflects an interest in the other human life, can stimulate a spectrum of reactivity in the other—none of which will yield the goal that was sought in the first place.

Contact-for-contact occurs during those times when planned communication (through letters, telephone calls, or visits) occurs without any attempt to deal with emotionally charged issues. Rather, the focus would be on the day-to-day facts in the other's life and upon an accurate reflection of one's own life facts. It is a process of getting to know and observing the other while avoiding the urge to seek approval for self or to avoid disapproval from the other. Contact-for-contact is crucial for the development of person-to-person relationships, as well as for the eventual discussion of emotionally charged issues.

Response to Nodal Events

Response to nodal events concerns the manner and quality of participation of an individual in the "major events" of his family. These events are part of the knowledge that is necessary in understanding one's system, that which is emotionally important to it. Such knowledge provides information about the system itself and is a reflection of the functional characteristics of the emotional system. Further, knowing which events are meaningful can act as a criterion for deciding what future events merit the effort of attending.

What makes nodal events significant is their impact, the increase of emotionality, anxiety, and reactivity within the individual and within the emotional system. A system that has increased anxiety will tend to be more open, family members more available for communication, and family history (past and present) more likely to be discussed. Members will be more likely to say what they think about the family and its history or, if responding with reaction to the event, more likely to function in an extreme manner.

There are several life events that are critical for all emotional systems, the most significant for most families being death of a family member. The more important the deceased member (i.e., either as a contributing leader or as a symptomatic focus), the greater the impact on the system. For instance, the best time to observe the birth order characteristics of a set of siblings is at the time of death of their parents (Toman 1969). Those siblings whose functional characteristics are like those of an eldest child (decisive, leader) will be those who are attending to arrangements and the multitude of tasks (related to the dying and death as well as the funeral structure). Siblings whose functional characteristics are like those of a youngest child (indecisive, follower) will be those who are *not* part of the decision-making team.

Surrounding nodal events or any significant change in a system one finds the human reaction to change. When life facts of a system change (through death, birth, change in job, change in location, etc.), there is enhanced anxiety about how, if at all, there will be a difference in the individual or in the system as a result.

The realignment in a system of the triangles and surrounding functional positions within the system following a death of one of its members is an example of the impact of change (Kuhn 1978). (Triangulation represents substitution of a cause, dogma, or relationship for an important other as a way to restabilize one's own emotion). This is not unlike the impact of a politician's unexpectedly announcing a decision to retire from office or not to run again. In the wake of the announcement, there often follows an intense time of anxious realignment, as potential new candidates and senior staff scurry to define the stronger position within their political party. In a family, the focus is not one of seeking votes. Rather, there is internal anxiety, within the individual, about significant relationships being different or about the lessening of his or her functional position within the system as a result of the change.

For the individual, family nodal events provide the opportunity to contribute to the system at an important time in its life. Such contributions occur on many levels. The fact of choosing to participate in an event or crisis defines to the system that the individual has a commitment to the larger system, something he has demonstrated through his actions. Knowing that a cousin, aunt, uncle, or other family member considers an event in one's nuclear family to be important enough for participation communicates commitment and can act to energize the system. The opposite outcome is true as well: if a system does not respond to an event (whether in total failure to make contact or in contact that is merely obligatory in nature), those who are directly associated with the event stand before the readjustment and realignment in the system in isolation from the broader emotional system. The impact of isolation can include a loss of energy, emotional paralysis, and heightened reactivity and anxiety thereafter.

Any time a family member communicates where he or she stands on any aspect of human life, the family system will be slightly calmer (following the initial reaction, which may be acute). If the position is one that defines contribution ("I will arrive by Tuesday evening and am prepared to help out in any way from then until Friday evening"), the impact towards calmness will increase; it is as if an emotional burden is held by many shoulders. Those involved stand to develop new potentials to develop person-to-person relationships and to be clearer about *who* self is in the large, extended emotional system and within self.

Issue Dealing

Issue dealing is a process by which an "issue—a family happening, family story, family secret—is brought into focus for the member or members of the family for whom it has emotional meaning. Ideally, issue dealing is meant to "open closed doors" in a family system, whether in a cut-off or simply a nondeveloping relationship. Issue dealing can be necessary in a closed system that resists all efforts of connection. At worst, ideal issue dealing can be an irresponsible "dropping of a bomb," the disclosure of an issue in a volatile way. Individuals who function in their family through exposure of highly charged issues yield little progress in building a position for self in family and, in fact, may permanently limit their effort. Rather than gaining respect in a family for being a significant contributor to the capacity of the system to cope with adversity (i.e., calm leadership) or to increasing its ability to be flexible and constructive (i.e., contributing through a successful event in the system), individuals who expose "issues" in irresponsible ways are frequently kept at a distance by the family thereafter. It is not possible to burst one's way into any relationship or system without the occurrence of substantial problems, perhaps total failure.

Vehicles in Family Work

There are numerous vehicles that can be utilized in family work to enable an individual to focus on family issues, make contact with family, and take advantage of family nodal events and their impact. Critical in any choice of action is that the base of decision be the theoretical foundation one has built about own family. What is it in the family's function or dysfunction that is being addressed? If it is possible to know what family process or pattern is being addressed, determination of an appropriate action is relatively easy. (For instance, in the case of a pattern of cut-off, the objective would be to establish contact). Determining *how* to act counter to the family's emotionality and the emotionality in self is quite another matter. It requires knowledge about the family and, particularly, about self; one's own reactivity level in taking a difficult action, one's own reactivity to having an action *reacted to* by important others, and knowing what actions self can carry through effectively. The process of evaluation runs: *Is* there a family process that is leading to immaturity and/or dysfunction (theory)? *Have* I acted in a responsible, defined way in regard to the family process? If not, *how* should I now act in order to do so (technique)? Therein is the balance of knowledge required for success in changing an individual's position within his emotional fields.

In a world in which families are spread far and wide, making contact of any nature is no easy or inexpensive thing. The avenues for contact include telephone calls, written correspondence, planned visits, and unplanned visits or actions. Each of these provides advantages and disadvantages in family work. Determination of which avenue to use would be based upon the theoretical knowledge one has of one's system, as well as from knowledge about events in the family that have emotional importance. More important than the nature of the response is the response itself. To be a contributor in one's family, it is necessary to leave one's mark of contribution on any family event, whether by an action of acknowledgment of an occurrence or through an action of doing or giving. Not to respond is a failure for self and to the family. Failure to respond to an event in the family may represent a major setback, because there will be reactivity in those family members for whom the event held importance. Therefore, when the individual makes the next contact with the involved family members, there may well be some degree of reactive distance that will once again have to be overcome to move forward again in defining self to the system and in developing solid relationships. This is not to say that any individual could attend *all* events in the family, even those occurring in his or her area of residence. It is to say that a *response* of some nature is critical, whether it be a telephone call, letter, or sending of food, flowers, or such. If it is important to self to be a significant contributor to the functioning of one's family system, it is mandatory to respond in a meaningful way to important developments.

Probably the easiest, yet perhaps, trickiest, vehicle for sustaining contact within family is the telephone. Easiest because it takes little effort and can be done quickly, trickiest because the individual calling can quickly become "caught" in the tone of voice, or other cues of emotionality, of the other. Calls that occur with family members without forethought of family issues and the position of self on those issues are likely to place self behind, not ahead, in the effort to define for self a position of clarity. This is so because of the emotionality that can be present, in each person, in the conversation. This emotionality is so powerful that if one calls another without knowing exactly what is an issue, it is unlikely that one's position will be heard.

Written communication has a major advantage over telephone contact: it can be rewritten and edited. The author can rewrite his or her communication as many times as it takes to eliminate unwanted emotion and subjectivity from the content of the letter. This provides the opportunity to be certain that the writer's principle of his effort has been clearly communicated, and that there will be a conviction about the communication. Such conviction will be important later should the other react to the communication, making it easier neither to attack the other's viewpoint or explain for self, nor to defend the action. A well-developed letter that defines where self stands towards important others can act thereafter as a guidepost. Thus, the hours it takes to write and rewrite a significant letter that clearly defines self on any issue provide an opportunity for greater clarity, which remains, now, within the self. The self, as a result of the extreme effort, has become more sharply aware of *who* he is, *what* he believes, and *what* he is prepared to do as a result of his beliefs.

Like every other part of family work, the planned visit will be as successful as the effort that precedes it: (1) knowing *what* the family processes and patterns are that the individual will be in the midst of, (2) *how* those processes and patterns exist within self, (3) *what* the objective is for self in countering participation in the family patterns that breed immaturity and dysfunction, and (4) *how* self is going to change functioning around the issues and relationships. The greater the planning and preparation, the more likely it is that the therapist will make progress towards change—not because events turned out as expected, but because the thorough planning and clarity built into the process act as a guide to help self remain on a thoughtful course no matter what, in fact, happens. Differing from a simple focus on technique (a specific plan around specific factors), preparation through knowledge (theory) prepares self, through focus on *principle* (i.e., family members do the best they can, therefore, I will take sides with no one) to respond thoughtfully to whatever turn of events may occur in the visit.

Success in changing self is so difficult because both the system and the self automatically expect that individuals will function as they always have within the system. Hence, the individual attempting to change must continually reckon with his or her own automatic processes in order to act differently, and then must reckon with the entire system, which expects the individual to function in the usual way. For this reason, it is often most productive in the beginning of work on self within the family to set easier objectives for visits, and to keep visits short. The longer the visit, the more difficult it will be to stay on course. Further, it may prove important that the individual take along materials that can act to sustain clarity once within the emotional field (literature on theory, letters written by self about issues, statement of goals, etc.).

Following a family visit that has included a focus on difficult issues and relationship contact, it is often productive to do follow-up contact around the work self has done. It is an opportunity to say again what self communicated through action, but with the advantage of editing and rewriting.

The final vehicle to be considered is *surprise*. Surprise in interacting with family in a different or opposite way from the usual patterns and processes of intereactions may at times be necessary if communication within the family is not open (e.g., an unplanned visit home). The objective in using surprise is to attract attention to a family member's functioning differently—it is not to act unexpectedly as a matter of course, so that the system begins to relate to the individual out of anxiety concerning the unknown.

Whatever vehicle one chooses, its success, and that of the entire effort at changing self through defining positions of rsponsibility in the family system, will be determined by the quantity and quality of theoretical preparation.

BUILDING A SELF

Knowledge of the System

Until an individual has built a foundation of knowledge about the functional characteristics and factual history of his/her extended family (multiple generations) and of his/her own functional characteristics and factual history, becoming a more emotionally solid human being will not be possible. Certainly, it is possible to become a calmer, "nicer," more organized human being through the myriad of stress-management, time-management, and behavioral techniques readily available today. None of these, however, provide a way to be a more solid human being, or a better therapist.

Increasing emotional solidness requires knowing the patterns and processes of one's extended family. Such knowledge would include consideration of demographic data of the family (e.g., length of life of family members, marriage/divorce/live-together patterns, thorough health history of members, work history/goals met and unmet, geographical closeness/distance from family of origin and nuclear family). The emotional patterns and processes of the family must also be known. These data, far more subtle, and prone to subjectivity, come from knowing not only *what* occurred, but also the conviction, reactivity, and anxiety that preceded and followed events in the family. These latter are learned through study of what happened, *who* participated, the manner of participation, and the outcome. For example: What was the nature of an extended family prior to a death? Once the death occurred, who participated in the burying process that followed? In what ways did family members participate (as leader, decision-maker, contributor or as a follower, present without definition)? What functional patterns followed? Did the family units pursue more contact after the death and funeral or, in fact, was there less or no contact? What emotionality was expressed by individuals after the event (positive/defined statements—negative/reactive–judgmental statements)—no mention of the event at all, or constant discussion of the occurrence? All this involves monitoring the details of the individual lives in one's system while simultaneously keeping the focus on the broad, long-term outcomes of the individuals and of the system itself. Out of such a thorough study of functioning and factual history comes the opportunity to build a reasonable understanding of the "fabric" from which one has emerged, and the nature of the environment created by such fabric that affected the functioning, ultimately, of one's parents and influenced the functioning characteristics that became self.

Knowledge of family history and functioning must be supplemented by the same body of knowledge about self; in other words, where is self in the functioning of the family? Once family patterns are known and areas of dysfunction discovered, it is possible to look for those same characteristics in self and the participation of self in the family's patterns. One can gain knowledge of the immaturity in self no better than in bringing to light such information. The study not only highlights the immaturities in self but also provides a factual framework upon which to begin the work of changing self towards more nonnegotiable solidness.

Determining *how* to begin to work towards change requires some good knowledge about human functioning and the ability to *predict the outcomes of action and reaction*. Once a body of data about the family extended emotional system is known, there is a framework for deciding what needs to be changed within self to bring to a close the part that self has been playing in the family dysfunction (e.g., making contact with a branch of the family with which one has not done so out of compliance with family emotionality about that branch).

Further, it becomes clear where work is required if self is to decrease the current quantity of immaturity that exists within. Such work would be grounded upon principles of responsibility and maturity that self has built concerning being a solid self. For instance, maturity does not take sides on family issues; rather, it knows that all humans carry a degree of subjectivity that decreases objectivity. Hence, there is a tendency to view what has occurred in the family system through one's own emotional lens. Knowing this, a self understands that one's viewpoint is not truth, but rather, opinion based on facts and mixed with emotional subjectivity—the more emotionally important the individuals involved, or the issue in focus, the greater the likelihood of increased subjectivity. Good functioning is not based on approval from others, but is based on clarity about where self stands on important issues, what one is prepared to do about those beliefs, and consistent follow-through. One seeks, thus, not to gain approval or avoid disapproval, but to follow one's own developed beliefs about responsible functioning. By following such self-discovered and developed beliefs, one automatically amends the tendency in self to participate and contribute to the family's dysfunction. Action now is based not on approval from others, but belief.

Human emotional process across the generations is neither insignificant nor easily countered. The clearest knowledge of personal belief by an individual and the cleanest action (i.e., factual, neutral, seeking neither approval nor avoiding disapproval) may end in failure if there is not also respect for and focus upon the family's likely reaction to those actions of an individual that make self separate from the system.

Prediction allows an individual to measure the degree of success of an effort to define self within family. Such measurement is crucial, for it allows the individual to evaluate whether a failure in an effort — an inability to define a position or to sustain the effort — was related to inaccurate theoretical postulation about family patterns and processes, or rather resulted from the manner in which the individual acted. Further on, prediction gives an individual the opportunity to prepare for the final and sometimes toughest part of any effort to change self within the family (basing behavior on belief and not relationships) — responding to the family's reaction to the effort. No matter how well an effort is executed, when family members react with hurt, anger, sadness, or threats (implied or direct) of termination of relationship, it is difficult not to respond. There is the drive to explain to them, so that they too will see the merit in the individual's actions. Barring that, there may be a pull to attack the reactive family member or to provide a defense of self. Should the individual explain, attack the other, or defend self, the purpose of the effort (to stay outside of the family's emotionality) will be minimized if not totally nullified. Having become reactive, the individual may now be viewed by his family system as lashing out, rebellious, somewhat strange, or at least likely to be unhappy in his own life — rather than being viewed as different from before, unpredictable in an uncomfortable way for the others, but nevertheless more worthy of respect.

In my opinion, it is *only* the capacity to predict the reactivity of others and the likely reaction within self to their reactions that allows an individual to sustain an effort to be clear about a position (i.e., outside the emotional field) and free of judgment toward others. It is this capacity that makes it possible to be at the center of the emotional system while not joining its emotionality. If there is reactivity to the viewpoint of others or reactivity to the response of others to self, it is not possible to remain in close proximity to the emotional field of the family; for to do so would increase the likelihood of defending self, attacking the other, or explaining in order to gain agreement with one's actions.

Emotionality Associated with an Effort to Define Self

Although individuals are different in a multitude of ways concerning reactivity, its onset, duration, and severity, there are, nevertheless, certain general phases that most will experience in one degree or another when attempting to become a more solid, nonnegotiable self within their emotional systems.

PHASE ONE

The first phase is marked by an intense level of anxiety as the individual contemplates countering the family's emotionality. There is an expectation of doom, some awful outcome for having done something "wrong." During this phase, one may wonder continually why such an effort came to be planned, and a thousand reasons why the effort should not be attempted at this time parade through one's thoughts.

PHASE TWO

A second phase occurs with the arrival within the family field when the forces for togetherness, approval, and habit are felt in numerous ways. The challenge of this phase is management of the pulls for togetherness, all the while maintaining the cognitive conviction about what is being attempted (reducing immaturity and increasing maturity) and why the actions are necessary (to become more responsible as a member of the multigenerational system and to gain greater ability to determine one's own future rather than automatically responding to the family's emotionality as one charts one's life); i.e., the challenge is to act on predefined conviction and plan rather than upon pulls for togetherness or approval.

PHASE THREE

The third phase is possible only when an individual has succeeded in the second. It occurs as the individual experiences a new functional and emotional position within the system and within self. It is as if one can breathe deeper, getting more oxygen than ever before, or can see sharper and wider than ever before. There is also an energy surge—as if one could accomplish anything. And there is more of a sense of self, who one is and is not, than ever before.

PHASE FOUR

The exhilaration of the third phase is followed by a predictable period of exhaustion. It is in this phase that the outcome of contemplating countering the family's emotionality, and succeeding in doing so, is felt in its physiological and emotional fullness. It is as if the self alone took on fighting Goliath. This is so, because defining a self, separate from the togetherness, runs counter to the resistance in all family systems to sustain members in their predictable positions. There is little wonder in such a total response, because an individual's sense of worth and belonging has come, in part, from dependency upon and connection to the individuals from whom self now tries to be separate at the risk of disconnection.

Following this focused and carefully planned effort to define self through action in one's own family come the days and months when all the pulls to return to the old, understandable position within family (in which self is not different, nor is there discomfort with important others) are strong. A *shift* has occurred when the individual sustains a separateness from the togetherness during an effort, but later lapses back into old functioning positions; *change* has occurred when the clarity of purpose, conviction, and action continue to chart one's course in the midst of important family emotionality.

FAILURE IN EFFORTS TO DEFINE SELF

As an individual moves through day-to-day life, he or she will be required to respond to functioning decisions, from minor tasks to major issues. At such times, the individual will act on the basis of forces for togetherness (acting in relation to the relationship system) or on the basis of individual forces (actions determined by facts and personal principle, regardless of the emotionality of important others). One force or the other will dominate.

Several factors will govern the interplay of the two forces. An individual's quantity of emotional solidness, free of the emotionality of important others, will be a major factor. The greater the quantity of solid self, the greater the likelihood that forces for individuality will dominate; and the smaller that quantity, the more the forces for togetherness are likely to dominate.

Levels of acute and chronic anxiety in the system constitute a major factor as well. When there is more anxiety, the forces of togetherness pull more strongly, regardless of the amount of differentiation. The same can be said for duration of anxiety; indeed, the longer anxiety remains high, the greater the pull from togetherness of the system and also the individual, the functioning of society, and the presence of nodal, anxiety-producing events.

Momentum

As an individual is buffeted about by forces of anxiety, he will define self *to* the force or will respond automatically, on the basis of emotionality. If a position is defined, the person will experience emotional grounding based upon personal belief. If positions continue to be taken, there will be established a momentum that will decrease vulnerability towards others' emotionality. If, on the other hand, an individual *fails to declare himself* around important issues, a gathering momentum will make it increasingly difficulty to detach self from the emotionality of others (Meyer 1982). Figure 2–2 illustrates the relationship between momemtum for defining self and the presence of anxiety.

An individual cannot come face-to-face with an issue and "duck" without losing some self in the system. Therefore, avoidance of issues—"out of sight, out of mind"—is not getting out of the emotional system. What I suggest is that defining or failing to define does not simply concern a specific situation. Rather, failure occurs in the midst of constantly changing shifts in the system, the interlocking triangles. Further, failure to define becomes the foundation for new spiraling forces.

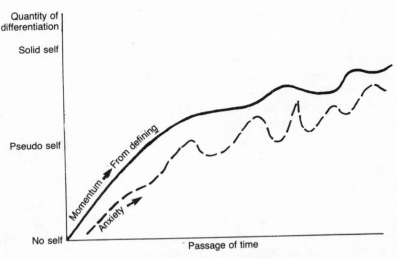

Figure 2–2. Functional momentum.

Even though there may be numerous new forces resulting from failure to declare self in a system, four will be discussed: emotional cut-off, increased vulnerability for triangulation, increased level of anxiety, and increased likelihood for projection.

Emotional cut-off can be expected to occur to some degree in any relationship in which an individual has not declared self around emotional issues. The impact of the failure to define on the relationship will include: a new level of chronic anxiety, acute anxiety if or when the issue is again raised, and increase in distance. Each impact will lead to an increased degree of emotional cut-off.

As a result of increased anxiety and reactivity, there will be greater vulnerability for triangulation. The individual may triangle with others in order to calm the anxious emotion or may be triangled by others in the same process. Triangulation increases anxiety within a system and makes it ever more difficult to become a self in a system.

Loss of self in a system will automatically increase the level of anxiety. Increases in anxiety can have manifestations in every conceivable arena of functioning, including, and in addition to, those mentioned above.

Projection to the next generation and elsewhere is likely to result when there is significant cut-off in a marital relationship or in a relationship to one's parents.

Undifferentiation

The second major impact of failure to define self is that the failure moves a person increasingly towards undifferentiation, further away from solidness. Hence, every failure becomes additional foundation for undifferentiation. There is no "standing in place" . . . no neutral. One defines self or becomes more and more non-self. It is the same for an individual who drives down the highway in the wrong direction, proceeding with momentum, and accumulates an increasing number of miles in the wrong direction. To move towards the goal would require driving back over the miles driven in the wrong direction. So it is with differentiation. Reactions and responses that "avoid" taking a stand for self move self further and further towards undifferentiation.

Failure in the Attempt to Define Self

Entirely different from making no attempt to define self with respect to an issue is work at defining that ends in failure. It is not possible to define self within the family field without failures of one kind or another. Failure, however, becomes a serious problem if the individual sees its basis in the other rather than in self. As long as the focus is on self as the source of the failure, the aborted effort itself is a source of new data about emotionality in the system and within self. It can provide knowledge and increase understanding of the system, as well as knowledge about the effort required to increase maturity and decrease immaturity.

Inability to define self can follow from numerous factors. One of the most potent is an overemphasis on a family's most intense emotional issues. When a defining effort includes family members with whom there is little or no previous relationship but, nevertheless, centers on those issues or relationships that carry the strongest emotional charge for a system, the likelihood of failure is great. The failure can include inability to build a person-to-person relationship with the individual as well as an inability to resolve the charged issue. Further, if the individual working to change self then responds to failure as indicative of the intensity and reactivity of the other or the system, the likelihood of continued failure is great. In time, he or she may decide that the family is too tough for one to have an impact upon it, and give up the effort. In truth, though tough indeed, it will have been that the obstacle was, instead, the attempt to present charged material outside the context of a personal relationship. The long-term outcome may be yet more significant, in that some individuals in the family may never choose to make themselves available for a relationship following the original, highly charged attempt. Hence, not only has the effort failed, but new, potent obstacles may have formed to stand in the way of a future success. The human does not respond well to a family member who, in the past, has demonstrated neither interest nor commitment to his extended family but suddenly enters the system carrying one of its most loaded emotional issues.

A second process that can lead to failure in efforts to define self in family is the tendency to undervalue or underemphasize the significance of contact-for-contact free of focus on loaded issues. It may well be that when a focus on issues is followed by, rather than precedes, contact with important family members, successful communication about important emotional issues may be easier to achieve.

Interviewing family members rather than *relating to* them is another possible pitfall. If the effort is simply genealogical in nature, a predefined interview may be useful and interesting. However, if the same discussion is to include highly charged emotional issues, the likelihood of success is greatly reduced. On the contrary, when questions about a life course are asked in the context of an active relationship, family data and memories often flow with ease.

The process of interviewing itself has several obstacles. The individual doing the interview may carry, without awareness, an intensity about "getting information." This is the case because a special time may have been set up to meet the other, and a plan to interview communicated. Therefore, once talking, there may be an intensity in "needing to get certain data," which is sensed by the other. Rather than the individual's defining to self that certain data will be necessary to obtain in time, it can be a process of attachment to another to learn new data. However, because the human is adept at sensing an "agenda" in another, success in obtaining those data may be minimal.

Another obstacle to success in efforts to define self is the tendency of some to leap into action, focusing on issues and charged material, before developing an adequate body of knowledge about the functioning of the emotional system and of the emotional self, perhaps because defining a self both connected to and separate from the family emotionality runs so counter to one's own emotionality. It is the deep conviction developed from getting to know one's own immaturity and its likely future that can keep self on course while the family's emotionality flows at an intense pitch. Without the body of knowledge (based on facts of the past and observation of the present) and the conviction towards maturity that can follow, the likelihood of a successful working towards self in the family without responding to the pulls of togetherness, explaining the effort, defending the actions of self, or attacking the reactive other remains minimal.

Another factor towards failure in changing self is the tendency to work in family that is "hit and run"; that is, rather than work at self in the family in a relatively steady, methodical way, an individual may complete two or three efforts at change within a year but commit little thought or action towards change the remainder of the time. Such a process creates an emotional ebb and flow that is emotionally exhausting. In fact, the individual may then have to build momentum against the reactivity to remain the same, not change, and not "begin the effort at all," each and every time.

The final factor that can lead to failure in efforts to change self to be discussed here is anxiety within the individual making the effort. If, as the anxiety begins to build within the individual, he or she was unable to contain the buildup and, rather, distanced from the family, then there would be as much or more reactivity in the family to the distance than to the data being focused upon. For the individual who is unaware of this process, the family is likely to react to the heightened anxiety without understanding its origin. In the meantime, the issue around which the individual worked so hard to communicate may have been "lost" in the exchange. Instead, mechanisms have to be developed by self to contain anxiety to make it possible for the issue to receive the focus that was the purpose of the effort in the first place.

These represent but some of the factors that lead to failure in efforts to change self in one's family. What is suggested is that the individual would do well to look first at his or her own reactivity in defined efforts that have failed and at the levels of anxiety engendered by such efforts. By doing so, it becomes possible to evaluate and understand how the failure came to be. How much did self "trigger" in the other? How inaccurate was the theoretical foundation upon which the work was planned? What data needed to be understood before attempting this particular effort? What individuals in the system need to be reckoned with or connected to before certain work can be accomplished? These questions are among those that would need to be understood in order to understand how a failure to change self came to be.

Hence, the therapist who does not initiate an effort to define self within his own family, or who attempted to do so and failed, will be vulnerable to several unfavorable outcomes: emotional cut-off, increased tendency towards triangulation, increased level of anxiety, and increased likelihood for projection (to own family and to those who come for therapy).

CONCLUSION

The task of developing an ability to bypass subjectivity in the therapy process is the greatest challenge of therapy. This is so because the forces of subjectivity are subtle, but powerful, and always present. If a therapist is not capable of deflecting subjectivity which leads to transference and to countertransference, the likelihood of promoting solid change in the individual is slight and the possibility that the therapeutic process itself will add to the individual's unresolved emotionality is, unfortunately, great.

An individual who selects the mental health field for his line of work acquires a responsibility to pursue knowledge than can promote excellence in work with other humans and ensure that his or her functioning will not interfere with the progress of those with whom the therapists works. A therapist's foundation must include knowledge about human functioning, the therapist's extended family system, the therapist's nuclear family system, and the self of the system if the therapist is to safeguard his responsibility to those with whom he or she works. At the same time, knowledge and skill in the therapeutic process are required for excellence.

My purpose in this chapter has been to explore the impact of immaturity on a therapist, and the opportunity provided by family systems theory to change self towards a more solid maturity. The outcome is a more mature *therapist* who knows his own emotionality well and who can, therefore, provide a therapeutic process in which objectivity and thoughtfulness are at a maximum and subjectivity and reactivity at a minimum. Therein lies the call of the self who chooses to become a therapist.

REFERENCES

Bowen, M. (1978). *Family Therapy in Clinical Practice.* New York: Jason Aronson.

Bradt, J. O., and Moynihan, C. J. (1971). Opening the safe: A study of child-focused families. In *Systems Therapy, Selected Papers: Theory, Technique, Research,* ed. J. Bradt and C. Moynihan, pp. 1–24. Washington, D.C.: Jack O. Bradt, M.D., and Carolyn J. Moynihan.

Kuhn, J. S. (1978). Realignment of emotional forces following loss. In *The Best of The Family (1973–1978),* pp. 178–183. New Rochelle, N.Y.: The Center for Family Learning.

Meyer, P. H. (1976). Patterns and processes in working with one's family. Paper presented at the 13th Georgetown University Symposium on Family Psychotherapy.

Meyer, P. H. (1980). Between families: The unattached young adult. In *The Family Life Cycle: A Framework for Family Therapy,* ed. E. Carter and M. McGoldrick, pp. 71–91. New York: Gardner.

Meyer, P. H. (1982). The cumulative impact of the failure to define a self on a life course. Paper presented at the 19th Georgetown University Symposium on Family Psychotherapy.

Toman, W. (1969). *Family Constellation: Its Effects on Personality and Social Behavior,* 2nd ed. New York: Springer-Verlag.

Family Life Cycle: Leaving Home, Marriage, Children, and the Family of Origin in Later Life

Chapter 3

THE DELUSION OF DIFFERENTIATION: NOTATIONS ON FAMILY PROCESS

Glenn N. Scarboro, M.S.W.

As I begin to write, I am aware of what may seem the false nature of what I am about to report. My understanding and information about family concepts and principles have been in operation for the past three years, yet I doubt whether family concepts and principles will assist me in making sense of the confusion when I meet with a family. R. D. Laing places my worry concerning the complexities of family process in perspective when he says:

> Two intrinsic difficulties face us in studying families. First, the time scale. Families (of some kind or another, all be it very different from ours) have existed, say, for a hundred thousand years. We can study directly only a minute slice of the family chain: three generations, if we are lucky. Even studies of three generations are rare. What patterns can we hope to find if we are restricted to three out of at least 4,000 generations? The second difficulty is that the more smoothly they function, the more difficult they are to study. [Laing 1969, pp. 84–85]

The purpose of this chapter is to evaluate differentiation, or the delusion of differentiation.[1] When I think of Laing's statement, it seems

---

[1]The essence of the title "The Delusion of Differentiation: Notations on Family Process" is summarized in a recent statement of mine that accompanied an exhibition of photographs in my hometown of Danville, Virginia: "As a child in Danville, trees, hills, people, family, values, ideas, and complexities were part of my life. I wanted to leave all

impossible even to consider the notion; however, for the past three years I have seen people devote much of their time and energy toward differentiating self, or changing their positions within their families. Needless to say, my present interest in these questions is a result of my being in my family, and wondering if there is a "self" independent of family process. Laing states the situation very clearly: "till one can see the 'family' in oneself, one can see neither oneself or any family clearly" (Laing 1969). Part I is a summary of my work in my family from a generalized state of amorphousness to a relative state of order. This description centers on two central patterns in my family, and the history of these patterns. Part II is a sharing of certain thoughts and ideas concerning family process that have emerged over the past three years.

PART I

Prior to February 1973, I had always viewed emotional and behavioral problems as being a result of intrapsychic conflict rooted in an existential–humanistic model. In February 1973, I began an elementary shift toward viewing emotional and behavioral problems in the context of the family. My family, in a holistic fashion, can be described as an overtly harmonious one that has demonstrated few signs of emotional and behavioral dysfunction. There were many indicators of dysfunction in the history of the family that were not being ameliorated in recent generations.

I was the second of four children, having an older brother and two younger sisters. I had an overinvolved, close relationship with my mother and a significantly distant and underinvolved relationship with my father. I experienced a considerable amount of anxiety and discomfort in the sibling subsystem of my family, but my efforts in my

---

this only to discover that I took with me trees, hills, people, family, values, ideas, and complexities. It is impossible to leave where you are from. It is not impossible to change where you are going. Going is the process of changing. Changing is the process of arriving at where you start. We circle the world only to end where we start. My pictures are facts that are part of the going, changing, arriving, and ending. Danville is where I am from and from where I am is where I go." I believe that people basically change very little, but are able to add to the basic beginnings.

family focused principally on my relationship with my mother and father[2] (see Fig. 3–1).

Before I learned about family concepts, I had considered most members of my family to be less than adequate people, and spent much time and energy trying to avoid them. At present, I do not see my family as being significantly pathological, or otherwise "sick," but rather as a "typical American family" living with the common vicissitudes and everyday struggles of human existence. In essence, I am beginning to see my parents, brother, and sisters as "people" with their own individual struggles which, in a conglomerate fashion, produced a family like many families in the United States today. When I was able to lessen the distance that I had maintained from my family, my anxiety about my family began to decrease. In some "metaphysical" fashion, this decreased distance increased my sense of self.[3]

I shall use the date May 30, 1969, as a point of departure. It was then that I made a suicidal gesture and was hospitalized for four weeks. Prior to this date, my overall functioning could have been described as being appended to my family, both financially and emotionally. I had not separated from my parents to the extent that I could live and work on my own. At the point of my hospitalization, I was still overly involved with my mother and significantly distant from and underinvolved with my father. When I was released from the hospital, I con-

---

[2]This discussion has been limited to a general description of family process taking five to six years out of the context of the total family process. In addition, it is generally limited to a description of process without reference to technique. The obvious omission is the detailed history of the Scarboro–Pedigo union and how the generational histories of each family played a part in the two family patterns described. Those interested in papers illustrating the importance of the extended family are referred to the following: "The Importance of the Extended Family," by Michael E. Kerr, M.D., and "In Search of One's Past: An Identity Trip," by Fernando Colon, Ph.D. Both were published in the *Georgetown Family Symposia*, Vol. 1 (1971–1972). The value I found in my research on my extended families was the discovery of *facts* that would not support the intensity of my feelings around certain issues in the family.

[3]Glenn N. Scarboro: "The Nature of Family: Minus 30 Years and Counting," unpublished paper, 1975. I developed a four-point criterion of self that was behavioral in orientation. The four points of self were (1) the ability to say "no" in a very intense emotional relationship; (2) the ability to learn how not to react to what other people say or do; (3) the ability to handle anxiety over key issues in the family or elsewhere without developing dysfunctional behavior; and (4) the ability to look at self less seriously and with more of a sense of humor.

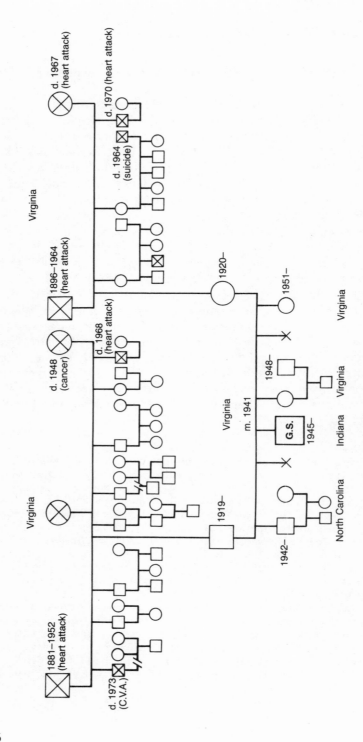

Figure 3-1. Family diagram.

76

tinued in individual psychotherapy for the next two years. This was my second experience with psychotherapy.

When I was hospitalized, I was 24 years old and had been living at home, with my parents, for almost a year. The actual hospitalization occurred at the end of a six-week pseudoseparation, in which I left my family and tried to function on my own.

While in undergraduate school, I had involved myself in two homosexual acting-out episodes; they were ephemeral but resulted in considerable worry about sexual identity. This behavior led to my first psychotherapy experience, at the counseling center of the university. When I left undergraduate school and took my first job away from home, I continued to be worried and preoccupied about sexual identity. At the end of a year, my anxiety had increased so much that, having made a plan to attend graduate school, I terminated my job and went to live with my parents for a month before I was to enter. At the end of a month's time, I had abandoned my plans for graduate school and decided to live with my parents.

During the year that I spent away from my parents after graduation, I continued to be excessively worried about sexual identity. When I walked through the front door of my parents' home at the end of a year of separation, the homosexual preoccupation seemingly evaporated, and was never in operation as long as I was in my mother's and father's presence.

While I was in individual psychotherapy following the hospitalization, this series of events, in addition to my individual struggles with my parents, was made part of the active exchange with the psychotherapist, in which I received support and reassurance. Even with reassurances from the psychotherapist, I was still very anxious about my relationship with my parents and experienced occasional anxiety about sexual identity.

I continued to live at home until September 1970. At that time, I entered graduate school and was able to put 150 miles between my family and me. Although I was 150 miles away, however, I still spent much time thinking about events back home in Danville (Virginia).

In February 1973, I began to see myself as an emotional appendage of my parents and started wondering how that had happened. I began to learn of family concepts and principles while a second-year graduate student by watching Murray Bowen do family therapy at the Medical College of Virginia. At the time I became interested in family concepts and principles, I also initiated my third psychotherapy experience with a psychoanalytically oriented therapist. During this time, the worries

and anxieties about my parents were beginning to reemerge and the issue of sexual identity was becoming a constant preoccupation. Thus,
in February of 1973, even though I was seeing an individually oriented
psychotherapist, and had been for several months, I was beginning to
close the distance that I had maintained from my family. Watching the
family sessions at the Medical College of Virginia, I had soon realized
that I was talking *about* my family and not *to* my family and, further,
that it was essential to talk to them if I was ever to improve my relationship with them.[4] I decided that month to go home for a week and
spend time with my parents individually.

In the course of trying to develop a relationship with both my parents, I learned from my mother that throughout her marriage she had
been worried that my father might be homosexual. Also during this
visit I learned more about her particular struggles with my father,
struggles with her mother and father, and struggles with my father's
family. In essence, my mother had attempted over the years to have
her emotional needs met through her overinvolved relationships with
my brother and me. During this trip to Danville, I related to my father
in a private conversation that my mother had been worried for a num-

---

[4]Frederick Sommer: An Extemporaneous Talk at the Art Institute of Chicago, October
1970." *Aperture* (16(2):1971). I use the word *confusion* with some trepidation. I believe the
social–behavioral sciences have made us victims of our own devices with the use of the
analytic–reductive method to tear down any, and all, experience to its essentials. Since
my introduction to family thinking, I have also had the pleasure of spending some time
with the photographer Frederick Sommer, who has a somewhat different idea about
"confusion" and how to approach "reality."

> We're not so damned inspired every day! If we rely on what we meet, some inspira-
> tion will arise. For example, if I go into a grocery store, no matter how beautifully
> stocked or lush it is in terms of display of fruit and edibles of all kinds, I would be
> smart to take home what is best that day. I will not say that I want to buy apples to-
> day or that I want to buy oranges today. In planning a meal, I plan from all the things
> I find there. I don't have a list with me even if planning a banquet (something I sel-
> dom do, believe me); nevertheless, I practice this every time I go into a grocery store.
> I buy the best of what there is that day. If the beef looks good, I'm not going to buy
> lamb. I buy the best of the beef. If the best of the beef is expensive, I buy less of it. I
> buy it carefully, so you can be sure I get a hell of a lot for my money; I always do. The
> store may have the kind of thing that you think you want that day. You are looking
> for pears. There may be pears, but those pears may not be at their best. Confusion is
> very enriching if you don't try to unravel it. It is unraveled confusion if you impose
> yourself upon what is available and come back with bad meat and bad fruit. You take
> the thing that is really there, and gradually build from it. You build your meal, your
> banquet. It is always a banquet when a few things are beautifully related.

ber of years that he might be homosexual. My father was somewhat astonished at my mother's concern but then went on to discuss a homosexual episode during his seventeenth year. It was this experience that my mother was using to feed her worries. I was able for the first time to discuss with him my concern about sexual identity and how it had affected my life. Even more amazing that evening was my father's approaching my mother and asking why she had not been able to tell him about her concerns for those many years. This active worry of my mother's seemed to function as an on–off switch that would operate any time I became too distant from her—If I attempted to increase the distance, the circuit would open. I felt such panic that I would have to return home to close the distance and eliminate the worry. Each time I returned home, the circuit closed and I felt bad about myself for not making it on my own. From this continuous process, the bond between my mother and me continued to grow tighter.

The obvious difficulty in this process was that no one knew what the issue was, since it was locked in the head of one. When I communicated the secret my mother had about my father, this information became part of the active exchange among the three of us, and it continues to be a part of the ongoing relationship.

In April 1973 I terminated my involvement with the psychoanalytically oriented psychotherapist and entered therapy with a family-oriented psychotherapist with whom I more closely evaluated the family process. From this work came the awareness of another significant issue in my family. In 1967, my father filed for bankruptcy. If I had not been careful, I would also have filed for bankruptcy in 1974. For my father the bankruptcy also increased his emotional distance from the family—his position throughout the life of the family. My mother's worry about my father increased at that time, which correlated with her overinvolvement with me. My brother filed for bankruptcy some two years later, and returned home with his family. Since his bankruptcy happened at the time that I was living at home, my brother and I were both back home for a six-month period. Initially, it appeared to me that the family had come back together to heal its wounds and lend emotional support to one another. The two bankruptcies, some two years apart, seemed to once again unite the family in a togetherness that accordingly perpetuated the issue of low self-esteem.

It was, and still is, difficult for the family ever to be together without money becoming the major topic of conversation. Through occasional letters and periodic visits, I started an effort to desensitize the issue of money for myself and to incorporate a less tense view of money into a more active, ongoing relationship with my father. Since that time, with the assistance of some carefully planned reversals, I have been able to actively engage my father in a whole range of experiences.[5] In addition, I have elicited far more information about his life, his thoughts, and his feelings. This activity has increased the closeness between my father and me, and it has also led to a decrease in my closeness with my mother.

In essence, a more reasonable balance between closeness and distance with both parents has gradually been achieved. The two issues in my family, homosexuality and the use of money, illustrate the way in which I was continually attached to my mother and father. As a result of looking at these two issues in a different way, I have been able to separate from my family more significantly. In March 1974, I took a job 600 miles away from my parents, the first time any family member has ever made an effort to separate with that much physical distance. By working on the denied emotional process among my mother, my father, and me, I have been able to "turn off the switch" that had operated automatically in my family for many years. Now my concerns and worries about sexual identity are not operative in an emotionally charged way and I conduct my financial life with reasonable responsibility. I am not as preoccupied about my mother and father as I once was, and I have been able to free most of that energy for pursuing my own goals and interests.

It is my understanding of family theory that has made the difference in my life. The difficulty in trying to generalize from my case to others is the difficulty that psychotherapy has always faced: the ever elusive desire to find and bring to some stable condition a conceptual

---

[5]The concept of the reversal is a well-integrated technique in the armamentarium of many family therapists. What interests me about the concept is the general reactivity that it arouses. It is most characteristically seen as hostile, or as inhuman, delivered to helpless victims. The paper by Richard H. Armstrong, Reversals: Their care and feeding, in *Georgetown Family Symposia*, Vol. 1 (1971–1972), defines the parameters of the proper reversal. I find it interesting that Victor E. Frankl develops a therapy technique from his experience in the concentration camps during World War II, which he called *paradoxical intention*. His beliefs about psychotherapy are rooted in humanistic–existential beliefs, which I think account for less reactivity to his method than I have seen to the reversal as defined by Bowen and Armstrong [V. E. Frankl: *Psychotherapy and Existentialism: Selected Papers on Logotherapy*, Chap. 12: Paradoxical Intention: A logotherapeutic technique. New York: Simon and Schuster (1967)]. Regardless of how the concept is identified, *Pragmatics of Human Communication: A Study of Interactional Patterns, Pathologies, and Paradoxes*, a book by P. Watzlawick, J. Beavin, and D. Jackson (New York: W. W. Norton, 1967), is one of the best sources illustrating the structure of interactions and how unpredictable behavior—the reversal—works to disrupt the established patterns.

model that allows for generalization and application to other, similar situations. If people were to ask me: "Are you more out of your family than you were?" I would certainly say "yes." However, I am willing to entertain the thought that this idea is pure delusion on my part. In other words, there may be yet another theory with adequate concepts and principles that would further clarify for me what has occurred, and is occurring, between my family and me.

In my lifetime, I have consulted four psychotherapists. The first was a Rogerian, the second a behavioral therapist, the third an analytically oriented psychiatrist, and the fourth a family therapist known as the "Metaphysical Onion" (Armstrong 1977). Obviously, I was having a difficult time negotiating relationships with people, experiencing anxiety about sexual identity, and having a difficult time separating from my family. Each one attempted to assist me with his own particular therapeutic "bag of tricks" to move further along the continuum toward being less amorphous, ill-defined, and chaotic, and toward becoming more defined and self-directed. During the first three psychotherapy efforts there was a diminishing of the multiple anxieties and conflicts which I had experienced for brief periods of time. Essentially, each one took me a step closer to the actual sources of my difficulty first, but actually dealt with content and not the underlying process. It became apparent to me that it was necessary to look behind the content to the forces that motivated the issues. Whether or not consultation with a family-oriented psychotherapist would have resulted in a more rapid change and alleviation of the symptoms when I was twenty rather than twenty-eight remains open to question. For any psychotherapy effort to be successful, the client must believe in what he is being asked to do. Even though I complained about my parents to the various therapists, I do not believe I was ready to go home and start working with the essential details of the situation. The first three psychotherapists were primarily implanting the seeds that would eventually lead me closer to home. It was almost as if I were searching, sampling the conceptual models that would contribute directly to the final outcome: talking *to* my parents, not *about* them. The most valuable result of my consultations with the Metaphysical Onion was *being less certain* and *wondering more*.[6]

---

[6]As I understand the process of the reversal as part of an active relationship between two people, it seems to call into question the commitment to old ideas and offers a fresh sense of wonder about old patterns. Hence, the rigidity in orientation changes and other possibilities are experienced. The similarities between the reversal and the creative process continue to be an interest of mine.

At this point I believe I am different in my relationships with my family. I am able to stay comfortably distant from old emotional issues and problems and yet maintain a reasonably active relationship with my mother and father. There still remains one big question: Will I, at some point in the future, go searching for a new theory? If I do, what will influence the active search for a new way to conceptualize and think about human problems? I am not sure whether I will or not, but in many respects I hope I do. I believe nobody can afford the luxury of thinking that he has a little corner of the universe that is complete and understandable to himself.

PART II

My major contribution to the present state of family theory is auto-biographical rather than theoretical. A free association of thoughts follows.

1.

At the midpoint of my 30th year, my entire family—mother, father, brothers, sisters, husbands, wives, and grandchildren—embarked upon its first total family vacation. As a child I remember being disap-pointed about not doing anything together because there was no "money." As we grew older, there were occasionally opportunities for a total family vacation, but they never materialized. I realized in the midst of the last outing that I was the one who had most recently said "no" to any opportunity to get together with the entire family. I would do anything to avoid my family's total presence, with accompanying headaches, stomach aches, and what I had considered to be a generally boring time. It would be simple to say that I did not experience any of the three above reactions during our recent outing—but I did. How-ever, I easily survived what I had thought would be an ordeal. I discov-ered that if I looked for different ideas and information about family members I would be able to confirm their differences rather than lump them together in a family amalgam. They are all people, with individ-ual thoughts and feelings, but with an overriding family stamp.

2.

The process between family members is what I called "the ultimate hu-manizer" in that if someone wants to discover his humanity, the discovery lies hidden somewhere in the heads of other family members. Re-engaging the family is the key to awakening a fresh sense of autonomy. The change from a generalized state of "uptightness" to a relative state of calm and direction is the by-product of a process that leads to a newly created sense of wonder about family, what it does, and what it can continue to do for a person who is questioning his identity and life goals.

3.

Periodically I try to evaluate what has occurred in relation to my family. From the description given earlier, it is possible to see that anxiety was very high in the Scarboro family, so tight and close at various points that at least one member would become dysfunctional. My suicidal gesture was an effort to get breathing room, but it served only to glue the members of the family more tightly together. By pursuing a family orientation, I have been able to leave home and achieve the essential distance. It is important also that the separation gave me the opportunity to pursue my own interests and goals without being totally preoccupied with family process. Being either too close or too distant from the family can increase anxiety to a debilitating point. Learning to increase closeness or distance is necessary for controlling the anxiety level.

4.

Family theory *seems* to imply that an active pursuit of extended family history and the reworking of existing relationships requires a total involvement. During the days in Richmond, Virginia, I found myself beginning to evaluate almost everything I did in relation to the monthly meetings of the Bowen group. In some ways, I do not now consider this preoccupation to have been any different from the preoccupation I formerly had with sexual identity. Both processes illustrate my lack of a self by my willingness to go along with existing patterns rather than actively work out a pattern of interests and pursuits unique to me. The less energy I spend being preoccupied with my family, the more time I have to stand on my own and think about what I want to do.

5.

It occurred to me some seven months ago that I was not Murray Bowen, Richard Armstrong, or Thomas Fogarty, but instead, Glenn

Scarboro looking and searching for answers to difficult questions.[7] So rather than tell you how difficult it has been without a support group or a supervisor trained in family behavior, I have considered the difference between what I think and what others think as the source of a growing edge of self. My ineptness in dealing with many people and families has taught me to evaluate, think, and be more curious about people rather than to approach them with a preconceived notion of what ought to occur between us.

For many years I had never felt that I had a father. I have seen four psychotherapists and have tried to make each one my father. Now I do not have a fantasy father: instead, I have a father who has values, opinions, strengths, ideals, disappointments, and hardships. It seems as though the more I talk to him, the stronger I become. It might be that the nourishment and the sense of relatedness that we all seek lies no further away than the distance between self and parents.[8]

* * *

This was written in 1975, after two years of work in my family and my subsequent relocation to another state. It would serve both practical and theoretical issues to comment on the state of affairs in my family and professional interest since that time. There has not been much additional work in the family other than continued contact and visits. However, a recent two-week vacation in Virginia has reminded me once again of an issue that I could not resolve in 1975: I was struggling over how much time one must devote to a differentiating effort and what is required in order to maintain that effort. My recent visit with my family again reminded me that it is impossible to assume that all

---

[7]I mention Bowen, Armstrong, and Fogarty, since they are the people I draw from when I meet with families. Influence does not determine outcome or behavior in the therapeutic encounter—it just seems to shape the boundary of possibility.

[8]Frederick Sommer: *The Poetic Logic of Art and Aesthetics*, published privately (1972):

Nourishment is to live things that are unsayable, that cannot be formulated. This is awareness other than by force of will. If this is what is in store for us, it will not be uninteresting. I say this not as a voyeur but as one whose empathy is to the cohesion of the voyage. I believe the sign is displayed in fragments already on the scene, but the picture has to be put together. The problem of modern man isn't to escape from one ideology to another, not to escape from one formulation to find another; our problem is to live in the presence and in the attributes of reality. Then we will be able to put the picture together. This picture can only be the outcome of all the empathy given to many things observed in common. When many things are observed in common by the many who constitute a society, we will have reached a condition worth celebrating.

will remain functional in a family after some initial differentiating efforts. The work must be continuous.

REFERENCES

Armstrong, R. H. (1977). The metaphysical onion: reflections on family technique. In *Georgetown Family Symposia: Vol. II*, ed. J. Lorio and L. McClenathan, pp. 78–102. Washington, D.C.: Georgetown University Press.

Laing, R. D. (1969). *The Politics of the Family*. New York: Random House.

Von Bertalanffy, L. (1974). General systems theory and psychiatry. In *American Handbook of Psychiatry*, ed. S. Avieti. New York: Basic Books.

Chapter 4

FREEDOM OF CHOICE VERSUS HONORING COMMITMENT

Robert J. Valentine, M.A., M.Ed.

The word *differentiation* confuses most people. I've dropped it in teaching—respect seems to be easier to comprehend. Not respect from the point of view of bowing to a higher authority, but rather as recognizing the space, the rights, the difference of the other. It means I can allow you to be you, letting you be different from my expectations of you. It also means I can allow me to be me, different from the expectations you have of me.

My initial attempts at differentiation from my family of origin involved some running away and then some violation of norms. My running away was accepted positively because it did not look like running away. I entered a monastery halfway across the nation. (If you want to diminish contact with and influence of your family, I would heartily recommend it.) My family did not understand my move, but in an age of war in Vietnam, which began some three years after I entered, and then at a time of student unrest on campuses, my family was happy to know I was meditating and singing the praises of God.

Then I was ordained and moved back near my parents' home. The monastic group I belonged to allowed a lot more freedom of movement when the priest was involved in ministry outside the monastery, and I made sure I was. The difficulty with that was that I was close enough, and free enough, for my parents to make demands on me in terms of contact. I became hostile to that, and somewhat rebellious.

Simultaneously I was studying counseling, full-time, at Columbia University. While I can say that those were the two best educational years of my life, as well as the most emotionally growth-producing, I must also say that I fused with the philosophies of my fellow students and my professors, and I had a very difficult time deciding where I wanted to be and what I desired to do with my life.

One of the men who lived in the rectory worked in the administrative offices of the diocese, particularly on paper work for men who were resigning from the priesthood. He used to kid me, saying, "Well, I guess you'll be leaving too. All you guys who go into psychology eventually leave." Actually, he did seem to feel it was inevitable.

I am not aware of any statistical analysis on men who leave the priesthood—that is, one to see if counselors leave in proportionately greater numbers than parish priests or teaching priests—but I have a hunch that a study like that would show that counselors become uprooted vocationally more often than do other ministers. Thinking back over periods of my own indecision about continuing in the priesthood, and recalling the experiences of several nuns and priests I have counseled through that same crisis, I have concluded that there is a definite connection between psychology studies and leaving.

The chancery priest who joked with me about eventually leaving proved to be right. Two years after meeting him I was out on a leave of absence, to decide whether or not I had made a right decision in becoming a priest. I remember that in leaving, the thought in my mind was, "If I had to do it over again, would I do it over again?" And, if not, then I should correct a poor decision and replace it with a better one.

Close analysis of my attraction to the priesthood convinced me that I was there for the wrong reasons, and I began to think about correcting the mistake and getting out. Briefly, I recognized that working for the church had an effect on my position in some family triangles. My mother's family was very religious and my father's was not. My mother's family was much more part of ours than was my father's family, and I always felt rejected by them. Only much later did I realize that it probably had to do with my looking so much like my father and his family. My mother's family looked down on my father's family, considering them low-class heathens.

Figure 4-1 is the family diagram. Becoming ordained shifted my position. I was the family priest, and my mother's family wanted to trot me out at every opportunity.

Then I hit my stage of rebellion, fired up by the psychology courses and the groups at the university. So I went on leave from the priesthood, fully intending to cash it in. I stayed out for three years, from 1972 to 1975. During that time I made a faint-hearted effort to be different from my family by joining another religion. That did not last long,

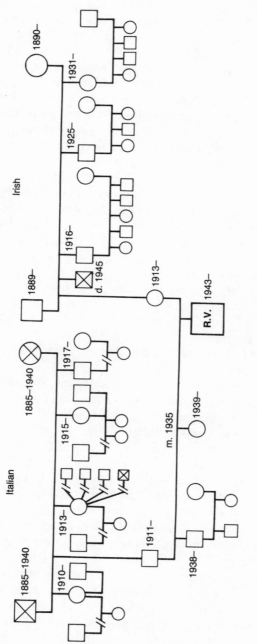

Figure 4–1. Family diagram.

89

because I found that the experience of other worship services left me indifferent, bored, or both. Within a short time I was back to attending Mass at a Catholic chapel in a local mental hospital. The chaplain was an older fellow who exuded a great love for the patients. There was something good and genuine about that man, and I was drawn back to prayer with him. It began to dawn on me that I loved the ministry, and that no matter what psychological weakness led me in that direction, there was also a natural predisposition in me toward prayer, toward ceremony, and toward ministry. I began thinking about all the years of study I had put into becoming a priest, and about how crazy it seemed for me to quit doing what I actually did best.

At the time I left I had convinced myself that I had to get out because it was, quite simply, impossible for me to be an independent human being within that powerful organization of the Church. When I returned to active, full-time ministry three years later, I had the belief that I was in charge of *me*, and that I did not have to fear an institution. In returning to priesthood, I made a decision based on two factors: commitment, and ability to survive.

I had written the commentary that was used at my ordination Mass, and in that commentary, I explained that the bishop would place his hands on the head of each man, and in that silent instant the man would be a priest forever. "And once it is done it can never be undone," I wrote. I did not make that life-long commitment easily; I do not break my word easily.

The strongest impetus I had for cancelling my commitment was the belief that I had made an immature choice; that I had been complying with my family's expectations, and that I now had a right to make a new choice, and this time—for the first time—a free one. Secondly, my counselor friends had fairly well convinced me that an interpersonal, heterosexual relationship would mature me and complete me. At the time I felt confused and decided "the Church" was to blame for this. When I returned, I had decided that if I was in emotional difficulty, I could accept responsibility for my own part in it. I also felt strong enough to live in the middle of the Church as an active clergyman without fear that being in contact with the institution would institutionalize me, or screw me up.

The person who was most instrumental in teaching me how to stay myself in spite of the pressure of others was Dr. Thomas Fogarty. My parents and I, as well as some other family members, worked with him in family systems therapy for six months shortly after I had left the priesthood. I remember an exchange with him in the first session: he had asked about how I saw myself as part of the family; I acknowledged great confusion. Then he asked about my membership in the Church, and again I acknowledged confusion. Then he said I should forget about figuring out my place in the Church and work on figuring out my place in the family, because "when you learn to handle the family system you'll find every other system is peanuts." He was right.

What was it that changed inside of me and enabled me to stay? I think I had gone from being a disciple to being a rebel in reaction to my family desires, only to find that, in the end, I was really neither. I was a me, and parts of me approached life in religion differently than they did; parts of me were very similar to them. I had taken the route of rebellion thinking that would make me free, but I had felt an emptiness after I had exercised my freedom and moved away from church life. As I reflect on it, perhaps what helped me attain the realization that I would not be done in by the powerful institution was that I had not been controlled by a powerful family. I remember so clearly the events of one evening in Tom Fogarty's office. He asked my parents how they would react if I decided to remain out of the priesthood. They both said they had gotten over the initial upset, and would be happiest if I would do what made sense to me. I had won. My freedom of choice was being respected, and I felt free. I also had a belief I could stay free there and in other settings.

Some years later, I do not think I was wrong. Staying free has never been easy, but how to do it has been clearer. The intellect has been fairly good at charting the course and has generally been followed even when the emotions have been troubling. Over and over again I have learned from the experience of leaving the monastery, when I followed my head even though I was terribly scared, just as in therapy I have often suggested to people that emotions are part of the person and help to reveal him, but conclusions are properly made by the intellect. I learned that not living up to other people's expectations can be very stressful but, as long as you are making an unreactive choice, it is, indeed, freeing.

Since returning to active ministry ten years ago, I have done a fair amount of therapy with priests and sisters who are questioning their vocations. Using my own experience and theirs, I wish to make the following observations.

Priests and nuns usually made decisions to work for the Church at an early age. Later, with the maturity that years tend to bring, they have looked back on the child who made that decision and wondered if it was the right one. If they have become involved in psychology studies, they may well spend more time than most people questioning why they did various things. They will also be inclined to cast off their chains of the superego and listen a little more attentively to the id in order to find their ego. If they also become involved in the study of family systems, they may start to wonder, too, what connection there was between their choice of vocation and their sibling positions, desire to get away from the family, and their fusion with their parents and *their* expectations.

Let us ask the question: if every married person now subjected his or her choice of partner to that kind of scrutiny, how many marriages would be in trouble today? If all social workers scrutinized their career choice, would they make the same decision if they were freshmen in college now, and if they would leave social work if the answer was no. I wonder how many of them would be out of work today? The point is, some of the assumptions made by clergy psychology students and their counselors may be questionable.

The first assumption is that an immature choice is an invalid choice. "If they entered for the wrong reasons, they should leave." I maintain that is no more true than saying if there were some wrong reasons involved in your choice of a partner, you should forthwith get a divorce. What must be researched is whether there were also some mature reasons, and whether this choice makes sense in the here and now.

A second questionable assumption is that if one finds that one has been fused into doing something compliantly, one automatically gets differentiated by rejecting the choice made when compliant. Thus, if a woman married her husband because her mother or father approved of him and she came to recognize that fact later, the best way to unhook her fusion is to chuck her husband.

I would be deeply misunderstood if I were to be interpreted as saying that one should never leave the priesthood or the convent. I *am* saying, though, that I have observed while doing therapy—as well as observing myself—that many ministerial people shift from one rigid stance to another and never give themselves the opportunity to make a full, integrated, free, differentiated choice. And what is meant by that? Going from black to white and never finding the gray area. For example, a man may begin with a rigid intellectual position, that it is good to become a priest, and it is bad to leave the priesthood; he gets involved in studying his motives and switches the rigid intellectual position to the other side: now that he has uncovered some of the function and immaturity involved in the initial vocational choice, it becomes "bad" that he entered the priesthood (and complied to the system's expectations) and "good" that he has the courage to divorce himself from that choice.

What then is the gray area? It is the point some ministerial people never get to, because they leave in the middle of their reactive distancing, fooling themselves and their therapists into believing they are differentiating. The gray area is the point on the other side of the reactivity. After I have pulled out and thrown out all the values that were fused into me by my parents, and have cleansed myself from all of that fusion, I decide which of those values I actually like and can claim for myself, even though by doing that I am complying to someone else's expectations. For example, Johnny's mother wants him to be a pianist, and so she forces him to practice. When Johnny gets too old to be forced, he stops playing the piano and wins the power struggle with his mother. But his mother keeps screaming at him, trying to convince him to go back to the piano. If Johnny decides at some point that he really would like to be a pianist, *one* of the difficulties he is likely to experience is his own internal resistance to giving in to his mother's demand. If he grows up, differentiates, he can decide to play the piano because he wants to, even though his mother thinks she is winning the power struggle. Given enough maturity (differentiation), he can allow her to interpret him any way she likes, without correcting her.

It is my experience that nuns and priests in vocational crises are often caught in the position of giving up their vocation and cutting off, and that most of the therapists they go to encourage that reactivity, mistaking it for differentiation. My impulse is to confront them with their blamecasting and their statements about inability to continue. They appear to have the need to get to the other side of an ocean of uncertainty to stand on firm ground again, where they can make a calm, differentiated, and free choice about their lives and continuation in their vocations. Is it possible to go as far as the integration process and still decide to leave? Of course it is—just as it is to make a differentiated choice to obtain a divorce. It takes a lot of work, a lot of quieting down of reactivity and weighing out of the value of continuing or ending a relationship at that time—and such scrutiny is painful, indeed. It is, I think, maturing, too. It allows you to become integral, if you last through the integration stage.

Chapter 5

BECOMING REAL

Stephanie St. John, M.S.

"Real isn't how you are made," said the Skin Horse. "It's a thing that happens to you. When a child loves you for a long, long time not just to play with, but REALLY loves you, then you become REAL."

"Does it hurt?" asked the Rabbit.

"Sometimes," said the Skin Horse, for he was always truthful. "When you are Real you don't mind being hurt."

- - - - - - - - - - - -

"Does it happen all at once, like being wound up," he asked, "or bit by bit?"

"It doesn't happen all at once," said the Skin Horse. "You become, it takes a long time. That's why it doesn't often happen to people who break easily, or have sharp edges, or who have to be carefully kept. Generally, by the time you are Real, most of your hair has been loved off, and your eyes drop out and you get loose in the joints and very shabby. But these things don't matter at all, because once you are Real you can't be ugly, except to people who don't understand." [Williams, 1958, p. 17]

Long, long ago, in a land far away I was the rabbit who was afraid to be real, in many respects because I had learned that it might hurt, or people might think that I was ugly. This is the chronicle of my begin-

---

In order to preserve the privacy of her family and to ensure confidentiality, the author is using a fictional name.

ning to become real, initially without my intention and only with the efforts and caring of a trustworthy Skin Horse.

* * * * *

In 1975, I entered the extended family course with Paulina McCullough, M.S.W. at Western Psychiatric Institute and Clinic, (Pittsburgh, Pennsylvania) with two goals in mind: to increase my skills as a family therapist by learning more about Bowen family systems theory, and to learn to cope more effectively in a conflictual relationship with my mother. The course met for one year in weekly two-hour sessions of a group of family therapists, who each presented their own families for consultation. In the succeeding two years, consultation sessions were held as individual members requested them. Although the issues which initially encouraged me to join the course involved the triangles of (1) my mother, my father, and me and (2) my parents, my in-laws, and me, my focus in the course rapidly turned to my marital relationship.

The same issue of "responsibility" that was so bothersome in my family of origin appeared in my nuclear family. Bowen (1974, p. 84) indicates that the "most productive route for change, for families who are motivated, is to work at defining self in the family of origin, and to specifically avoid focus on the emotional issues in the nuclear family." My personal experience, however, was that focusing on the nuclear family first can be more helpful. For me, the anxiety was less since the marital discomfort was great and I felt I had little to lose. I suspected that work on my family of origin might result in permanent cut-offs that would be less tolerable than a cut-off from my spouse. The beginning signs of success in the area of marriage then gave me courage to go on and tackle the more difficult task in my family of origin. I have yet to explore the issues dealt with in this paper in my broader extended family; that is my agenda for the future.

The term *real* has for me many elements of Bowen's differentiated position. It is being free to be oneself and acknowledge oneself as an individual with both positive and negative characteristics. Prior to the course, I had spent so much time and energy attempting to do the "right" things in relation to my parents and people in general that it was difficult to be sure of what I thought, felt, or believed; so much depended on what would be approved of and accepted. This often resulted in feeling like a hypocrite, since I was unable to freely risk being entirely myself—real. The differentiated person is able to be real and to feel unthreatened by someone else's reality.

(In order to preserve the fluidity of this chronicle of my work in the course, I shall not expound the theory that accompanies the steps I took, but will instead refer to the appropriate literature.)

REDEFINING — "WHERE ARE THE CLOWNS?"

Who would not agree wholeheartedly that difficulties in a relationship are mutually contributed to? A statement such as this, though, intellectually acceptable, has the potential to create panic when its truth becomes apparent at a gut level, particularly to an individual who had essentially made it her life's goal to avoid being wrong, doing the wrong thing, or appearing silly. It was incomprehensible to me how one who seemed to think things through carefully, attempt to anticipate *responsibility* the outcomes of alternative modes of action, and carry tasks through to completion, in short, one who seemed to be dependable and trustworthy—could be involved in another's seeming carelessness, irresponsibility, undependability, and untrustworthiness. I had made many fumbling attempts (in my responsible way) to right things in my relationship with my husband, Adam, but generally my attempts all involved a new plan to get him to change, to "shape up," become more responsible. It was not until I began working in the extended family course that I was forced to look at how I needed to change the focus from my husband to my self. As I recollect, my initial reaction to group members' questioning me and seeming to be quite taken with my husband was to assume that they simply did not understand the situation. We were firmly entrenched in roles of "responsible and intelligent" versus "irresponsible and intellectually dull." Waterman's (1972, p. 114) statement that "most dilemmas cannot be solved in the context in which they are stated" described the situation accurately. I was feeling quite frustrated and hopeless without realizing that my definition of the situation made a solution impossible. Waterman continues (p. 115): "The quagmire has a base of emotions which is self-pity, a martyred feeling, pompous self-righteousness, helplessness, despair, panic, hatred—but none of these emotions give firm footing."

I was unaware of the important purpose Adam served in being the repository of all the disowned parts of myself. As I reflect on this responsible, logical, intelligent, efficient role I was playing, it becomes apparent how out of character as a younger of two sisters was my behavior according to the prototypes Toman (1969) describes. Likewise,

Adam, as the oldest of three brothers was functioning more like a youngest. I remember, in my bitterest moments, feeling as though my husband's entire family had deceived me. They all knew these many secrets about Adam's defective functioning, and had purposely hidden them so as to have him off their hands! It was not until recently that I realized that I had been looking for someone to take care of me (not so out of character for a youngest), and had felt cheated and foiled when the "oldest" I chose refused to fit the plan. I berated his immaturity—his not having grown up to take care of me (I shudder to think where I would be if I had managed to hook up with an individual who would have agreed to make my decisions, handle things for me, and take care of me.) Rather than differentiating from my extended family, I seemed to be attempting to transfer that lack of differentiation into the relationship with Adam, to attempt to fuse with him—and he re-fused.

The marital system, of course, was homeostatic. The more cautious I was with money, the more foolhardy Adam seemed to be in his spending, and vice versa. The tidier I attempted to be, the sloppier he became. The more responsible I was, the more irresponsible he seemed to be. I could see no way out. Although I had attempted, on numerous occasions, to be less tidy or less responsible, the motivating force was anger and revenge, with no clear understanding of the part my behavior played in keeping the system going. I feared that unbalancing the system would create a runaway. If I were to spend money more freely, along with Adam, we would be ruined financially. I did not understand balance, homeostasis, or deviation amplifications (Hoffman 1971). As I view it now, Adam and I both had our doubts about our capabilities of handling our lives on our own. As he gave indication of his self-doubts (something I was not free enough to do openly), my own self-doubts would begin. I would work extremely hard and efficiently to counter my own doubts, but only succeeded in further stimulating Adam's doubts about his capabilities and, at the same time, stimulated feelings in myself of being overworked and abused. In my anger and resentment, I would chide Adam for his lack of hard work, which created the necessity for my overwork. He would then further doubt his own capabilities, as well as become angry at my nagging and, of course, behave even less responsibly. I would work harder and more efficiently, and so on. We continued to trigger emotions in each other and to reinforce, unwittingly, behaviors we objected to (see Fig. 5-1).

When the tension in this whole sequence would become too great,

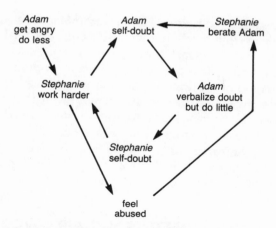

(After the example by Feldman, 1976)

Figure 5-1. Performance of the clowns.

or stress external to the marriage impinged, Adam would often suffer a breakdown of some physiological system—he was even less able to carry on his responsibilities, and I would attempt to pick up more of his functions. In these cases, however, much of the affect involved went underground, since, after all, Adam *was* suffering physically and even I am loath to berate under such circumstances. It reminds me of Stephen Sondheim's "Send in the Clowns."*

> Isn't it rich?
> Are we a pair?
> Me here at last on the ground
> You in mid-air.
>
> Where are the clowns?
>
> Isn't it bliss?
> Don't you approve?
> One who keeps tearing around
> One who can't move.
>
> Where are the clowns?
> Send in the clowns.

---

*From *A Little Night Music.* Copyright © 1973, 1987 Rilting Music, Inc., and Revelation Music Publishing Corp. International copyright secured. A Tommy Valando Publication.

Now it seems incredible to me that I was unable to see the similarity of my behavior to that of my mother (also a youngest), which I had resented for many years. In fact, the issue that initially encouraged me to join the family course was on my own difficulty with my mother's accusations that I showed little responsibility and love toward her and my father. Having joined the extended family group and presented my family system, the tremendous desperation, depression, and anger I had felt about the issues with my mother seemed miraculously to dissipate, while at the same time the ongoing conflict in my marriage heightened. Of course, I felt there was no relationship between the two; the shift of feelings was coincidental.

MARITAL MOVES – "GETTING MY HAIR LOVED OFF"

Since the tension was high in the marital relationship, my work began there. With the support of the extended family group, I was able again to attempt to stop filling the role of the person to worry about bills, see that things borrowed were returned, take care of obligations for gifts and letters to grandparents and parents, attempt to keep the house organized, and generally be practical. This time I was committed to maintaining this new stance for however long was necessary, not out of revenge, but in order to get in touch with these aspects of myself as well as allow room for the responsible, logical, practical characteristics of Adam to show themselves. The steps I took involved changes that individually seemed inconsequential, but which en masse began to get the message across that I simply wouldn't – rather, couldn't – handle all these functions any longer. For me, to present the image of being unable to cope, and really get in touch with my inadequacies initially caused feelings of panic and shame (the latter rampant in our family). In time, however, and not too long at that, I felt as though a great weight had been lifted from me – a real freeing up – a certain relaxation, of which I was actually proud. It had never occurred to me that I would one day find pleasure in my own "frailties." During an argument with Adam I began to let go and act berserk, which I had often felt the impulse to do, but had been unable to fit in between my logical arguments. I ran up and down our hall, slamming my fists into the wall and crying hysterically. The anger seemed to be as much at myself as at the situation, for somehow, in that argument, something "clicked" for me in a new way, and I became aware in one overwhelming rush of how I had contributed to the state of our marriage and, much more, how I had treated Adam and what type of person I had been. From that point on, the changes came somewhat more easily.

I needed to establish myself as an individual differentiated from Adam and to detriangle myself from all the attempts of others to get me to be responsible for him. I informed Adam's parents that I no longer was able to handle letter writing and that, although I enjoyed their letters, they would receive no more from Pittsburgh unless they could encourage Adam to write. I ordered some lamps I had wanted for a long time, bought myself a few things without consulting Adam (something he never demanded or wanted anyway), and began to look into the cost of going on a vacation by myself (Adam was unemployed at the time—a furloughed pilot for a small charter company). I began to let dishes and dust pile up, doing them when I felt like it, and taking more time just to enjoy myself (Bowen 1971).

As messages began to come in from family members, particularly Adam's parents, about things I should remind Adam about or things I should see that he got done, I declined, saying that I realized my mental health was failing and since I was having a difficult enough time coping with myself, it was "every man for himself." Adam's parents were startled, even mildly annoyed, but very concerned about me, and quickly redirected their messages to him. In accord with their style, though, there was little reaction if he failed to follow through on tasks he offered to complete, information he planned to obtain for them, letters he promised to write. They humorously mentioned such things, but there was no discord, no shame, as I had been used to in my family. My inner reaction was anger, for their part in creating such an irresponsible person (plus envy for having parents who always treat one with respect). My overt response was to write to Adam's mother, expressing admiration for her ability to stay off Adam's back, lamenting my own nagging behavior, and requesting advice on how to be more like her. The message filtered down to Adam's youngest brother (aided by a letter I wrote telling him of my difficulty in coping lately), who wrote him a letter urging him to look more vigorously for a job (something I had *not* been worried about!). This same brother wrote to the middle brother, chiding him for not being more responsible in visiting his parents, a battle cry which Adam quickly picked up, putting him in the role of keeping someone else responsible! When I *did* feel like writing letters to Adam's grandmothers, I did so for me with news only about me. Initially, I planned rather illogical, impractical, irresponsible things to do, but once I freed up those aspects of myself, planning was quite unnecessary. I knew I had made progress when

Adam told me one day—in no uncertain terms— how stupid some action of mine was, and we both stopped short and dissolved in laughter (Bowen 1971). Being me, being real, was not shameful and not devastating.

In essence, the message from my family had been: "You cannot be a good person if you do not do everything right. If you do anything wrong, you shall feel very ashamed." Adam's family, on the other hand, promoted the view that "no matter what you do, you are a good person; it doesn't matter that there is *a lot* you probably can't handle—do not distress yourself; you (we) can't handle distress."

There are many signposts by which I measure the changes in my functioning and the reverberations in my relationship. Things improved, I became pregnant, and I was able during the pregnancy to let myself be taken care of (at least a little). I was able to trust and depend on Adam as my Lamaze coach during the difficult delivery of our son. Adam and I are both involved in the care of our son, Jed, as well as household and financial management, without which I would not be able to coordinate my career, our home, and parenting. In fact, we work together as a team in a more satisfying and effective manner than I had imagined possible. In the fall of 1977 I made the decision, monumental for me, to cut back to part-time employment. It meant that I would be the one throwing a crimp in our budget and that I would depend largely on Adam for our financial support (he changed jobs frequently and had been unemployed for a total of 16 months during recent years). In addition, as I began the second draft of this very chapter, Adam was asked to resign from his job because of financial cutbacks by his employer. When a friend questioned whether I would return to a full-time schedule and I realized the thought had never even occurred to me, I knew I had come a long way.

EXTENDED FAMILY – "THE ORIGINS OF IT ALL"

The work in my extended family has been much more difficult for me (see Fig. 5–2). The issue of responsibility that emerged in my marriage needed, predictably, to be traced to its origins in my extended family, where the distinction was never clearly made between being responsible *to* others and being responsible *for* others. In my family, being "responsible" often meant taking on the responsibility (whether or not it was requested) for doing another's thinking, feeling, speaking, and decision-making rather than being defined as meeting one's own

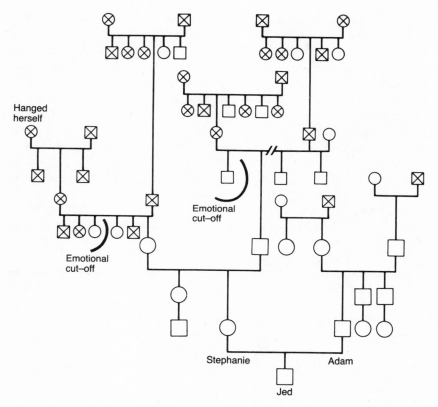

Figure 5-2. Family diagram.

needs, setting one's own goals, and accepting the consequences of
one's own actions or lack of action. Conflicts between individuals, in
which one appeared to be the one who is "doing the right thing" (i.e.
responsible) and the other appeared to be the "neglectful, selfish" one
(i.e., irresponsible) were frequent in my family. These conflicts were
overtly between my mother and one of her children or between my
mother and one of either her or my father's sibs, and they centered on
responsibility toward one's mother. There was no overt discord between my parents—as there was in my marriage—around the issue of
responsibility, despite the fact that my mother is, as I was, "responsible." The operating principle in my parents' marriage was "Never
present your spouse in anything but a very positive light, particularly
with the children." It is apparent that for my parents the arena for conflict was with sibs and offspring, not spouse; while I seemed to react in

the direction of preserving the relationship with sibs and offspring (this, until recently, in fantasy), opting for marital discord and spouse dysfunction (Bowen 1971). It occurs to me that the mode of dealing with one's immaturity may demonstrate predictable shifts from one generation to the next in reaction to the effects of the mode used in the previous generation. I have not yet explored this issue back to my grandparents' generation in my plodding efforts to differentiate.

Both of my parents were the sibs in their generation most devoted to the theme "Do not abandon your mother." In the early years of their marriage, both mothers-in-law took up residence with my parents. The exact details of these decisions are unclear, but I understand the major aspects to be: (1) other sibs of my parents were not eager to have their mother live with them; (2) my parents each felt responsible to have their mother live with them; (3) my parents each felt responsible to their spouse's mother, and (4) "one does not abandon one's mother." This theme seems likely, in my mother's family, to have had some relation to my maternal grandmother, for as a child of preschool age she had discovered her mother after she had hanged herself. I don't recall my grandmother's discussing this experience, but its impact may be assumed to have been great. My mother and father lived with my maternal grandparents for a time early in their marriage, and next door for another period; they often took my grandparents with them when they went out. When my grandfather died, my grandmother came to live with my parents, at my mother's request. My grandfather had often commented that upon his death, my grandmother *would* live with my parents.

My paternal grandfather was a colonel in the U.S. Army, and was transferred frequently. My father, therefore, moved often as a child, and while my grandfather went on ahead to his new position, my grandmother and her sons (my father was the middle child) stayed behind and fended for themselves. The message I always heard clearly about those days from my father was that my grandmother depended on "the boys" quite a bit to handle things; further, his older brother was not too dependable in this regard, leaving my father as the next oldest and therefore responsible for managing things. An anecdote I often heard concerned my grandmother calling the three boys for some help, with one running right, one running left, and my father remaining standing in the middle and thus the one who inevitably ended up doing whatever was to be done. My paternal grandmother came to live with us when finances became difficult for her some years after my grandparents became divorced. An interesting side-light here is that my paternal grandparents were divorced for several months without informing their children. My father, in high school at the time, was enlightened when he went to visit his father for the summer. (I discovered this in gathering information for my extended family work.)

There were years of bitter arguing between my mother and both her and my father's sibs (while my father largely observed) over the care of their mothers. The arguing seemed to consist mostly of my mother's attempting to berate the sibs' lack of responsibility and effort, and her own feelings of being overworked and abused. There were three total family cut-offs and one partial cut-off that eventually resulted at least in part, from this issue (see family diagram, Fig. 5–2). My mother's oldest sister and her only brother, as well as my father's older brother, dissociated themselves from my family completely. My father's younger brother continued to argue and occasionally distance himself, but has remained affiliated with the family. I now see a strong need to reconnect with these cut-off relatives; however, my first efforts were in my relationships with my parents.

Crises arose in my extended family when I attempted to make what appeared to be fairly typical moves, such as deciding to go to college, accepting an offer to live free of charge on campus as a college senior, considering reconfirmation in my husband's church, and making plans for allotting time with in-laws on trips home. As I attempted to make each of these "crisis" moves, I always wanted – and expected – my parents to be pleased with my decisions. They never were, at least overtly. I was always subjected to a harangue from my mother, while my father quietly listened, never disagreeing with her. His philosophy was that she knew what was best for "you girls," clearly leaving her responsible for us. My mother labeled each decision as a direct move against her, which indicated my lack of concern for her. I always reacted to this, initially by trying to explain logically to her how her perceptions were inaccurate, and then with quickly rising anger to match her emotionality. She made absurd statements and accusations, which I found intolerable. When the extended family group questioned why statements had to be true and logical, I couldn't answer. What else was there? She periodically threatened to forbid me ever to return home and generally stated she would "never forgive" me. I never thought to question what that meant. My mother did, however, become the recipient of the resentment of my sister and myself, since she was the disciplinarian and the tier of the apron strings as we tried to separate. I never perceived that she was representing my father as well as herself, and that some of the bitterness I felt belonged to him for giving all such responsibility to her and for not helping tone her down when her "responsibility" nearly overwhelmed me.

THE PARENTAL TRIANGLE – MOVING IN TO MOVE OUT

All along I had felt so stuck, so unable to do freely what I thought best in my life. I was well into my extended family work when I realized that although I felt so "in" I would never get out, my parents viewed me as so "out" they would never be able to get me back in. It had not occurred to me that in spite of the harassment involved with most moves I wanted to make, I had *always* made them. How would my mother know I had always heard her? She didn't, and she spoke more frequently and more intensely with each new decision I made. I needed to (1) reverse the process and do less of the adamant pro-claiming of my separateness from her and (2) establish more extensive individual relationships with each of my parents rather than have my mother be the hub of communication (Bowen 1974).

Among my first steps were attempts to stand back and observe the sequence of interactions, program some neutral statements to help me through generally emotionally reactive times, and get out of the bind of needing to be logical. Although I had feared the predictable reaction from my parents, "You're not much of a psychologist; you need one yourself," I was much less reactive than I thought I would be, particu-larly following my self-awareness in the marital work I had done. (Evi-dently my message of not being able to cope was getting across. There were no expressions of concern from my parents – just accusations.)

I began to ask my mother advice more often, let her know more of the internal emotional turmoil I experienced, and attempted to draw my father into discussions in a more active way.

FAMILY FLOW – BIRTH AND DEATH

In the two following years there occurred major events that provided opportunities to continue the above-mentioned efforts:

Spring 1975   Issue of reconfirmation raised – attempt to put the issue of religious differences back between my parents

March 1976   Announcement of my pregnancy

April 1976   Father's first heart attack
October 1977   Birth of first child (Jed)
March 1977   Father's second heart attack
May 1977   Father's death

When the issue of my reconfirmation in my husband's church emerged, my mother saw my in-laws as having won some ground in the competition for "best-liked in-laws." She saw the reconfirmation as a move against her and her church, and began making comments and asking questions about how Adam's mother would react if she were "treated" similarly. I detriangled here (Bowen 1974) by passing the questions along to my mother-in-law and requesting she answer them, since I was at a loss to do so (and wanted to be out of the position of being responsible for answering for everyone). I passed on to my husband all the accusations my mother made about his tearing me away from her and controlling my life. These were the sorts of statements I would formerly have kept to myself, hoping that others would not be aware of how illogical my mother could be. I was no longer responsible for her behavior. She was busily trying to convince me that I was not responsible for my own—Adam, or the church, or friends were controlling my mind. I did not reconfirm, hoping that for once my mother would become aware of her influence on me. I admitted my gullibility and admired her ability to "see things so clearly." I requested she not try to cut the apron strings from me too fast.

As for the issue of religious differences, I decided to put it back with my parents, where it belonged. My father, a disenchanted Catholic, and my mother, a part-time overtly practicing Lutheran, never resolved the issue of religious differences between themselves. My father left the church and declared himself an atheist, and my mother sent my sister and me to Lutheran Sunday school. Whenever I approached my father about his religious beliefs, he would respond briefly and factually, and my mother would write to tell me to let him alone, since he wished not to talk about religion; then she would go on to tell me what God and she wanted for my life. I remember remarking in an extended family group session, that I had convened for some help in dealing with this issue, that my father would rather have a heart attack than deal with my mother on an important issue such as this. A few weeks later, I announced my pregnancy and he had his first heart attack. I am not relating these as causal connections, but I am noting that they coincide.

The pregnancy was a time during which I had many opportunities to move into my family of origin. My feeling was that my pregnancy was more difficult for my father to accept than for my mother, and that he saw it as an indication of my increasing separation from *him*, in particular, and of my decreasing need for him. When my father heard of my pregnancy, he had little to say. My mother questioned him about his silence, and he said he wasn't eager to be a grandfather; but he would not elaborate. My parents arrived to "celebrate" the next day, and my father's greeting was to hug me and smilingly (?) say, "You traitor." It was then that I recalled his continuous "joking" as I dated, questioning why I would want to marry when I could stay home with him. He had shown he loved and enjoyed my husband throughout our courtship and our seven years of marriage. I felt that perhaps the baby signified physical separation from him and uniting with another male, and this would be too difficult for him to accept. I began a campaign during my pregnancy of letting my father know how much I still needed him — admitting my ambivalence about being pregnant and my fears about parenting, opening up the topic of "how does one define being a 'good parent'." My father, predictably, did not answer my letters, but evidently he had my mother read them (as she always shared with him my letters to her), for she generally responded to the issues raised. One year later, as my father and I were dealing with his impending death following his second heart attack, we had the opportunity to compare notes of his fathering, his regrets and my perceptions.

As other family members were busily talking with my father about how he *was* going to recover, my learning to be less responsible to others and more to myself, allowed me to speak directly to him about the possibility of dying, my fears about how I would manage without him, and my sadness. Arranging time alone with him was a major challenge, not only because of the policy of the intensive care unit, which allowed only fifteen minutes of family visitation once every three hours, but also because it made my mother very anxious. She had difficulty tolerating not being privy to our conversations and seemed threatened by my irresponsibility in not saying "the right things" to my father. I was able to arrange time alone with him, however, through letters, telephone calls, early-morning trips to the hospital while other family members were still sleeping, and a "God-send" of a trip to visit by myself.

A few weeks after my father's second heart attack (and six months after the birth of my son), I was overwhelmed by a last attempt at maintaining my position of responsibility. I felt as though I were doing nothing well, not having enough time for my son, or my husband, or our first "child" (a German shepherd); not doing my job or my house-keeping and homemaking well—there just was not enough time. None of these victims complained, though, and that bothered me too. A consultation about my family helped me put my feeling of lack of time back where it belonged, with my father. I accepted the advice given me to go back home, minus husband and child, to spend time with him. My father died one week later. In the past I would never have done such an "irresponsible" thing, making a trip without planning ahead, with no connections, creating further trouble with our budget, and leaving an "undependable" husband to care for the baby for a weekend. (It is interesting to note here that my solitary arrival, unannounced, late at night, evoked fantasies in my father that I had separated from Adam and "come home." His response was to be glad that he still had the house, with a room for me.)

FAMILY CONFLICT: AN ILLUSTRATION

The specific circumstance that prompted my interest in extended family work illustrates most of the issues mentioned and the differentiating techniques used over the course of my work.

There were, for years, annual Christmas battles between my mother and me over the allotment of time spent with each set of in-laws. Despite all our neurotic efforts to see that all were fairly treated, often involving over-compensating by giving my mother more time, my husband and I were generally accused by my mother of not thinking enough of her feelings, not doing enough with both my parents, and, finally, with giving Adam's parents "prime time" (better hours)! Generally, the questions would begin some weeks before Christmas: "Where are you going to sleep when you come home?"; "how many nights with 'them'?"; "where will you eat meals?"; "who will you go to church with?," etc. On one plane trip home with both families meeting our plane, my mother looked at me, almost demanding "who will you hug first—her or me?" The issue "whose car will you ride in from the airport to the house" was blatantly discussed. In all the situations, my mother would raise the issues and argue the points while my father listened, saying essentially nothing, my in-laws making it known that whatever we did, they would support. No matter what we planned, my mother would find something that displeased her, and on Christmas Eve she would sniffle in the kitchen over how we had "hurt" her, would get quite cold toward us, or comment on our behavior, to which I would react with rage.

The issue of church attendance was particularly troublesome for me. My mother, who seldom attended church while I was growing up, berated my husband and me for attending church with my in-laws rather than with her on Christmas Eve. She would have no one to go to church with, since my father would not attend. Rather than dealing with him about this, the responsibility (which I always "shirked") fell to me to accompany her. My sister was spared this, since she chose never to arrive in town until Christmas morning. I did not want to lay on someone else the guilt my mother laid on me (and I certainly did not want to recreate the cut-offs with sibs that occurred in my mother's family); thus I never tried to enlist my sister in taking some of the heat. Directly approaching the issue of my father accompanying my mother generally resulted in further harangues from my mother concerning my lack of respect and her policy of never forcing my father to do anything against his wishes. Somehow, I could not simply do what I thought best and ignore her reaction. I responded not with guilt, but with anger that her attitude destroyed any Christmas spirit I arrived with. I experienced little anger with my father for not helping me out in all this. On a few occasions, when I tried to get him to take a stand, he would noncommittally say both "you have to do what you think best" and "your mother knows what is best for you, girls." On some occasions he would make a more pointed remark, such as, "If they don't want to come around, I wouldn't coax them."

Having learned about triangles in the extended family course, I tried a number of techniques to extricate myself from this triangle. I suggested to both mothers that they get together to plan our schedule, since we seemed to do such a poor job of it. My mother declined, indicating this was my responsibility, not hers. Adam's mother was confused, since she thought we were managing our time adequately. Adam became anxious with this suggestion. He had picked up my concern about how illogical my mother is in discussion of such things and wanted to protect is mother, since "she wasn't complaining" anyway. One Christmas I did nothing about the scheduling and let Adam handle all of it. I redirected to Adam any question, from either family, concerning arrangements. Adam's family, again, was confused, but was becoming accustomed to my taking responsibility no-longer and said little. My mother, of course, saw this as further evidence of my lack of concern for her, since I was not going to "fight for her side." I wrote a letter requesting advice from my father on how to stay out of the middle and how to improve my success in getting others to make plans. Of course, he didn't respond. I, like my in-laws with my husband, would make humorous responses about his not following through, but put no pressure on him. I knew I was making some progress, when two years later (Christmas of 1976) Adam and my mother were the "Christmas Eve arguers" while I stayed upstairs. When my mother attempted to pull me into the argument (asking why I was not supporting her and how I could let my husband say "such things" to her), I directed her back to Adam, pointing out that I did not control his behavior.

That was to be my father's last Christmas, and for the first time I experienced real annoyance with him for having such a "humbug" attitude and dampening Christmas spirit. I never realized in my push for "spirit" that he was, perhaps, dealing with his own approaching death. In spite of the similar efforts I was involved in, I did not expect his death to occur so soon. The overriding emotion I experienced with regard to that Christmas was sadness, not anger, as I finally recognized that I had been trying year after year to fit my parents into my expectations, and they were never going to fit. I entered the first Christmas without my father, with few expectations other than that it would be sad without him. I was determined not to be concerned about Christmas spirit, to deal with whatever occurred, and of course, the holiday progressed with ease. My mother made few comments about our behavior, and I was not reactive to those she did make. Although my mother and in-laws spent all of Christmas day together, I did not feel drawn into my usual position of helping my mother feel and appear comfortable in the presence of my overconfident mother-in-law.

CLOSING REMARKS – THE BEAT GOES ON

There have been changes in my extended family system. Most notably, the tension between my mother and myself has lessened. I have put much thought into trying to understand the relationship between the work in my nuclear family and that in my family of origin. It seems to me that I grew up with the threat that any acknowledgment of irresponsibility towards one's mother (abandonment *of* her) could result in abandonment *by* her and, therefore, I learned very early on not to acknowledge or accept irresponsible aspects of myself. It is not difficult to conceive of this as projection through two generations of the theme of "abandonment of and by mothers" relating to my maternal great-grandmother's hanging. Rather than dealing with my own irresponsibility, which would risk my being cut off, I dealt with Adam's irresponsibility and often threatened to cut off from him. The extended family course work began with the marital situation. The risk was less with Adam because (1) I was feeling quite bitter toward him anyway, and (2) he never threatened a cut-off. When I was able, with the aid of consultations, to deal with my own irresponsibility in the marriage and discovered it did not result in the feared cut-off, I became a bit better able to be irresponsible in my family of origin. Some of the lessening of the tension between my mother and me since my father's death seems related to my feeling of less risk that my mother will cut off from me without her husband to turn to. I see both my mother and me as interfering in some way with others' attempts to be responsible (my mother's sibs with regard to their mother's care, Adam with marital responsibilities) because of the possible effects:

1. My mother would have to share her mother with her sibs (abandonment of and by her mother?).
2. If my marriage were successful, I would be moving more away from my mother (abandonment of and by her?).

I realize that my father remains curiously outside most of the affect that accompanies my thoughts about my attempts at differentiation. In my family, fathers have always been presented in glowing terms and have generally been outside areas of conflict. This is not clear to me. Abandonment of and by fathers has not been as overt an issue, although it did arise for me when I was pregnant.

With my father's death, the issue of my mother's residence arose. My parents had sold their home and were planning to move into a new house they were building. When a family conference was held to elicit the thoughts of all, I alone leaned in the direction of her continuing with the plan for the new house. I would have predicted prior to the extended family work that I either would have responsibly taken over arrangements, as my mother had done in her generation, or I would have refused even to consider the possibility of her living with me. Surprisingly, my sister offered to have my mother live with her, and I was able *not* to feel drawn into making the same offer. Later, when my mother directly questioned me concerning her options in deciding where to live, I included living with us, but declined to encourage her in *any* particular direction. She chose to live in the new house and has adjusted well.

I am trying to keep track of the ways in which my son, Jed, is triangled into the system. He has "eased" many difficult times. My mother makes fewer demands on Adam and me, prefacing most of them with concern for the baby's convenience and well-being. He entered all of our lives when we were faced with sadness and loss.

It seems that my next steps will need to be in the direction of renewing contacts with cut-off family members and exploring the issues of responsibility and abandonment of and by mothers, fathers, and husbands back at least another generation. For the time being, I am enjoying not feeling driven to responsibly continue working daily on family. I am not overworked or abused. I am rolling with what life presents, and when the next crisis comes, I'll call my coach, and the extended family group, and ask them to take care of me.

REFERENCES

Bowen, M. (1971). The use of family theory in clinical practice. In *Changing Families*, ed. J. Haley. New York: Grune and Stratton. pp. 159–192.

Bowen, M. (1974). Toward the differentiation of self in one's family of origin. In *Georgetown Family Symposia*, vol. 1, 1971–1972. ed. F. D. Andres and J. P. Lorio. Washington, D.C.: Family Center, Department of Psychiatry, Georgetown University Medical Center.

Feldman, L. B. (1976). Depression and marital interaction. *Family Process* 15(4):389–395.

Hoffman, L. (1971). Deviation-amplifying processes in natural groups. In *Changing Families*, ed. J. Haley, pp. 285–309. New York: Grune and Stratton.

Toman, W. (1969). *Family Constellation*, 2nd ed. New York: Springer-Verlag.

Waterman, C. E. (1972). Dilemmas, paradoxes and family quagmires. In *Systems Therapy*, ed. J. O. Bradt and C. J. Moynihan, pp. 111–116. Washington, D.C.: Groome Child Guidance Center.

Williams, M. (1958). *The Velveteen Rabbit,* p. 17. New York: Doubleday.

Chapter 6

EFFORTS TO MODIFY ONE'S POSITION IN INTERLOCKING TRIANGLES

Jack T. LaForte, Ph.D.

My interest in family of origin work dates back to the autumn of 1976 when I was an intern in the Family Therapy Training Program at Bristol Hospital, in Bristol, Connecticut. At that time I was introduced to Bowen theory and the concept of extended family work. One of the requirements for the first-year intern was to make a family diagram of his or her own family and present the family diagram, along with other material about own family, to the group of interns.

I live approximately 225 miles from my parents; it would have taken four to five hours each way for a visit. At that time, it was not possible to make a trip until later on in the winter; so I asked my parents to select 50 to 100 pictures of family over three generations. I also thought it would be interesting to see which ones they selected. From the group of pictures they were to send I planned to select twenty to thirty for a presentation.

Within three weeks a package arrived containing a couple of hundred pictures of family members, a list of names, and dates of births, deaths, and other nodal events. I went through the pictures and laid out the family diagram. As I did this I saw some interesting facts emerge, of which I had not been conscious. Some were obvious, such as the fact that both my parents were the oldest siblings of their sex in their family—so two "oldest, responsible" types married each other. Another obvious fact, of which I had not really been conscious, is that both of my parents' families of origin contained two parents and five siblings (see Fig. 6-1).

A less obvious, but interesting, thing I realized when reviewing the

115

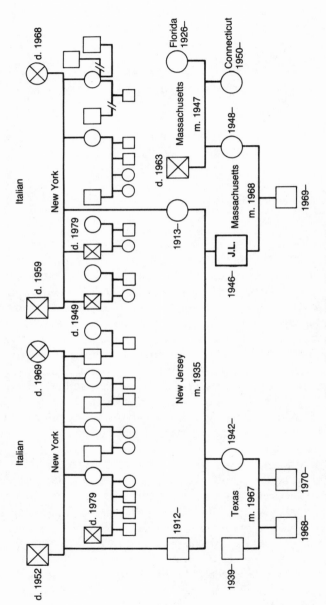

Figure 6–1. Family diagram.

family photos was the fact that my paternal grandfather was seldom in a picture with the family. He was usually photographed alone, at some activity. I did not realize to what extent he may have been a distancer. The other pictures of my father's family usually consisted of my grandmother and her three daughters, a "close bunch." In those pictures with my father, grandmother, and the three sisters, my father looked more like one of the parents, rather than a sibling. In viewing these pictures I got a better idea of how my father had been in a "parentified" role in his family of origin.

As I continued with the process of preparing a presentation of my own family for my intern group, I realized that I was seeing my family and myself from a different vantage point. This subtle activity of linking names and dates of nodal events, and viewing old photographs, had a profound impact on me, which I had not expected. I began to see how I was a part of a greater whole: my family system. From this perspective, I was not unique, or so separate as I had imagined myself. I was connected to themes and patterns, much like the threads woven together into a tapestry. My behavior had purpose and was not completely spontaneous or idiosyncratic. Paradoxically, this realization was freeing. Through this process one becomes a better observer of oneself, as if from a distance.

During the fall of 1976, I put together a booklet of photographs of my family, along with a family diagram. During the presentation I discussed some of the themes in my family and what the process of preparing the presentation had meant for me. In doing so I realized that I found a great resource for understanding of self and of families. I also was aware that I had just scratched the surface in terms of understanding my own family system. It was from this initial experience that I decided to continue my extended family work for the next several years and to include family of origin works as part of my doctoral training in counseling psychology at Union Graduate School.

THE THREE PHASES OF MY EXTENDED FAMILY WORK

Phase I

The experience that I have just described represents what I consider to be the beginning of the first phase of my extended family work. The first phase began in the fall of 1976 and extended to the spring of 1979. It consists of my introduction to the concept of extended family work; my introduction to Bowen theory; the activation of the flow of information regarding family from parents to self; the identification of some themes and patterns of behavior in family, including the major triangles in the family, and the beginning of consciously seeking to differentiate a "self" from my family of origin.

The concept of *differentiation of self* is the cornerstone of Bowen theory. According to Bowen (1976, p. 362), "the concept defines people according to the degree of fusion, or differentiation, between emotional and intellectual functioning"; those persons with a low degree of differentiation fuse emotional and intellectual processes. These persons' lives are dominated by the automatic emotional system. They are less flexible, less adaptable, and more emotionally dependent on those about them. Those persons at the other end of the continuum, who have a higher degree of differentiation, find it possible to separate emotional and intellectual functioning to a satisfactory extent. People in the latter category can retain relative autonomy in periods of stress, are more flexible, more adaptable, and more independent of the emotionality about them. They cope better with life stresses; their life courses are more orderly and successful, and they are remarkably free of human problems. In between the two extremes are an infinite number of mixtures of emotional and intellectual functioning. Thus, it was my general goal to decrease the degree of fusion between my emotional and intellectual functioning.

Phase II

After my initial exposure to, and experience with, my extended family work I decided to enter a second phase in which I had a specific focus for my family work. This second phase began during the spring of 1978 and continued to the fall of 1979. The focus I chose was my nuclear family, with a specific goal of lowering the level of reactivity between myself and my son.

It was during phase II that I actually began a systematic approach to my extended family work, with the coaching of Peter Titelman, Ph.D.

SPECIFIC FOCUS OF MY FAMILY WORK DURING PHASE II

The focus during phase II of my family work was on my own nuclear family: self, wife, and son, with the specific goal of lowering the level of reactivity between self and son. From my earlier family work I had become aware of the pattern of the projection process in my family. The family projection process, according to Bowen, refers to the process through which parental undifferentiation impairs one or more children and operates within the father–mother–child triangle. He says, "It exists in all gradations of intensity, from those in which impairment is minimal to those in which the child is seriously impaired for life. The process is so universal it is present to some degree in all families" (Bowen 1976, p. 81).

In my own family the transmission of the projection process over four generations went from maternal grandmother to mother to self to son, as illustrated in Figure 6–2. The undifferentiation would be most apparent during times of stress and would manifest itself in struggles relating to control versus autonomy, reactivity versus calm, and emotional distance versus closeness. With my grandmother and mother, the projection took the form of parentification of my mother in relation to my grandparents, and strong social prohibitions, which impaired my mother's social development to some degree. With my parents, the projection took the form of control in terms of emotional and geographical closeness versus autonomy and some emotional distance. Problems associated with such differences became greatest when I left home to go to college, after I completed college, and at various times during the establishment of my own nuclear family. Arguments would

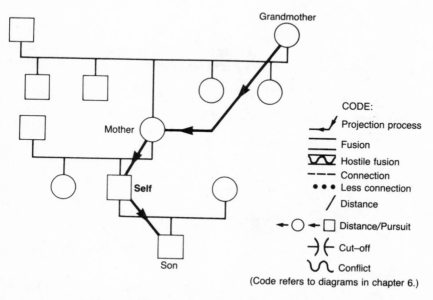

Figure 6–2. Four-generation projection process.

center around my not calling or writing frequently enough. The more demanding my parents were for communication, the stronger was my desire to distance myself from them. During periods of stress and reactivity with my parents there would be an increase in the levels of reactivity between me and my son. My reactivity took the form of controlling, i.e., correcting behaviors or criticism, with ensuing emotional distance. However, during phase II of my family work I tried to be less distant and controlling with my son. I also tried to be less reactive and distancing with my parents.

In Bowen theory the basic emotional unit is a triangle. Bowen (1976, p. 373) contends that a two-person emotional system is stable only during calm—it becomes unstable during stress. Therefore, a third person is needed to stabilize and complete the unit. Bowen (1976) calls this three-person emotional configuration a triangle. He says, "When tension in the triangle is too great for the threesome, it involves others to become a series of interlocking triangles" (p. 373).

In the following series of diagrams I present my conceptualization of the triangles in my family, the emotional flows during periods of tension, and the series of interlocking triangles that form in the emotional system during periods of tension.

Figure 6–3 illustrates stable fusion, or comfortable twosome in parents' relationship, and sister and self in distant but connected relationship with parents.

Figure 6–4 illustrates the stable fusion turning into hostile fusion as couple has conflict over issues concerning closeness and distance. Son (self) becomes triangulated by mother, but son resists and conflict ensues.

Figure 6–5 illustrates the development of the interlocking triangles in the family system. Parents join against son, son joins with wife against parents.

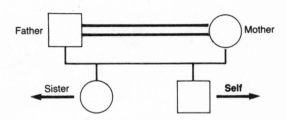

Figure 6–3. Emotional configuration of family of origin during periods of calm.

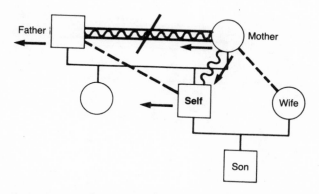

Figure 6-4. Emotional configuration of family of origin during periods of conflict.

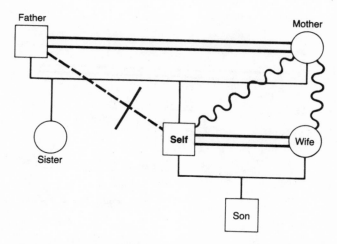

Figure 6-5. Development of interlocking triangles.

Figure 6-6 illustrates the following flow: tensions increase, distance is sought, and temporary emotional cut-off takes place.

When there is stable fusion in a marital relationship, tension from family of origin gets projected onto child in nuclear family by most stressed parent. Reactivity becomes manifest in controlling, correcting, and distancing. This process is shown in Figure 6-7.

In the nuclear family, during period of increased intensity father distances from wife, father becomes reactive with son. The father–mother–child triangle shifts, as mother counterbalances father's reac-

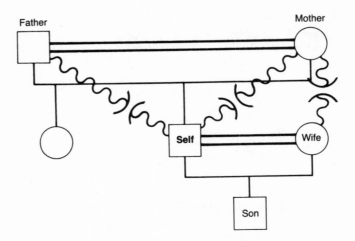

Figure 6-6. Interlocking triangles and emotional cut-off.

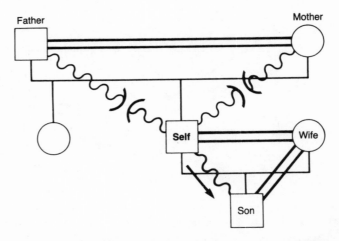

Figure 6-7. Interlocking triangles and projection to the child.

tivity with child with more closeness. This process is illustrated by Figure 6-8.

Mother disagrees with husband around issues concerning child. Father replicates pattern from family of origin, and uses emotional cutoff to distance from son in situation. This process is illustrated by Figure 6-9.

The goal of the second phase of my family work was to get out of this "stuck" position of emotional cut-off, and to try to reduce the family projection process through differentiation of self. The following is the strategy that was developed while I was being coached by Peter Titelman to deal with this problem.

STRATEGY

1. Stay in contact with parents even after arguments (shorten cooling-off periods). Talk with both parents during telephone conversations. Work on having more of a one-to-one relationship with father. Concentrate on trying to be less reactive with mother.
2. Make greater effort to be more involved with son. Try to spend more time together on a one-to-one basis: take drives together, play ball together, sign son up for soccer league, go to games, be supportive of him. Concentrate on being less critical of him. Do not

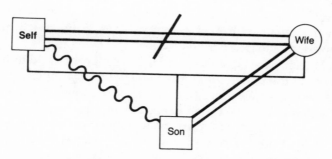

Figure 6–8. Primary triangle in the nuclear family.

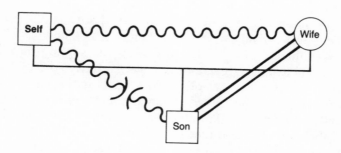

Figure 6–9. The nuclear family triangle and emotional cut-off.

enter into disagreement between wife and son, particularly siding against son. Persist with effort even if it is initially rejected.
3. Anticipate higher levels of reactivity after contact with parents. Arrange get-togethers with parents for reasonably short periods of time. Slowly increase the length of time together as situation improves.

During this phase, I made a sustained effort to implement the above strategy. Periodically I consulted my coach, Peter Titelman.

I planned activities with my son, and I worked on having more of a one-to-one relationship. I made a special effort to sign him up for the local soccer league and go to as many of his games as I could. I also tempered my reactivity and criticism of him, and tried to stay out of arguments between him and my wife. After about six months I felt that things between us began to improve. If I felt stressed, I would state it rather than act it out. I also felt a decrease in wife–self–son tension.

As for my relationship with my parents, I tried to be less reactive to my mother's demands and criticism of me. In this, I was moderately successful. At times, I would become enraged and go on the defensive, or even the offensive if mad enough. At other times I would stay unreactive for increased periods.

I felt I met resistance when I tried to have more of a one-to-one relationship with my father. Attempts to talk with my father on the telephone were often awkward and short-lived. My mother usually talked in the background while I tried to speak with him, or he would make the conversation short and turn the telephone over to my mother. I found this frustrating. During visits together I had a little more success in talking with my father. We would be in the garage/workshop, or take a short trip to the store and be able to talk a bit. The visits that took place at their house were less conflictual than at our house. When my parents visited us, my wife was more stressed and a bit more reactive. She was sensitive to my mother's unsolicited advice about housekeeping and her desire to take over the kitchen and cooking.

My relationship with my parents improved slightly during this phase. We still had disagreements and were reactive with each other; however, rather than conflict followed by emotional cut-off, there was conflict followed by short-lived distancing and continued contact. I would call them in two weeks rather than a month. In these situations I initiated the contact. I also made it a point to see them at least four times a year, whether or not we were on good terms. My wife also made it a point to write to my parents on a fairly regular basis. Thus we both tried to maintain contact.

Figure 6–10 shows the rebalancing of the triangle in the nuclear family: self in close relation with wife, self in mildly connected relation with son, and wife and son in close relation.

The relationship between self and mother alternated between conflict and calm: parents in close relationship, self and wife in close relationship, and self and son in a mildly close relationship. Figure 6–11 illustrates this process.

Phase III: Fall of 1979 to Fall of 1982

Having experienced some movement or progress in my efforts to lessen the level of reactivity between self and son, and between self and parents, I decided to focus more directly on my family of origin — mother-father-self-sister — rather than on my nuclear family.

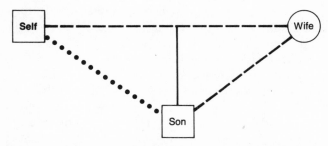

Figure 6–10. Modified emotional configuration in the nuclear family.

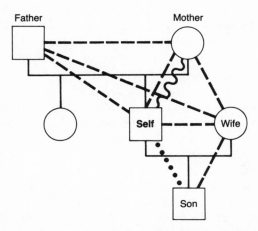

Figure 6–11. Modification of interlocking triangles.

BACKGROUND

In my family of origin my parents were both responsible "oldests." They both grew up as the parentified child in their respective families. My sibling position in my family is a younger brother to an older sister. Between my mother, father, and sister all the tasks at home would be taken care of. My place as the youngest put me in a passive position, with fewer demands or responsibilities in the household. Although I was given chores to do around the house, they were pretty minor ones. Being the youngest, I also had the least say in the decision-making process of my family.

I did not like the passive/dependent position, nor did I like not having a greater voice in the decision-making process. Thus, as I grew up, I concentrated most of my energies on activities outside the house, where I could be active and have power to influence the situation. During periods of tension in the family, my outside activities gave me a vehicle to distance myself and also stay calm. It was usually during periods of stress that my mother (who was usually the most stressed person) would become critical of my outside activities and tell me that I never did anything around the house. She would try to pull me in; I would resist, and a conflict would result.

My older sister was the compliant one. She did what my parents expected of her, and more. She studied hard and got good grades throughout school; she helped around the house, even prepared meals when my mother was too busy; and she smoothed over conflicts by being a mediator or a bridge between family members. When it was time for college, my sister went to a college in the city in which my family lived, she stayed at home and commuted to school. I, on the other hand, decided to go to college out of town, managed to get a football scholarship, and went to college in New England. My sister lived at home until she married in her mid-twenties. Eventually she moved out of town with her husband and two children. Once I left home to go to college I never moved back. The realization that I had left home unstabilized my relationship in the family. For several years this was a source of conflict, especially between my mother and me.

Figure 6–12 shows my father and mother joining against me in a triangle. My mother would be stressed by my absence. She would complain to my father, who was in a more passive position. He would eventually agree with her and become active; then they would both attack me for not writing or calling. I would become defensive, and then reactive, and a big argument would result. The argument was followed by a period of emotional cutoff. The cut-off would last one to two months, until some nodal event or holiday would open things up again. My sister, who had her own family and was in a more outside position, would help to smooth things out by encouraging each "camp" to understand the other "camp's" feelings. However, not much changed, and the cycle was repeated time and again from 1964 to 1979, with varying degrees of intensity.

GOALS

To have more of a one-to-one relationship with each member of my family of origin, especially father and mother.

STRATEGY

1. Use reversal technique. A reversal consists of doing or saying the opposite of what one would usually do or say in relation to someone else. This technique is used to change a habitual pattern and shift family patterns.
   a. Be more emotionally available to parents.
   b. Initiate contact at times: phone calls, letters, visits.
   c. Work on agreeing with parents on some issues.
2. Use soft paradox and/or humor when encountering strong resistance from parents over an issue.
3. Increase contact with sister.
4. Don't triangulate nuclear family, wife and son, in differences with my family of origin.

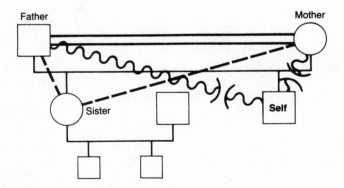

Figure 6-12. Primary configuration pattern in the family of origin: 1964-1979.

During the early part of phase III, the major nodal event was my acceptance and then participation in a doctoral program. My parents were very pleased to learn of my interests and efforts to pursue a doctoral degree. My parents have always encouraged both my sister and me to do what we could to reach our potential and be successful. My initiative to pursue the Ph.D. fulfilled my parents' wish for my success. It signaled that I had complied with their hopes for me to be a high-level professional. They were excited, and they supported my efforts. In their support they placed less of a demand on my writing or contacting them, knowing that I was occupied with my graduate activities.

Even though I was busier than I had been in the past as a result of my graduate work, I managed to maintain contact through telephoning; and I continued with the regular visits during the holidays and the summer. As a matter of fact, there was an increase in the amount of contact that I had with my family of origin during my time in the doctoral program. As a learner in an external degree program, I had to be mobile in order to attend graduate seminars in different locations around the country and, later in the program, in order to attend professional conferences. Whenever I had occasion to travel to geographical areas near my family, I made it a point to arrange to see them. Those visits were in addition to the regular visits, and had the advantage of spontaneity.

In June 1980 I attended a seminar in Philadelphia. My parents live in southern New Jersey, about an hour's drive from Philadelphia. I arranged to visit with my parents the day before the seminar began and stayed overnight with them. In a sense it felt like a visit home from college. It was very pleasant to visit both parents, and I enjoyed the spontaneous get-together. In the fall of 1982, I was invited to present a paper at the National Conference of Marriage and Family Therapists in Dallas, not far from the home of my sister and her family. Again, I made it a point to spend time with them as part of my trip.

In February 1981, early in phase III of my family work, I traveled across the country with my nuclear family to visit my sister and her family. We drove to Texas during a school vacation. We had not visited them for five years—not since they had moved to Texas; it always seemed hard to get motivated to visit Texas. But as part of my family work, the trip had more meaning and we decided to undertake it. My goal in visiting my sister, from a family perspective, was once again to initiate contact rather than remain distant; to take an active role rather than passive; to be in relationship with my sister; to be open to having her share part of her way of living with me and my family; and to stay detriangled from taking sides regarding my parents. When we were alone and the conversation shifted to my parents, I purposely stayed neutral and did not make my usual complaints regarding the demands that my parents make, or our differences concerning their life-style.

REGULAR VISITS

During the first two years of phase III, the frequency of regular visits with parents and my nuclear family remained constant at four visits per year. In the third year, the number of visits increased to six. I believe the increase in the number of visits is a sign that the quality of the contact was improving. With a better quality of time together there is a greater desire to spend time together.

In my regular visits with my parents I used the following strategy to differentiate a "self." Once again I concentrated on becoming less reactive with them. When I encountered resistance, I used "soft" paradoxical techniques to express my point of view without arguing. One technique was "reframing," in which I would say it was good that we do not always agree, that it shows that we can have different points of view and not become angry at each other. Another technique I used was "reversal": My father had gained several pounds since his retirement, and his being overweight was a family concern. Whenever someone expressed concern over his weight, he became defensive and denied that he was overweight. So instead of telling him he should lose weight I told him that he should continue to gain weight and should grow to well over 200 pounds. Having a shorter but fuller life was probably a good choice for him, even though we would miss him when he passed away; at least he would not have to deprive himself of anything now. The use of this paradoxical technique allowed me to be neutral on this issue. In the past, on an issue like this I would have joined the effort with my mother against my father. I am sure he felt then that we had ganged up on him, making him even more stubborn.

I also tried to plan the details of our visits better than I previously had. If it was my parents who were to visit my nuclear family, I would plan to take them on a short trip in the area each day. The trips got us outside and shifted the focus from meals and other issues to doing something together. I also let my parents know before the visit that we were planning to have certain foods, that food should not be brought because we already had it. Occasionally, though, I would ask them to bring something we would like to have, such as Italian pastries. This planning and communication before the visit contributed to a more relaxed time.

One of the goals of my family work during phase III was to play a more active role in activities between parents, sister, and self. As I mentioned earlier, the pattern had been that my parents and sister performed various necessary tasks, and I was in the passive role. During the summer family gathering of 1980, I decided to try and alter that pattern. My sister and her two sons were visiting my parents at their home, in southern New Jersey. I with my nuclear family came for the weekend to visit my parents and see my sister and her children. We arrived Friday evening. During the evening we discussed going to the beach on Saturday. We all agreed it would be fine to go to the beach, but in order to get a parking space we should have to leave rather early. In the past, on Saturday morning my parents would prepare a big breakfast, and then, while my parents cleaned the dishes, everyone else would get ready for the beach. My parents would then want to bring lunch, and so they would prepare the lunch. Meanwhile, everyone else would be ready for the beach and would grow anxious about the time. My parents had to finish getting lunch together, get ready themselves, and then discuss what we should have for dinner in the evening. The whole process took three hours. It would be at least 11 A.M. by then, and the beach was already getting crowded. By the time we would actually get to the state park beach that we liked, the sign would say **CLOSED**. We then had to go to the crowded public beach and endure the crowds and noise and commercialism.

However, this time I volunteered to make the lunch while my parents got ready for the beach and my wife and sister cleaned up after breakfast. It was also decided that my sister would prepare a special recipe for barbecue sauce for dinner and I would actually cook the meat. My parents hemmed and hawed, but agreed to the plan, and then off we went to the beach the next day in time to get into Island Beach State Park.

Another aspect of the strategy to differentiate a "self" involved making an effort not to triangulate my wife or son against parents. After a visit we might discuss the visit, but tried not to make negative judgments about them or to join in a negative feeling that one of us had at a time during the visit. We allowed expression of feelings, but tried not to let it turn into a triangle. This was very helpful in preventing a me-against-them attitude, with its escalation of negative emotion and perpetuation of bad feelings.

There were a few situations in which I used humorous paradoxical techniques to bring about a certain change in my family in areas where I had been frustrated in my attempts to modify a pattern. Once again, food is involved. With my Italian background, many issues in family relate to food and the rituals around eating. My parents are basically generous people, but in the case of food, they are excessive. I had been unable to get them to stop offering me food when I did not want it. After hundreds of attempts that failed, I decided to try a paradoxical approach to deal with the problem. During the spring visit to New Jersey in 1981, I reversed my position regarding the consumption of food. Instead of saying, "I don't want any more," I began saying, "What else is there?" When we (my wife, son, and I) arrived at my parents' home on Friday afternoon before the weekend, I told my parents that I was really hungry and asked what they had to eat. They told me what there was. I then proceeded to go through the refrigerator and pantry closet to examine their supply of food. I noticed that they did not have potato chips, so I asked, "Where are the potato chips?" No potato salad! "How come you have no potato salad, you usually have potato salad!" I then ate four sandwiches and some leftovers that I found in the refrigerator. My parents finally commented that I might get sick if I ate so much.

During that weekend my parents were reluctant to urge me to eat more, but I continued to ask for food. At each meal I had an excess of at least one course, such as meat or dessert. Before the main dinner of the weekend I asked my parents why we were having only one entrée instead of two, as we sometimes had, such as turkey and lasagna.

Since that weekend my parents have backed off a lot in offering me food when I do not want it. They *still* offer an abundance of food, but can accept my refusal, or at least my second one.

AN OPERATION

The major nodal event that occurred in my family of origin during the period from the fall of 1979 to 1982 was my mother's operation to remove her gall bladder, in January 1982. Nodal events, according to Bowen (1976, p. 172) provide the family with an opportunity to enact change in the family system. The family system is less stable and can be mobilized more readily than during a period of calm. In my family, during this nodal event a significant change did occur in the family's transactional pattern and in my efforts at differentiation of a self.

The preferred family pattern, which I have described at various times, became altered. The pattern involves my parents, who are both "eldests," and my sister, who is also an eldest, in an active role, close to parents, and myself in a passive role in a distant position. The following is a description of the sequence of events that led to the eventual shift in my family's transactional pattern:

My mother had had trouble with her gall bladder, with very painful attacks from time to time, during a six-year period, as well as continued minor digestive problems. She had to change her diet and live with the fear of an attack at any time. During the fall of 1980, after consulting two physicians, she decided to undergo surgery to remove the malfunctioning gall bladder.

While my mother was in the process of making her decision concerning the surgery, I expressed my concern for her well-being and offered her my support should she decide to have it. I also let my parents know that I would be available to help out whenever she decided to schedule the operation. My willingness to help and be available was a result of progress that had been made in efforts to lower my level of reactivity, and my desire to play a more "adult" active role in my family of origin. I also was aware that my parents would need and appreciate my support, and so I was explicit in telling them that I would be there. My mother proceeded and scheduled the operation with the surgeon for January 4. The plan was that my parents would spend Christmas with my sister and her family in Dallas, and after the holiday my mother would have the operation. It was all well planned and handled except for the fact that my parents decided not to tell my sister of the exact date of the surgery. Their rationale was that my sister would only worry and be upset. They didn't want her to have the expense of flying from Texas to New Jersey, or take time from her job as a school teacher. Besides, I lived nearer and would be available.

When I was told of my parents' decision not to tell my sister, I indicated that it was my opinion that it would be wrong not to tell her. She would be angry when she found out—and she did not need to be thus protected. My parents had already made up their minds and felt in some strange way that they were doing the right thing. I decided that my position was to (1) encourage my parents to tell my sister and (2) not agree to keep the secret from her. During the Christmas visit to Texas, my parents told my brother-in-law about the operation and asked him to promise not to tell my sister. Figure 6–13 depicts who knew about the date of the operation and who did not.

During the Christmas vacation, my brother-in-law telephoned me to discuss the situation and his dilemma. My advice to him was to tell my parents that he could not agree to keep the secret. If they didn't tell

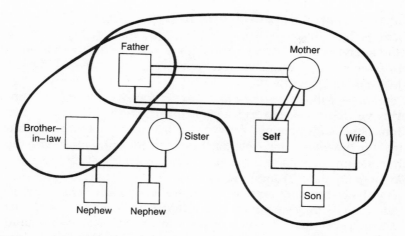

Figure 6-13. Inclusion-exclusion pattern of communication regarding mother's operation.

her, he would have to. We agreed that it would be best to wait until after Christmas day, but not just before they left Texas.

On Sunday, January 5, 1982, I drove from Massachusetts to New Jersey to meet my parents and go to the hospital with them. My mother checked in at 3:00 P.M., and was in good spirits; my father was more anxious and emotional. During the evening at dinner I asked my father if my parents had told my sister about the operation. He replied that they had and she had gotten very angry at them. As a matter of fact, it had turned into a terrible scene, with my sister and her two sons very angry and upset.

The operation the next morning was successful. My sister called to find out how it went. My father became upset in talking with my sister. I picked up the telephone to reassure my sister that the operation was successful and that my father was really fine, even though he didn't sound as though he was at the moment, and that if the situation changed, I would let her know.

My mother began a good recovery, and I stayed for a few more days, confident that my father could handle things until my mother returned home, and left for Massachusetts. I came away with a good feeling that I had been supportive of my parents in their time of need and that I could be emotionally available by playing an active, responsible role. I came away feeling more of an "adult" and no longer the younger passive son.

After the operation, my sister and my parents got along better. My parents agreed that they would not keep secrets from my sister and would keep her informed of any health developments. As a result of this nodal event, a reorganization took place in the transactional pattern in my family of origin.

Figure 6–14 illustrates the old configuration of my family of origin during periods of tension. Figure 6–15 illustrates the present configuration of my family of origin. Everyone is in clearer one-to-one relationships, my parents in close relationship (calm fusion). I am in relationship with my parents and in relationship with my sister. She is in relation to my parents and to me.

A year after my mother's operation the "new" balance in the organization of my family's emotional system has been maintained. I have continued to be active and emotionally available to my parents without becoming reactive. During the year since the operation I visited my

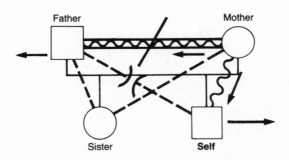

Figure 6–14. Original emotional configuration of family of origin during periods of tension.

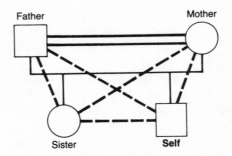

Figure 6–15. Present emotional configuration of family of origin.

parents six times—an increase over the past few years. During the past summer my sister and her two sons came east for ten days and stayed with my parents. My wife, son, and I joined my parents and sister for a weekend during their stay. The family get-together was the best it has ever been, and there was a feeling of calm togetherness throughout the weekend. Our plans to go to the beach on Saturday worked out beautifully, and we actually arrived two hours earlier than ever before. We all prepared for the trip to the beach, and each person did his or her part. The children were even willing to get up early without fussing.

When we arrived at Island Beach State Park, we just drove in and had our choice of parking. Only a few people were on the beach at the time, and we could choose whatever spot we wanted. It was a lovely day, with a lot of fun and relaxation for us as a family. It was typical of the whole weekend.

During the summer of 1982, my wife and I bought a house in a pleasant residential area. My parents, after learning of our plans to make the purchase, felt that we could use some money to deal with the expenses one encounters in buying a house, and they gave me a substantial financial gift, which was designated part of my inheritance. It was well appreciated.

At the end of October, I attended a professional conference in Dallas. During the trip I visited my sister and her family. After the visit I realized that my sister and I talked only briefly about my parents, and then only lightly and in passing. The stay with my sister was quite pleasant.

Later in the autumn my parents went to Texas to spend Thanksgiving with my sister and her family. From all reports the visit was a good one: no secrets, no arguments, no triangulations. My parents are scheduled to spend this Christmas with my wife, son, and self. It will be a five-day visit, the longest time that my parents have stayed with me at my house or apartment since I left home in 1964.

REFERENCES

Bowen, M. (1976). Theory in the practice of psychotherapy. In *Family Therapy: Theory and Practice*, ed. P. J. Guerin. New York: Gardner Press.

Chapter 7

DEFINING A SELF AFTER THE LAST CHILD LEAVES HOME

Susan S. Edwards, A.C.S.W.

This chapter is about my effort to define a self (Bowen 1978) in my family of origin after my two children, who were young adults, had left home. My husband and I were a couple again, each with a range of feelings and thoughts about the future of our family, our relationship, and our respective careers. My parents were living about 400 miles away in their own home. Although my father had recently developed Parkinson's disease, my parents were independent and both functioning rather well.

A few years prior to the departure of my youngest child, I undertook the project of "fixing up" my nuclear family. At the time, I was guided by the principle of resolution of emotional attachment before separating from one's family of origin (Carter and McGoldrick 1980). I knew that theory holds that family therapy and self differentiation are most effective when the emphasis is directed toward the parental generation (Bowen 1978). It soon became evident that the project was a belated and futile attempt to resolve emotional issues that had been left unattended between my parents and me, and were replayed with my husband and my children (Bowen 1978). I abandoned the project and began to consider my relationship with my parents and my one sibling, an older sister. The result was a shift in focus away from my children and my husband toward my parents, from whom I had merely physically separated.

The idea for this chapter came out of the Fifth Pittsburgh Systems Symposium, 1982. During one of the discussions, questions were raised about the advantages to children of having parents who were working toward differentiation of self in their respective families of origin. The comments addressed the idea that parents engaged in this effort might, unintentionally, modify the family projection process in their own nuclear families. At the time I was struck by the notion that the resolution of emotional attachment between the second and first generations could alter, in some fundamental way, the relationships between the second and third generations. While this idea comes from Bowen theory, it is a slightly different perspective from that which is usually discussed at family symposia and conferences. After thinking about it, I realized that a secondary gain of the self-defining process in which I had been involved had, indeed, left its imprint on my relationships with my two adult children.

My story is set in a multigenerational framework and a family life cycle context. It will illustrate three main ideas from Bowen theory (Bowen 1978):

1. Physical separation, including death, does not resolve the emotional attachment to parents or create a differentiated self. Emotional systems merely lie dormant until the combination of players reconvenes to activate the old triangular processes.
2. When either spouse or both set out to define a self in relation to their respective parents, there is a beneficial spin-off to the nuclear family system, including the younger generation.
3. Studying one's family system and the emotional processes in the family of origin increases one's ability to observe and to control reactivity when stress in the family is high.

THE SETTING

The family life cycle is an intergenerational process. Combined and separate family histories are created as the living generations move together through time. The inner connectedness across generations is immune to distance and emotional cut-offs; the older, the younger, and the new are inextricably linked to one another, to the past, and to the future.

During the various stages of the family life cycle, each generation must deal with a number of family-related changes (Carter and McGoldrick 1980). These changes are both stage-specific and cross-generational, and are concerned with the shifting of roles and status at the time of the separation of the young adult, marriage, birth, and death. The more open-ended a family system is on the vertical and horizontal axes, the more able the members of the system are to negotiate the emotional processes and second-order changes necessary for ongoing family development and continuity (Carter and McGoldrick 1980).

The events that are pertinent to the central points of this chapter will be told from the view of the second generation in a four-generation family system. The family is in the period just after the youngest child has left home. There is some anxiety between a husband and wife during this transition, particularly if parenthood has been the main focus of the marriage (and, for that matter, even if it hasn't). Being parents for twenty-five years with all of its vagaries can stabilize a nuclear family and submerge emotional stress. (In many cases this stress goes unnoticed except, perhaps, in one or more of the children.) The process of separation between children and parents is an index of the ongoing quality of relationships between the young adult and his or her parents and also of how the parents together will manage the transition and that stage of life. It is also a reenactment of the same process in the family of origin of each parent a generation earlier.

Provided the marriage of the parental generation is not interrupted by divorce or the death of one spouse, this stage is today the longest period in the family life cycle (Glick 1977); it may continue for twenty years, or more, depending upon the age of the parents when the last child leaves home. It therefore behooves the spouses—now that they have a sense of being a couple again—to take up whatever issues from the past have not been resolved and examine those yet to be experienced.

Speaking from a middle-class perspective, there are many delightful features to this stage. Some of these are the result of a longer period of good physical health and a degree of youthfulness that past generations did not enjoy. Furthermore, there are opportunities for women to reenter the job market and for men and women to shift careers. In addition, there is less financial strain, which allows for more leisure and diversified cultural pursuits. For those who have reached a reasonable degree of resolution of emotional attachment to their parents and have the makings of a person-to-person relationship with their children, this period can be exciting and fulfilling, and certainly less stressful than the stages of the family life cycle that involve young children or adolescents.

THE EMOTIONAL SYSTEM INITIALLY

I shall now describe the three-generational emotional system at the time I decided to work toward the differentiation of self (see Fig. 7–1). My father had been retired for seventeen years, and my parents were living in their home in New Jersey. Although my father had developed some early symptoms of Parkinson's disease, he had not shared this information with his children and had spoken lightly of it to his wife; otherwise, he was in good physical condition. Except for a severe hearing deficiency and hypertension, which was controlled by medication, my mother was also in good health.

My older sister, her husband, and the older of their two adult children, a daughter who lived in separate quarters, were residing 800 miles away. Their son had joined the Marines. My husband and I were living where we always had since our marriage, about 400 miles away from my parents and 800 miles from my sister. My sister and I had tried to persuade my parents to move close to one or the other of us, but my parents did not want to leave their friends and the area in which they had spent all of their married years. At various times, my sister and her family had lived near my parents and, during one period, had stayed with my parents in their home. Close or distant, my sister, her husband, and her children were very involved with my parents. Uncomplimentary stories (usually about my sister's and her husband's parenthood) were passed on to me by my parents. Derogatory tales about my parents (their harsh natures and their punitive measures) were relayed to me by my sister. I was always available to listen, being careful (most of the time) not to take sides.

My sister and I visited our parents either with family members or alone, and my parents visited both families in return. By the time my children had reached adolescence the visits to my family were less frequent, and after my children were about seventeen and fourteen years old, they did not see my parents unless my parents visited my home.

Throughout my childhood and adolescence, my mother and I had been very close. As a young adult I made efforts to pull away emotionally. Living 400 miles away and being occupied with family life provided boundaries that I was unable to establish for myself when I was in close proximity to my mother. She, like me, is a youngest and had been well taken care of by my father, who is a middle child and older brother to a younger brother and a younger sister. When I was in my parents' home, I usually "took over" for my father, who distanced himself and remained in the background. I was the child who could do

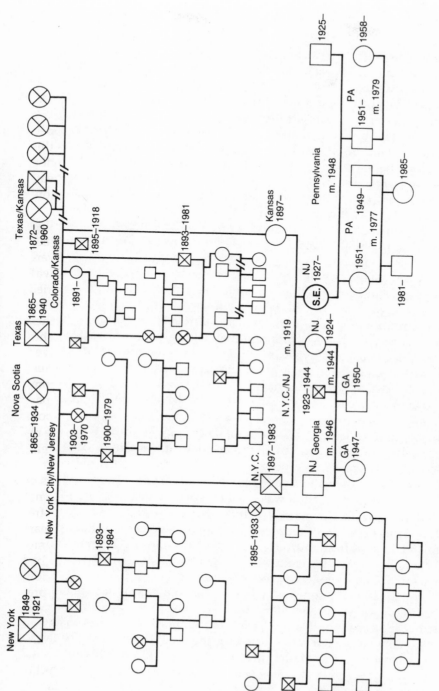

Figure 7-1. Family diagram.

141

nothing wrong, in contrast to my sister, who could do nothing right. I took advantage of this family set-up which favored me until my children were older.

My son and my daughter were both developing identities that were very much in opposition to my parents' beliefs about how children should behave. Rather than risk the kind of criticism that had been directed toward my sister, I made excuses for my childrens' absence at get-togethers with my parents. During my visits to my parents' home without my children, I was generally warm and loving and avoided opening up issues that would tarnish the congenial relationship between my parents and me, or alter their perception of my sister.

What I learned from my sister, and eventually from my parents, was that my mother and father were critical of me, my children, and my husband for not visiting them more frequently. By this time I could not even *entice* my children to take one step in the direction of their grandparents' home. Thus, an emotional cut-off was in process. No matter how often I visited, I could not narrow the huge gap between my parents and my children. I took comfort in the knowledge that my mother and my maternal grandmother, who at one time had been very close, had spent twenty years without seeing one another. My mother always claimed that she could not afford the 2,000-mile trip. (In reality, she experienced herself as having been betrayed by her mother, who retained a piece of very valuable property, which rightfully belonged to my mother.)

My husband and I had a warm relationship. We dealt with fusion, some by distance, some by the over/underfunctioning process, and more by the projection process, of which our son was the object. This was similar to the way in which my parents absorbed fusion. My husband was distanced and I was emotionally involved with my son. My daughter was on the periphery of the process, and has been the more functional of the two children. It was not until sometime after I shifted my focus away from my nuclear family to my family of origin, with the idea of dealing with the unresolved emotional attachment to my parents, that I noticed any appreciable difference.

By the time my son was eighteen years old he was having noticeable social and scholastic difficulties, which were more severe than the usual adolescent problems. He left our home several times to live on his own. It was after he returned for the second time that I began to think more in terms of family process and less in terms of his individual dynamics. However, my view was narrowed by my own discomfort in imagining myself disturbing a homeostasis that had served my family well for three generations if not more. I convinced myself that although the evidence did not support my plan, I would attempt to make changes in my nuclear family and somehow be the one exception to the idea that moving up the system (working on family of origin issues) is always more profitable than looking down (working on nuclear family issues).

A SHIFT IN FOCUS

Nodal events are predictable happenings that signal a period of transition and a new stage in the family life cycle. Reactions that cover the range from mild to incapacitating anxiety are dependent upon just when the transgenerational (vertical) stressors intersect the normative (horizontal) stressors, and how loaded one or both of the axes are (Carter and McGoldrick, 1980). At these junctures, most families experience some degree of stress but negotiate the transition without incident. However, a few families reach a point beyond which they cannot move until obstacles from the past have been cleared away.

By the time my husband and I had fully realized that both our children had left the home and that their returns would be as guests, I was about forty-nine years old and my husband was fifty-one. Fortunately, we were able to share our private thoughts and feelings about our current life situation. We spent many evenings talking about ourselves, our relationship, and how we wanted to live the rest of our lives. I was four years into a new career, and my husband was considering retirement at the age of fifty-five.

Having experienced the nodal event—the last child leaves home—I reminisced about my own departure from my family and, most particularly, my parents' reactions. Although the circumstances of the separations were quite different, the underlying emotional processes seemed to be the same: youngest children in an overly close relationship with mothers who were also youngest children, in combination with somewhat distant fathers. I could not exclude the close relationship between my mother and her mother, an oldest, and the ensuing emotional cut-off of twenty years. Nor could I stop thinking about my maternal grandmother who overfunctioned, my mother who underfunctioned, myself who overfunctioned, and my son who underfunctioned in mother–child relationships. Although my son and I had formed a satisfactory relationship, in which there was mutual generosity and good will towards one another, the signals and predictors of a poor life adjustment were obvious.

I had been made well aware through my study of Bowen theory

and my consultation in a group on extended family that a history of emotional cut-offs and separations without differentiation portends emotional dysfunction. As I thought about these similar happenings three generations apart, I was struck by the notion that, except for my being older now, my position in relationship to my parents was not much different from what it had been at the time of my marriage. Were I to change that position, other relationships would change as well. The time was ripe for a serious effort toward self-differentiation.

THE IMPORTANT TRIANGLES

Three-person relationships (triangles) in any system are a phenomenon that people seem to understand without much thought. In the course of a clinical interview, triangular relationships are fully described by clients who have never read any of the family therapy literature. The popular belief is that one can remove one's self from triangles at will and that work on internal symptoms is more productive than the modification of triangles in which the client has been involved for many years. What most people do not know, is that vulnerability to symptoms is directly proportional to participation in emotional triangles, which restrict the capacity for the differentiation of self.

After I read Bowen's theory (Bowen 1978) for the first time, I became more consciously aware of myself in triangles in my family of origin, my nuclear family, and my work system. The awareness motivated me to take a course on the modification of one's function in the family system with the emphasis of the work being the family of origin. My hidden purpose, however, was to straighten out my nuclear family. After I shifted my focus from my nuclear family to the differentiation of self from my parents, it became clear to me that I was important in a number of triangular relationships, of which some were transgenerational, while others included only the members of my family of origin.

THE EFFORT

Out of the many interlocking emotional triangles in my family of origin, I shall discuss three, describing the emotional issues related to them and the effort I made to modify my functioning in these triangles.

Depending upon the level of anxiety in the family and which issues were in the forefront at the time, a visit to my parents guaranteed a degree of involuntary emotional involvement with my mother and my father, and also with my sister, whether she was present or not. Learning to observe the process—and myself in the process—helped me control my reactivity and freed me over time to develop a person-to-person relationship with each one of my parents and my sister. Visits to my parents' home with some thoughtful planning ahead of time about particular emotional issues and my position in relationship to them were the most helpful events in my project. Letters and telephone calls were also useful, especially when the drama became intense and an on-site visit might have resulted in self-defeating reactivity.

The First Triangle

The central and most seductive triangle, in that it has the longest history, was the one in which my mother and I were close and my father was distanced. At times this triangle worked in the opposite direction, with closeness between my father and me while my mother was distanced. My mother ritualistically confided in me a list of worries and complaints about my father. When my father and I were alone, he recited his litany of worries and complaints to me about my mother. Concerns about money, my mother's hearing impairment, and what my mother would do were my father to die first were at the top of each list. What seems obvious now, seemed at the time an almost insoluble problem: how to alter a familiar process, as well as the substance of the relationship, so that issues would be about and between ourselves.

I became much more of a talker and a discloser than a listener and advisor, which had always been my trademarks. I recommended, with some trepidation, that each one take her or his worries and complaints to the other. Although this shift left a void in the respective relationships, it was eventually filled with content of a more intimate nature.

The triangle is not totally inactive. My parents, who are elderly, incapacitated, and isolated, have an intense relationship, with little outside relief. During my recent visits, the emotional forces have been readily rekindled and the old processes have again been set into motion. The difference is that I am aware of the history of the triangle and my participation in it. Knowledge and observation of self have helped me to control my reactivity and to accept the triangle as a necessary function of my parents' life situation.

As the distance between each parent and myself has shifted and the respective relationships have evolved into person-to-person contact, my perceptions of my mother and father have changed considerably. I discovered my father's desire for support and closeness and my mother's impressive strengths. My parents, each from a different perspective, discovered an adult behind the daughter who had always been a "good little girl."

The Second Triangle

In the second important triangle, my sister and I each had a positive, albeit gossipy, relationship with my mother and a competitive relationship between ourselves. My mother spread uncomplimentary tales about one daughter to the other daughter, and vice versa. My sister and I at times gossiped about my mother. Generally, the content of my mother's stories had something to do with her feelings of having been injured by my sister or me, and her disappointment in her daughters' skills as parents. My mother was critical about the appearance of my niece's nose, which blighted an otherwise lovely face. She and my sister had battled for years over the issue of a rhinoplasty to change a too-long nose into one more in keeping with my mother's aesthetic sense. My mother had attributed my niece's personality deficiencies and lack of male attention to an unattractive nose, which, if repaired, would resolve her "problems." (My niece had her first birthday on my wedding day and replaced me as the focus of the family projection process.) An interlocking triangle sprang up when my brother-in-law and my niece were eventually recruited into my sister's camp against my mother, who had by that time been joined by my father. Later my niece vacillated between her mother and her grandmother; eventually she had plastic surgery. It was not easy for me to maintain my objectivity in the heart of this battle, and many times I lost completely. My sister and my mother were looking for loyal troops and spies, whereas I was looking for a person-to-person relationship with each.

On the other side of the triangle, my mother complained to my sister about my son, who had to have something wrong with him, since he had not visited his grandparents for a number of years. After my son reached late adolescence, I had lost my parental leverage regarding family responsibilities and accepted the condition that he would see his grandparents on his own schedule, and not on mine or my mother's. In my effort to differentiate, however, I had stepped up my own visiting timetable. Eventually, I recognized that no matter how often I went to see my parents, it would never be enough for my mother.

During the process of developing person-to-person relationships with my sister and my mother, I often suggested that each would derive more personal satisfaction by speaking directly to the other about her particular concerns rather than to me. I avoided entanglement by keeping my contact with each on an intimate basis, which diffused the tendency to gossip. I had several long talks with my mother about her grandson, and I finally confessed to her that he was just like me—so what could she expect anyway?

The project did not run a smooth course. At times I wanted to quit and luxuriate in the safety of fusion. However, once I had accepted that my wish for instant change and success would not be gratified, I reduced the intensity with playfulness and humor, which lowered my anxiety.

A Triangle Deactivated

One piece of information that recently surfaced is that my mother has been giving money to my sister and her two adult children. The justification for this financial support is that my brother-in-law has not been working for the past seven years and, as a result of his lack of employment, is depressed. My mother is empathic towards my sister, who has a talent—picked up from my mother—for decorating her home with objects purchased at junk shops and flea markets. However, my sister's natural gift is seen as a signal of financial distress rather than as a superior ability.

When my feeling system takes over my thinking system, I am, at the very least, disturbed by the evidence that my mother considers my sister worthier than I. Why shouldn't I feel slighted by such discrimination? My husband hasn't worked for three years, and during that time he has been going to law school at no small expense. Isn't this deserving of something?

A more accurate understanding of my mother's unequal distribution of her income hinges on the family history of money and its symbolic meaning. Money not only represents prestige and success, it translates into emotional support, love, and happiness; lack of money equals unhappiness.

My maternal grandfather left his entire estate to his fourth wife. My maternal grandmother—my maternal grandfather's first wife and the only wife to bear him children—left a sizable estate, which she divided equally among her three children. Because my maternal grandmother was partly Cherokee Indian, she secured homestead land for herself and her children from the American government. Being a resourceful businesswoman who wanted to increase her net worth, my maternal grandmother persuaded my mother to turn her property over to her with the idea that she would deed it back to her when my mother turned twenty-one. My grandmother, however, never fulfilled her agreement with my mother and until her death, continued to collect revenues yielded by my mother's property. Under the conditions of my grandmother's will, my mother's property was included in the estate and divided equally among the three children. After my grandmother's death, in 1960, when my mother was sixty-three years old, my mother's older siblings deeded their portions of what had rightfully belonged to my mother back to her.

My mother had been excluded from her father's will, a symbolic cut-off, and had been betrayed by her mother. She and my maternal grandmother remained cut-off from each other for a period of twenty years. My mother had struggled with a hearing deficit since she was twenty-six years old. She always claimed that a lack of money and her hearing impairment prevented her from involving herself more fully in life. As I look back, I realize that during my childhood and adolescence my mother was unhappy, if not depressed, much of the time. After my marriage I moved 400 miles away, obtaining for myself physical separation and relief from her many justifiable grievances. My sister and her family took up where I had left off by becoming entangled with my parents, particularly my mother.

Financial issues are of great importance to both my mother and my sister, and these formed a strong bond between the two families. In addition, my mother has an emotional identification with my sister. My mother's favorite brother was killed in World War I. My sister's first husband was killed in World War II. My mother's husband was unemployed for a period during the Great Depression. My sister's husband has been unemployed. Both have similar interests in music and artistic expression in the home. Both can make a dollar do what most people do with two dollars, and both would complain of poverty with a million dollars in the bank.

Again, a generation later a youngest daughter has been overlooked. By informing my mother and sister that I objected to being left out, I reactivated an old triangle, the central theme of which is "who gets and who doesn't." My mother has learned one thing from her younger daughter: how to keep issues where they belong. She told me that it was none of my business what she did with her money and that, if she wants to give money to one daughter and not the other, she will.

Every time I question my mother's and sister's sense of justice, I feel like a grain of sand in an oyster, which eventually, I hope, will yield a pearl.

Although establishing person-to-person relationships and differentiating from triangular emotional systems with their time-honored and ritualistic processes may appear to be simple maneuvers, they are not. The risk of rejection and isolation and the loss of the comfort of fusion keep people locked into unproductive relationships, which are eventually passed on to the next generation. From a transgenerational viewpoint, the modifications I made are barely noticeable. For me they were like moving a monolith.

THE EMOTIONAL SYSTEM NOW

Each generation has its own developmental tasks to work through during the various stages of the family life cycle. The more open families are across generational boundaries, the more competent they will be in dealing with these tasks and the related stresses introduced by nodal events and unpredictable life situations. With this in mind, I shall attempt to depict my four-generational family system as it is now.

My father took a downhill turn after his younger brother died three years ago. Since then, the spreading paralysis of Parkinson's disease has affected his body to the extent that he no longer has control of his bodily functions. He is depressed and wishes to die. My mother, who has a spirit as strong as any pioneer woman's, attends uncomplainingly to my father's needs. Although she appears worn and tired from her daily vigil and housekeeping chores, and gets about only with the aid of a walker, she seems to have endless energy. About a year ago, my mother, who throughout my father's illness had done everything herself, relented and hired a twenty-four-hour nursing service.

During this difficult stage in their lives, I have spent short periods in person-to-person conversations with each one of my parents. I have had the experience of taking "I-positions," which did not come out of reactivity, but out of what I think and believe.

Death, usually a forbidden subject, has quite naturally come up in these conversations between me and one parent or the other, but not between them. While they have been mutually supportive and adaptive throughout the course of their marriage, the structure of their relationship prohibits the discussion of many intimate and intensely emotional issues. Therefore, in a collusive effort to spare each other, little is said between them about what they both know is there: the imminent death of my father. My mother operates on the fictitious assumption that my father will someday get better. She tries to encourage him by turning each tiny evidence of improvement into a sign of hope. Likewise, except for two occasions when he made attempts to commit suicide, my father rarely complains to my mother. She interpreted his suicidal threats as the irrational ravings of a sick man, and not the genuine expression of his suffering and his desire to die.

As a child, and even as an adult, I too had operated on a fictitious assumption. This fiction, also shared by my parents, was that it was my obligation to make things better for my mother and my father. In my mother's case, my being close and empathic seemed temporarily to relieve whatever unhappy feelings she was having. In my father's case, my being close to my mother provided him with the distance he needed to be comfortable when she was not. A degree of differentiation from my parents has made it possible for me to witness the physical deterioration and emotional suffering of each while experiencing less of the emotional pull to perform an impossible task. Occasionally, when the stress level, which is always high, escalates, an old triangle is reactivated and the familiar processes take over. I am reasonably quick to recognize the regression, but am unable to change the direction until the triangle is no longer necessary.

My husband, an engineer by training, was forced to retire from a career of thirty-five years in barge-line operations and three years later, he has finished law school. At the age of fifty-six I am busy in the practice of psychotherapy and in writing papers. My competence and flexibility in psychotherapy have improved substantially. Together my husband and I are making short-range future plans. Although less grandiose than those of thirty-five years ago, they are more in keeping with where we are in the upward movement of the generations and the forward movement of the family life cycle.

My children have each found suitable pathways that lead away from and back to their family of origin. My daughter, her husband, and their son live nearby. The comings and goings between the two families are open and fluid, and my daughter and I have a warm relationship in which the process of differentiation ebbs and flows.

My son, a truck owner–operator and an entrepreneur, and his wife live about sixty miles south of our home, on a 40-acre lot with a farm. Although he has many educational deficits, his level of functioning has improved, and he seems to be happier now than I have known him to be for many years. Our two families are friendly and open to each other. The relationship between my son and me is warm. The more differentiated I become, the less distanced he becomes.

As I predicted, both of my children in their own time made contact with their grandparents and reestablished bonds without much difficulty. Had I tried to encourage the reconciliation, it might never have taken place. After my son's most recent visit to his grandparents' home, my parents called to report about him in the most enthusiastic terms.

About a year-and-a-half ago, the social order of our family changed when our daughter and her husband became parents. Each family moved up one rung on the generational ladder to make way for the beginning of a new era. Family relationships and familiar roles shifted with the birth of the fourth generation. Although my husband and I are still parents, we are now grandparents, and my children's grandparents are great-grandparents. These changes remind us that time never stops and that the passing of generations is inevitable.

The relationship between my sister and me has changed; we no longer discuss our parents except out of concern or when the anxiety level is high. There is less "one-upmanship" between us and, instead, a degree of empathy and compassion that has been missing in the past. Recently, in making plans to meet, she did not once bring up money as an obstacle.

Emotional triangles outlast people. They are passed on as legacies from generation to generation. Even though differentiation is never finished, each slight modification—each increment of change— broadens a vision once limited by family processes that long ago had ceased to be useful.

* * *

My father died in December 1984. My sister and her husband supported my mother through the last few days of my father's life. My mother continues to live in her house, with a nurse. We talked together about her living in my house and I decided that, because of her several physical impairments, I did not want to have her live with my husband and me. As an alternative I suggested a nearby retirement facility in which she could live with a considerable degree of independence while being able to avail herself of medical care when required. She was hurt when I wrote her a letter explaining my position on having her live in my home, and she has rejected the idea of moving close to me but under another roof. My son and his wife have visited my mother; and my daughter, her husband, and their three-year-old son have also visited her.

My son—the one who received the heaviest dose of the projection process—is now functioning better than he ever has in his life. He and his wife both want to have children, but have not been fortunate in that endeavor. Together they are building a business and have successfully worked through a number of risky and stressful situations. My daughter and her husband have a second child, a girl. My husband and I enjoy being grandparents to our two grandchildren. I have a warm, friendly, and, at times, intimate relationship with each one of my children, as does my husband. The effort to differentiate from my parents has had noticeable, positive spin-offs, two of which are some modification of the projection process in my own nuclear family, and the pleasure of having an improved, person-to-person relationship with each of my adult children.

REFERENCES

Bowen, M. (1978). *Family Therapy in Clinical Practice*. New York: Jason Aronson.

Carter, E., and McGoldrick, M., eds. (1980). *The Family Life Cycle: A Framework for Family Therapy*. New York: Gardner Press.

Glick, P. (1977). Updating the life cycle of the family. *Journal of Marriage and Family*, February.

Chapter 8

TAKING A GIANT STEP: FIRST MOVES BACK INTO MY FAMILY

Blanche E. Kaplan, C.S.W., A.C.S.W.

This chapter covers extended family work done over a decade ago, in 1973–1974. I was an extended family initiate in a heyday of excitement and optimism. It was for me part of an effort that has no end.

More than a year of moves back into my family of origin has culminated in results beyond anything I imagined when I began. In what follows, I review the circumstances of my trip: whys, hows, and whats, beginning with a description of myself and my family of origin, and then shifting the focus to my attempts to make changes, especially in my relationships with my parents.

MY FAMILY AND ME

I am the fourth daughter, and fourth child, of seven children, with two younger brothers and a youngest sister. My father, who is eighty, and mother, seventy-six, still live in our hometown in upstate New York. We children, who range in age from thirty to fifty, live everywhere in the country and world but our hometown. My husband and I and our son, seventeen years old, live in a suburb of New York City. Our daughter, now twenty, lives in New York City, where she attends college.

My family background is working-class, fairly religious Jewish, with much of our early lives centered around my father's fruit store. My parents were born about 100 miles from each other in Europe. They met and married in America in 1922. We children held a fiftieth anniversary party for them in 1972. I never knew any of my grandparents. All died in Europe.

I became interested in family systems theory and therapy in the course of two years of family therapy training. I have sculpted my family of origin and nuclear family and have been painfully impressed with the persistence of unsatisfactory old roles despite previous therapy. I became increasingly unhappy at the extent to which my mood swings controlled my life. Although somewhat satisfied with myself as a parent, I disliked the fact that I kept running from closeness in my marriage and looked for it everywhere else. I hoped that working on myself in my family of origin might address these concerns. Later, I began to want more in my family for its own sake.

I have had a jumble of positions in my family of origin. I was overresponsible in assuming family chores. I asked for nothing, took up little space, and made little noise. My rewards were mostly for scholastic achievements. I won many scholarships, and was Phi Beta Kappa at an Ivy League university. I have only recently ceased being embarrassed about these. I was also praised for being a good helper, at home and in the store. I was a "nice," quiet, Jewish girl.

Last year I sculpted myself as in constant motion in my family of origin, always trying to give, not knowing how to get, unable to stop moving. My youngest sister's birth, when I was fourteen, seemed a signal that I had to leave the family if I was ever to get anything. I cried (privately) for many hours. (My mother, interestingly, left her family in Europe in very similar circumstances.) I left at age seventeen for college out of town and have never since lived in my hometown. Contacts in the years between have been largely pleasant, ceremonial, and distant. Large family gatherings have frequently been a lot of fun, often to the point of stomach aches and tears. These have seemed the only safe tears in each other's presence. I have lived near New York City since college, and have felt somewhat close to several brothers and sisters who have lived in the area from time to time, but this has usually included considerable anxiety on my part as to my right to be "me."

The following is a description of my family of origin in 1972, at the time of my parents' fiftieth anniversary party (see Fig. 8-1, the family diagram).

Dad was the second oldest son and child in his family. He left in his teens, and has been angry at them and cut-off all his life. An older brother survives in Paris. His mother and five younger brothers and sisters died in concentration camps. My mother handles rare contacts

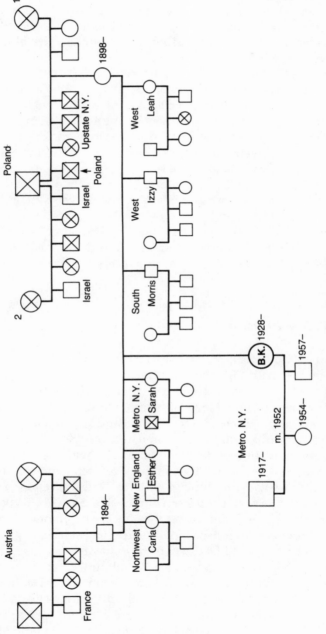

Figure 8–1. Family diagram.

155

with his brother and paternal cousins. As a child I was terrified of Dad's anger. I tried desperately to win his approval, mostly through studies and work. He has referred to himself as a "black sheep," and is the outsider in a triangle consisting of my mother, her older sister, Rosie, and himself.

Mom was the fifth of seven children by her father's first wife. Five of these children settled in our hometown. Her mother died when she was five, and her father remarried shortly thereafter and had five children with his second wife. Her father became a distant, revered figure, struggling to make a skimpy living. Mom became a maid to her stepsisters and brothers, a sort of Cinderella who *never* got to the ball. In my strongest memories of Mom are of her in the basement, ironing, sitting on the radiator, or eating soupmeat. She remained in the corner, a stepchild all her life. Mom *was* available when one was sick, and I loved her special rituals of camphorated oil and hot lemonade.

When I was growing up, most of the time I felt sorry for my mother, and only much later connected her withdrawal and my father's rage. Until recently I felt that I could drown in my mother's needs if I got close.

TRIPS TO MY FAMILY

I decided in September 1973 to use a coach for my work with my family. I have met with him about six times altogether. With his help, I made plans for a series of trips to my parents, at approximately six-week intervals. My initial idea was simply to start gathering information. I knew very little about either parent and so had many questions. I made my first trip, with my husband and children, to coincide with my father's eightieth birthday. I got time alone with Mom fairly easily. Dad still worked during the day, and my husband and children were cooperative. It was more difficult with my Dad. He tends to settle in front of the television set and seem immovable. He likes to take walks, however, and I joined him, somewhat anxiously, on one of these.

Mom was very responsive. With surprising honesty, she told me she had not really liked Dad when they married, because he was so stubborn. She married him because she felt unwanted in the home of her older sister, Rosie, and her husband. Mom thinks Dad is easier to get along with now. She also told me of the difficulties she had over the years being between Dad and Rosie. She never complained to anyone, because adults "aren't supposed to," but she resented how much she had listened to *Rosie's* complaints. Mom's responsiveness to me was such that I felt as though she had been waiting for years just for someone to ask her.

Most poignant was my mother's description of her own early family experience. She told of a time when she was sixteen and alone in the house, with her stepmother in labor. She felt helpless and cried for hours for her stepmother—whom she had thought she hated—the new baby, and herself. She felt there was no more room in the house for her. While telling me this, Mom started crying and left the room. I spent several seconds debating whether to follow. I did, found her crying in her room, and took her in my arms. Within a few minutes she stopped crying, composed herself, and continued as before. It was lovely to hold this little woman and then be able to let go. She had never cried in my presence before. Crying, to her and me, had been "for babies."

I had notably less success with Dad. I asked him question after question, feeling ridiculously like an interrogator. His answers were mostly unresponsive or tangential, but I did find out some interesting things. When he was courting Mom he felt closer to her family than to her. In response to questions about his anger and unhappiness during my childhood, he blamed these on my mother's "trimming the lettuce in the back of the store." He clearly meant her failure to share responsibility with him out front in the store *and* at home. (Now that lettuce comes all trimmed and wrapped, I wonder how *that* would be expressed.) This of course has been a central issue in our family.

I felt good about connecting with Mom, but uncomfortable about Dad. I decided to make the next trip at Thanksgiving, with my husband and my son. Returning so soon was news in my family, and I heard in letters from my sisters of their pleasure in our attentiveness to Mom and Dad. Mom's letter responding to mine indicating our plan to visit opened, "We want you to know that this is your home and you are welcome to visit anytime." Considering that we previously visited about once a year, I imagine she was uncomfortable, if also pleased.

My main effort for the second trip was to see if I could do better with Dad. He has an album with a few pictures of his family, and many of his days in the Austrian Army in World War I. I planned to try to get involved in conversation about the album. My coach thought that might take several hours. I was not quite convinced, but determined to try.

The night of our arrival for Thanksgiving I asked my father to show me the album. He agreed pleasantly, and we must have spent some twenty minutes going through it. Dad was most enthusiastic about pictures of himself in an Austrian hospital. He had very little to say about his family. A question such as "What was your sister like?" got the reply, "She was a sister." I wasn't alone with Dad again on that trip. He was either at work or—seemingly—cemented to the television. At one point I complained about this to my husband, and he said I should get off *my* ass. I certainly wasn't going to let *him* tell me how to work with *my* family!

On Friday night Mom asked me to go to temple with her. I have consistently refused in the past, out of an acute allergy to the Jewish religion. I felt engulfed by it as a child. Prior to adolescence I was very religious; I used to pray to God in both Hebrew and English to make sure She (or He) understood. Dad used to predict I'd marry a rabbi. Mom hoped so. Now, on this Friday night of this visit I went to temple, just with my mother. I enjoyed it; enjoyed being shown off, and I was comfortable, and even nostalgic.

Shortly before we left for home Mom approached me and observed how flat-chested I was. She suggested I get some padding. This once would have driven me wild. Now I was, somehow, able to thank her for caring and also to say that I really liked my little breasts the way they were. Mom was uncomfortable about giving advice, especially since I didn't take it. I said it was fine, that I felt free to follow it or not.

I was still unhappy about Dad and pleased about Mom. I decided to make my next trip alone, in mid-winter. The idea of two whole days, mostly indoors with two old parents, was alarming. My coach suggested I approach my father directly and tell him I wanted to get to know him before he dies. My stomach hurt just thinking about that! I became increasingly anxious about the trip. I decided my coach was pretty inadequate in having only one lousy idea—any *decent* coach would have *several* lousy ideas! I wrote my parents that I wanted to have time on my trip to spend with each of them alone. My mother's only response was, "We want you to know that this is your home and you are welcome to visit anytime." As I got closer to leaving I felt *sure* they thought I was crazy, and I began to think so, too.

I flew to my hometown, and on landing began to shake all over. I arrived to find both parents home and seemingly very happy to see me. Dad was grinning all over; Mom gave me lunch, and they both showered me with attention and seemed so lovely that I wondered how I was ever going to discuss death. With such nice parents, who needed to?

After a while Dad invited me to take a walk with him. We tramped in the snow, and Dad then said, "Well, I guess there must be some-thing personal you want to talk about." I was overwhelmed and barely able to mumble something about just wanting to know better . . . nothing special, really. Dad said *he* had something he wanted to talk to me about. He was concerned about what would happen to Mom when he died. I then began to experience a great excitement, an urge to run and tell someone. I controlled myself by self-lectures about "keeping it in the family." (I needed many such lectures.) Dad continued with his concern about Mom's ability to assume responsibility if he died first. He was concerned about his will. Mom knew nothing about his fi-nances and didn't write checks. I told him I would be glad to help if I could, and he said he would like me to call Cy, a lawyer friend, about changing the will. Mindful of triangles despite surging emotions, I said I was sure Mom must be concerned about the same things, and I thought she should be involved. Dad was afraid to upset her and asked if I would talk to her. I agreed, and said I would then talk to both of them. I hugged Dad, and said I'd be around if *Mom* died first, too. He didn't hug me in return, but I knew it was all right.

Later I sat in the living room with Mom and Dad and the TV. It took fifteen minutes to be able to tell my Mom I wanted to speak to her pri-vately in a bedroom. I had never done *that* before. I told her that Dad had spoken to me about things that concerned them both. As soon as I mentioned death she started to cry, and said she could not talk about it. I hugged her briefly, told her that crying was no big deal, that I did it all the time. Mom said she couldn't talk to Dad because he would think she was already planning his death. She worried most about *his* man-aging without her, especially because none of us lived nearby to help out. I assured her I could be available quickly and would be upset if not called upon. I thought others in the family probably felt the same. She said that made her feel good.

The next day, after a sleepless and agitated night, I lingered in bed, reluctant to return to the family intensity. Finally I did, and spoke to both parents before calling the lawyer. At one point, Mom looked at Dad in amazement and said, "You told her *that?*" I felt somewhat like a family therapist, keeping things open. My head was extremely clear. I called the lawyer in my parents' presence. He was helpful and under-standing, and offered my parents an early appointment. They have since made a new will and named me as co-executor, with my oldest sister. The *previous* executor had been another lawyer.

Other things happened on that weekend. I went to temple with both parents and was introduced as their new daughter. I found out for the first time that I was named after an aunt of my Dad's. I became aware of a "family flow," whereby my mother would push me toward my father; I'd stay a bit, come back, and get another push. They asked me to write to my brothers and sisters about what happened and I agreed to. Carla called while I was there. I spoke to her after Dad did, and she told me he seemed pleased about my coming, that he said I'd come to take care of their future, and he thought it was "wonderful." Carla did too. Just before I left, both parents flooded me with stories of their early lives in Europe; it was more than I could begin to absorb. Our joint excitement was very high.

I left feeling that I had "tripped" on two little old Jewish parents. Nothing had prepared me for it. My husband met me at the airport and I cried all the way home while telling him about it. My coach was away; so I debriefed instead to several friends. I had a great need to talk. When I did speak to my coach, he said that I, like Columbus, had discovered America, and that *was* something to get excited about!

After the "high" of that trip, I experienced a period of letdown, because everything was not different now between me and my family. We still lived far away from one another, and I still initiated most contacts. For a while I felt angry at my in-laws for living a half mile away and not being *my* family.

In the following months I had contacts with Izzy and Leah on the west coast; with Sarah in the area, with Carla in *her* town, and with everyone else in more frequent calls and letters. I emphasize frequency, because *infrequent* contacts of all kinds seem to have helped maintain our family distance. I have carefully created my own frequency, nonreactive to that of others as much as possible. I have visited my parents three more times. There have been no more dramatic breakthroughs; rather, a gradual accumulation of information about them and myself. For example, I have learned of my own intolerance for the tedium (as I see it) of their lives. I have experimented with both "leaving the field" and reducing the tedium by "feeding in" new experiences. This has helped me deal with my intolerance of tedium generally. (Life is only *sometimes* a cabaret. I still have some regrets about that!)

My husband and I spent one week of our recent vacation in Paris, partly in order to visit my father's brother. I knew he was eighty-four and very ill, and I wanted to see him before he died. I hoped he might also be an important link to my father. I was concerned about communication, since he spoke only French and Yiddish (unfortunately not the same ones as God), and I was proficient in neither. When we arrived he was in a nursing home. We met my aunt and my cousins at their home in Paris and went with them to see my uncle. I had met him just once before—twenty-two years ago—when I was wholly uninterested in uncles. As I entered my uncle's room and saw him, I was overcome with emotion. He is the image of my father, although now much older-looking and frail. He understood who I was, and was warm and gracious despite extreme weakness, near-blindness, and acute breathing difficulty. I cried, and felt like I would explode if I touched him. He seemed to understand my meager French, and seemed moved at my being there. Before I left I took his hands and we embraced. I experienced an availability I've never known with my father.

In the hospital room I also discovered the difference between the way American and French Jews feed their sick family members. My aunt was feeding my uncle a napoleon during most of the visit. And my uncle, with all his disabilities, managed to eat it.

CONCLUSION

Here is what I see as the impact on me and others of my work in my family. While it is impossible to *prove anything*, it is tempting to take credit for *everything* that has happened since I began.

I no longer search desperately for closeness everywhere. I *am* searching for it in my family. More important, I no longer *feel* desperate about closeness, and yet have more satisfying relationships than before. I have worked a great deal on my marriage; I had done so before, but without the same results. This time I had made up my mind to try to be responsible only for myself, and to stop trying to make my husband change. That has been very difficult. My first attempts to make my own statements ended up sounding like the same old blame. For a while, I saw with painful acuity all the things in myself I had pointed out in my husband. For example, I found out *I* was sometimes boring and dull. This seemed impossible at first; eventually it seemed not so bad. My marriage appears better now because it and my husband are *less* important to me: they are no longer the equivalent of my personal survival. And when we *are* close together, it's much nicer. Marriage for me must include a lot of separation, and I have learned to achieve it without feeling blamed or blaming—some of the time.

My recent visit to my uncle seemed to eliminate some intrinsic "badness" I have always carried with me and never succeeded in concealing. I also think it has given me a more solid base for connecting with my father. His family is no longer unknowable.

Mom seems more vivacious in recent telephone calls than she ever used to be. She told me she is very happy to have a daughter like me. Dad has written his brother since I wrote my parents about *my* visit. Izzy has made his first visit alone to my parents. Morris wrote recently that he cannot understand how he can like me better every time he sees me, yet still write so little; he planned to change that. There seem to be many more family contacts generally, although I have no exact count.

Professionally, the past year has been the most productive of my six-year career, and the succeeding ones promise to be even more so. I am writing, speaking, and practicing more and, I think, better. An increasing number of people who come to me for help develop an interest in their families. Part of my private practice is derived from a women's psychotherapy service. Women come to me seeking a "nonsexist" therapist, and often end up doing family work. The combination seems to work very well.

Chapter 9

THE BIRTHDAY PARTY REVISITED: FAMILY THERAPY AND THE PROBLEM OF CHANGE

Edwin H. Friedman, D.D.

It is almost twenty years since "the Birthday Party" (July 14, 1968); sixteen years since the following essay describing that nodal event in my family was reported (Friedman 1971). At the time of its appearance, almost a full generation ago, only Murray Bowen's anonymous article on his own family of origin had preceded it. Over the years it became good fare for clients and supervisors who wanted to learn or teach about the "family of origin approach." As I began to reread the Birthday Party for inclusion in this anthology I started to ponder the change and lack of change in my family, in my thinking and even in the movement during this past generation. Those thoughts and some conclusions about multigenerational transmission appear below as epilogue both in Joycean style, to capture the flavor of the process, and in scientific notation (family diagram), to portray its existence. I have left the original, which follows, intact, so that the reader may come to his or her own conclusions.

THE BIRTHDAY PARTY: AN EXPERIMENT IN OBTAINING CHANGE IN ONE'S OWN FAMILY

It is thought by many that anyone who engages in the practice of individual therapy would benefit, both personally and in his work, from experiencing such therapy. Can the same be said for those who practice family therapy? My guess is that, in fact, many who practice family therapy with their patients are often tempted to use their skills and insights to try to obtain change in their own families. Perhaps the family therapist may be said to be in a perpetual multiple family group as he draws parallels and refers insights back and forth between relationships in his own family and those in the families with which he works.

To work therapeutically with one's own family could be the concealed expectation of the family, and a major force in drawing the therapist to that kind of professional work. After all, if patients are to be seen as symptoms of their family networks, why not therapists? We talk about *identified patients*, why not talk about *identified therapists*? I shall come back to this idea more explicitly later.

This essay will describe a studied, carefully planned attempt to obtain change in my own extended family over a two-year period, the focal point or fulcrum for the whole process being a surprise birthday party for my mother on the occasion of her seventieth birthday. The work was done in consultation with Dr. Murray Bowen under whose supervision I received my general training in working with families.

The format of this paper will be as follows: first, a brief description of the extended network in which I wished to see change occur, pinpointing those areas where I felt dysfunctional symptoms of the network could be identified; second, a description of the way I tried to encourage the process of change with some exposition of the theory on which I based my own actions; and third, some afterthoughts and general conclusions about how the professional person may work within his own extended family to obtain change.

Figure 9-1 describes my extended family on my mother's side. My mother is represented by the circle which occupies the next to the last position in the third generation (containing the number 70); my own position is represented by the square containing the letters "E.F." The diagram represents five generations, though only the third and fourth (with one exception) are relevant to the experiment carried out. As the reader can see, the first generation had three children, two girls and a boy. They were born in Europe and came to America where they produced fourteen offspring (all first-generation Americans). The sisters each had five children, the brother had four. My mother's generation of fourteen cousins, on the other hand, produced only twelve offspring, primarily in multiples of one! Four of my mother's cousins had no children (one never married), and only two of the remaining had more than one child. In each case, the two cousins who were the only members of their generation to have more than one child were the siblings who became most involved in their spouse's extended family—that is, they were most out of the system.

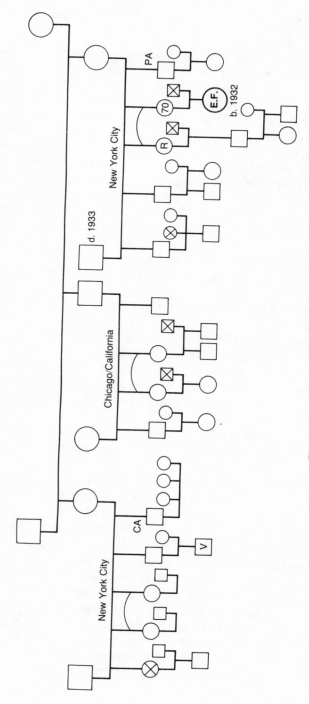

Figure 9-1. Maternal family diagram.

Some other interesting attributes of the system are these: every one of my mother's first cousins at the time of the party (July 1968) was alive and in his seventies except for her younger brother who was sixty-eight, and the woman who had been the oldest. She had committed suicide twenty-five years previously. Secondly, in each of the three sets of siblings that made up my mother's generation, the sisters had stuck together. My mother and her older sister (R) live on the same floor of the same apartment house in New York City. The two sisters in the Chicago group live in the same apartment house. All four are widows, having lost their husbands around the age of fifty-five to sixty. None remarried. My mother and aunt, however, had had almost no contact with the Chicago cousins and never met the younger one. The other two sisters from the group on the left have lived within walking distance of one another on the northern tip of Manhattan throughout their entire lives. They have never had children, and they have never become widows!

It should be noted also that in the middle set of my mother's cousins, the two boys have always lived together, the youngest of that set living with his married brother in California. In contradistinction to this pairing off among siblings in my mother's generation, their children live almost totally separate lives from one another. It is true that they are cousins and not siblings, but generally speaking it can be said that the cousins on my level are almost never in communication with one another.

There were three points in the network where I wished to see change; that is, where I felt pathological symptoms of the network were showing up. One was my own relationship with my mother, which I felt was distant and rigid despite many efforts on my part to be closer to her. The second concerned my oldest cousin's son (the male member of the fifth generation indicated on the chart), who started taking drugs at thirteen, was obese and doing poorly in school, in contrast to his older sister, who was bright, witty, and charming. The third place I wanted to see change was with regard to the younger of the two New York City cousins (V), who, despite the fact he was an extremely successful professional person, was nearing forty and was unmarried, indeed the only unmarried member of my generation. At the time of this writing (two years and three months after the party) not only has my relationship with my mother changed considerably, but my younger cousin has just been enrolled at a Washington-area university and allowed to take honors courses, and my older cousin has been married for more than six months.

The Process

Since my own work with families is at the systems end of the continuum rather than the analytic, I should like to begin this section by indicating my conceptual approach to family systems. By *systems* I mean a set of relationships which, upon achieving homeostasis, functions to maintain that homeostasis through inner-adjusting compensations. Change in one relationship of a system so defined will usually bring about change in another relationship.

When it comes to family systems, I do not equate the degree of physical distance with the degree of emotional distance. People certainly are involved in important non-family relationship systems, but I think those other systems are rarely as intense emotionally as the family system so that a family relationship that is physically distant can be much more influential than a non-family relationship of greater physical proximity. The potential for becoming free from the influence of one's family system, however, is much greater in an approach that brings one towards the family than in an approach that takes one away. I think, therefore, in terms of differentiation of self *within* the system rather than independence of it, and do not believe it is really possible to become independent of one's family system except by becoming intensely part of another system (and then all one has succeeded in doing is transferring the dependency).

Success at achieving such differentiation of self can be measured, I believe, in the extent to which one can be a part of the family without automatically being one of the "emotional dominoes." The path towards such a goal can be achieved best not by a process of internal analysis of oneself but through a process of external perceptions that analyze the system. In other words, I do not think in terms of a *sense* of self, which seems too unverifiable, but in terms of a *position* of self.

In my work with my family of origin and with clinical families, my primary orientation is Bowen theory. Also, I have been influenced by an approach to general systems thinking known as "black box" theory. As computers and other sophisticated electronic equipment became too complex to take apart when they dysfunctioned, an attempt was made to deal with this by inserting new inputs into the system instead of trying to analyze the dysfunctional elements. The method is not all that hit-or-miss, since one always knows some of the major characteristics of the system (contained, but unseeable) within the "black box." Some of the ramifications of that approach are to see dysfunctional parts as always symptomatic, to define dysfunction always in inter-relational terms, to note that the definition or label of dysfunction also includes a large measure of perspective and to diminish the distinction between essence and function.

One other fact has influenced my decision to apply black box theory to human beings and their family systems. Miniaturization with computers has reached the point that ten thousand elements can be put on a disk one-tenth of an inch square. By the end of the decade that should be increased to one hundred thousand. To achieve the density of cells in the human brain one would need a cubic inch of the latter. Thus I have been asking myself if less complex systems than human relationships are now being considered too complex to change through methods that analyze the components (or even the relationships sometimes), surely a similar approach is worth considering in trying to obtain change in families.

The Birthday Party

Applying black box theory to my own family, I began asking what seemed most to characterize the program of my own family system's set of relationships. How could I go about changing some of the most significant inputs, at least some of my own most significant inputs?

What struck me most about my mother's extended family was the set pattern of relating; the isolation of the cousins, the closeness among my mother's cousins of the sets of siblings—with little crossing of lines there. Within my mother's sibling group alone I was struck by the fact that my mother herself was like Cinderella before the ball—she had been given the job of taking care of *their* mother in her seventies, when she was old and feeble and defecating in our bathtub because she was too blind and unaware to know where she was. I also decided that the biggest "no-no" in the family—perhaps because no one was dying—was age; I took note of my own relative disengagement; I noticed also that I was almost the only member of my family with a "helpful" title.

In these terms the question was, what would be the most "unthinkable" event one could carry out in this family system? Obviously, to give a birthday party—indeed a surprise birthday party—a ball for Cinderella, so to speak, outside of New York City, and given by the last person the family might have expected to throw a ball.

For three months, therefore, I set about calling every one of my mother's cousins and siblings—from top down, in deference to age. Her sister, as you can imagine, was against it—until I put her in charge of something. Added and unexpected benefits came during this phase, as in conversation with each relative I had to ask information about the others, received the information in the form of opinions I did not expect but made sure to pass on to the others when I called them. It was as though there were little light bulbs connected into each circle and square on the family diagram that were either all out or all on (steady state sort of thing); the day I started telephoning those bulbs started flashing—out of phase—for the first time in many, many years. Something dormant (and apparently dead) came to life.

One interesting detail during this part of the process may be mentioned. When I called the oldest group of cousins, living in Manhattan, the brother said they couldn't come because one of his sisters was very sick but he would tell his sisters for me and I needn't call. I called the sister who wasn't sick and she said she couldn't come because her sister was very, very sick, and she would tell her for me; I needn't call her sister. Now remember it was the brother's son who was unmarried. When I spoke to the sick one, I found her much brighter and much more knowledgeable about the family than the other two—this certainly fit all my ideas about families, namely, that it couldn't be clear at all who was sick for whom, that indeed the symptomatic one was often the most aware and responsible one. So I wrote her a short note saying I was sorry they all couldn't come down for the day and I realized that she had a responsibility to keep the family together, but how would we ever get Vicky (my unmarried cousin) married? As I calculate, that letter arrived in New York on a Friday and the following Monday Vicky called to accept the invitation and asked if he could bring a girl.

With the exception of Vicky, none of my mother's cousins was able to come nor did any of her close friends whom I called—all, however, kept the secret, and all sent good wishes. To each person I had sent a list of the names of everyone invited. There were twenty-six people at the party, and the surprise was total. Only one of her siblings did not come, the next oldest brother. He, incidentally, married secretly when young, fifty-five years previously, and came back to live with the family for six months before he announced he was married. He was the only sibling who had two children, the one from this group as I mentioned before, who was more a part of his spouse's system. I point this out because it has become my experience generally to note with families that brothers and sisters will carry out inter-relational inputs at age seventy as though they were still viewing one another as age seven.

There is one other grouping I should like to mention before talking about the party itself. One of my mother's intimates was not a blood relative but her sister-in-law on my father's side; that is, my father's brother's wife. My aunt and uncle had lived in Canada with their only child, a son, for forty years, had been extremely successful in the retail business and were perhaps my nuclear family's closest relatives second to my mother's sister's family. In recent years this aunt had been sickly, alcoholic, depressed, and had growths on her feet that necessitated repeated operations. At any given time, however, she was liable to recover completely from everything and take a trip half-way around the world. When my father died, this aunt and uncle had begged my mother to move to Canada to be near them.

This group also would not come to the party because my aunt had become phobic after she finally stopped drinking. And like the group on northern Manhattan none dared fly away for a day "to the heat of Washington." I learned as much about those who did not come to the party as those who did. For example, the absurd excuses given by this group and the one on northern Manhattan made their own stuck-togetherness stand out in relief and pointed out directions for follow-up in the future.

The party itself was a complete success, especially considering the logistics. People came from four cities and had to meet at one place at precisely the right hour while my mother was bluffed into going out for an hour. The caterer was precision itself, arriving and setting everything up during the same time. Actually, I felt the success at keeping the secret—that is, the ease with which I was able to get my family to gang up in a conspiracy against my mother—did not speak well for my family. Her total surprise, however, confirmed my feeling that I had done something truly unthinkable.

At the party one event in particular was significant. My next older cousin, my mother's sister's son, had been like a complementary sibling to me. Although Walter Toman in his work on sibling constellations recognizes the complementary aspects of sibling relationships, he says only children are "wild cards." It has been my experience generally that if there is enough feedback between their parents, two only children from the same family will produce some kind of complementary system. My cousin is an accountant, very proper in all ways, no maverick opinions, and super-responsible for our two mothers. He became totally, helplessly drunk within one hour after the party started and was walked around outside by his wife for the next three hours. During this time, his son, whom I knew only to be obese and failing in school, told me he had been on hard drugs for the last two years. In the middle of the party when I investigated a strange tinkle of breaking glass downstairs, I found my aunt, seventy-one, who in her concern for her son, had given our glass sliding door something that must have been a karate chop with her knee as she went to look for him. She was uninjured but the entire door had been shattered. Rushing in to keep the party going, I told everyone upstairs that they would never guess what my Aunt Rose had done to upstage my mother, her younger sister. Strangely, maybe because of the way I put it, nobody believed me, and everyone went right on eating and drinking while my unmarried cousin, the dentist, applied iodine.

In the months that followed the party, the following events occurred in rather rapid succession: one month later my conservative cousin had grown a beard; for my aunt, who will clean an ash tray before you have finished your cigarette, this was truly earth-shaking. I wrote him a letter telling him I thought it was a terrible thing to do to his mother and whom would I look up to now? I also wrote my young cousin a letter asking him seriously what his trips were like and received a long exposition about the effects of drugs on *coitus*—to use his word. He also announced that he had given up drugs because he wanted whole children. Two months later my mother's younger brother, the youngest in this line of cousins, the only one who was not seventy, dropped dead of a heart attack. His wife thereupon came to Washington six months later to live with her married daughter, and the younger cousin enrolled at George Washington University the following year. Precisely between those events my dentist cousin married a Gentile divorcee with two children, the granddaughter of a prominent New York Protestant clergyman. They were to come to Washington for a private marriage ceremony by me, but his father had a heart attack, and they haven't made it yet.

During the following year my Canadian aunt made an unsuccessful suicide attempt with drugs. I wrote this aunt a letter, having been told by my uncle and cousin that she couldn't come to the phone. In the letter, I told her that I had always thought of her as my most competent aunt, considering her success in business over the years, and I couldn't understand how she would do such a sloppy job of committing suicide. I followed those lines describing my own life in the most depressing terms I could think of. As I say, I was encouraged to do this by what I had seen with the other group. The reaction of my aunt was most interesting.

As it turned out, my mother arrived in Ottawa two days after the letter. My aunt never revealed the contents, and to this day everyone is saying what a wonderful thing my mother did for my phobic aunt, who had not left the house in two years, and was now, "as a result of my mother's visit," back to her old self. Indeed she has since struck up relationships with other relatives in the States and relates to me entirely differently than to anyone else. (It never ceases to amaze me that those who think of "systems" as a "cold" approach usually resort to electrical means when it comes to shock.) My aunt has reestablished contacts with her own family of origin from which she had become increasingly cut off over the years. I paid a visit to her during the summer two months later, during which time she gave me "hell" for writing such a nasty letter; she came down to Washington in September to hear me preach (for the first time) during the High Holy days; she went to some weddings on her side of the family the following month. And in December she told my uncle that she could no longer take their forty years of a battling marriage, their separated vacations, etc., and that this time she really was going through with their ten-year-old, suspended, but constantly threatened separation agreement. My uncle went off to the West Indies for a month and came back with cancer of the liver. He died two months later.

I have, since the party, kept up my own interests in the extended network, paying a trip to Chicago, for example, to visit my mother's and aunt's two girl cousins, and wound up in the ridiculous position of having my mother and aunt question me about the family for a change; they never met the younger one, age seventy-two.

The Hangover

In this last section I should like to describe some of my thoughts and conclusions about doing work in one's own family. I shall subdivide this section into two parts: technical and personal.

From the point of view of technique I would say I consciously tried five different varieties. Listing them in order of *least* effectiveness, I would say they were (1) being straightforwardly analytic about people or relationships, that is, being the expert; (2) telling them a story about one of my clients; (3) performing verbal reversals; (4) performing behavior reversals, and (5) being stupid—this one has to follow, if being expert is at the other end of the scale.

Regarding the straightforward analytical approach, I found that the reaction was almost always one of denial. I was told I didn't understand, or a comment would be made about my playing therapist. On the other hand, when I went to Canada after my aunt's suicide attempt and spent one week with the family, never once making an interpretation, I found by the end of the week they got so scared by this that they began to talk to me in a way that showed they knew more, and maybe thought more, in analytic terminology than I did.

Telling them about a client had some limited effectiveness. On several occasions since the party, when members of my family were deeply distressed about something, I found that telling them about a similar situation from my practice helped de-personalize the situation for them. It reminded me of what had worked and not worked with the client and thus helped me know how to behave at that moment. But most of all, I think, it enabled the conversation to continue with me in the position of experienced relative who was not trying to change them but who, from their point of view, despite his experience, didn't seem too anxious about it, either.

For example, for about a year my mother's older sister had been obsessed with anxiety about gastrointestinal problems. In her concern over the doctor's failure to find something specific, she had not been eating and was thus losing weight. The loss of weight contributed further to her worry that something sinister was at work. Everyone including the family doctor had been at a loss to reassure her. I had treated a similar case with a "paradoxical intention" barrage: did she know where the cancer was, what progress did she think it had been making and, finally, people didn't just get cancer—she must have done something wrong, perhaps God was punishing her.

Thus I dealt with my aunt by: (1) not attempting any reassurance; (2) figuring, but not mentioning, that it had something to do with her son's involvement elsewhere (which indeed turned out to be the case); and (3) telling her as coldly as possible that I still needed her help in getting my mother straightened out, and I would appreciate it if she could just hang on a bit longer.

The third technique is verbal reversals. The two kinds I have employed most have been to out-kook and to go contrary to my instincts. An example of an out-kooking dialogue might go like this (with my dramatic aunt from Canada and in front of my mother who always feels so sorry for her):

Aunt: Eddie, what do you think of me?

Me: I never analyze my relatives.

Aunt: I have opinions about you.

Me: Well, maybe you can get more distance.

Aunt: You must have some opinions.

Me: Okay, I think you're crazy, but it sure keeps you from being boring.

The other form of the verbal reversal is to follow one's instincts and then do the opposite. Thus when my aunts, who are in their seventies, complain about their sundry ailments, and I find myself thinking "they're old, afraid of dying, lonely, etc.," I immediately tell them they're getting older, or nobody lives forever. Sometimes before they get a chance to complain, say on the phone, I tell them they sound terrible. And then we usually have a delightful conversation. As my mother got close to retiring (at seventy-two), I would take her for a drive and point out the new old folks home and describe how secure she would be there. She is now looking for another job and applying for unemployment insurance!

The effect of the verbal reversal on these relationships is, I believe, that I convey I won't play their games. Consequently they relate in a much more adult manner to me than to those who take the so-called compassionate approach. I believe I sometimes set an example for other members of the family and make unthinkable actions do-able.

The fourth technique, the action reversal, is more effective, I believe, though I must admit that this dichotomy between verbal and action reversals is somewhat artificial. There are two kinds here, also. One is to behave in a situation the way no one in the family ever does, the other is to behave the way you yourself never do. The party was so successful, I believe, because both things happened. I have been doing a lot of research on how widows should invest their money, and sending advice to my mother. My CPA cousin has always done my mother's income tax—for free—and she naturally takes my very professional-appearing plans to him, who admits to my mother he hasn't done much thinking about this area. My final recommendations are always overly conservative, and he winds up having to suggest something more speculative in comparison.

Switching means of communication is another good behavior reversal (say phone and letter), but reversing whom one talks to about whom is better. Throughout my life I have had gossipy talks with my mother about my aunts; recently I have been doing this with my aunts about my mother. For example, my mother always took a highly sympathetic and supportive position toward my Canadian aunt despite years of my telling my mother that I thought she was selfish. I got a juicy tidbit from my aunt about how she thought my father secretly liked her and passed it on. My conversations with my mother now are filled with my mother's diatribes about my aunt as I try to explain that you have "to understand her." I find that the more I do this the freer my mother seems to be with me. (My grandfather died six months after I was born, and I believe I replaced him in some original triangle with his two daughters.)

The best reversal I have found, however, is to refuse to be serious about what the family is most uptight about. I would add, however, that being exaggeratedly overserious sometimes seems to amount to the same thing. (I am also coming to believe there would have been much less possibility that my hypertensive father would have died at fifty-six if he could have taken my mother's "goodness" less seriously.)

This brings me to the fifth and I believe most powerful way of inducing change in one's family, and primarily I believe because it focuses one most on his own inputs, and that is what I call being stupid. At the beginning of this essay I raised the question if patients were to be considered symptoms of their family system, why not therapists? Maybe the same processes that produce dysfunction create other kinds of functioning. Or, since we are talking about process, if when a member of a family becomes the patient, the other members respond in a way that keeps that person in the patient role even though it is ultimately to their own detriment. Maybe a similar process goes on regarding professionals and their families: that once someone becomes a member of the helping professions the effect on the family is to have them adapt to that person in ways which are not necessarily helpful to that person or themselves. If this is true then the way to get the most change in the homeostasis of such a system is clearly never to play therapist in the system, that is, therapist as they would think of therapist, indeed to play anti-therapist. (Stirring up trouble, not being helpful or responsible, giving pain or at least not rushing in to relieve it.)

All forms of reversal help in this matter, of course. I asked my formerly alcoholic aunt to take back a bottle of unusual Scotch as a gift to my cousin. She "forgot" it at my mother's in New York. Until my dentist cousin got married I never missed an opportunity to remind him of his responsibility to his aunts and parents as their only offspring. I have found, however, that asking stupid questions or making obvious common sense interpretations of equally obvious pathological behavior turns relatives into very insightful people. And that gets me asking, "Well, if they knew the answers all along why the hell are they asking me about the problem?"

For myself as rabbi another way I have found to be unprofessional is to fail to go, no less to perform, weddings and funerals for members of the family. This is producing a very strong reaction: on the other hand you can almost watch the shifts in responsibility among my cousins when I force my family members to find their own rabbis. For example, when I just couldn't make it to an uncle's funeral, another cousin (the oldest in the line) who went, took charge. This has changed his relationship with that uncle's family and I believe had corresponding salutary effects on his own nuclear family.

I find this quite a paradox: that is, by *not* helping precisely where because of my professional expertise I could have been most helpful, I *may* have been more useful.

Now I should like to conclude with a few personal observations. This whole paper has been framed in terms of obtaining change in one's extended family. Yet I am quite sure that the person benefitting most from any attempt to induce such changes, at least in the ways I have been describing, is the person doing it. In fact, it would be my guess that if one sets about trying to induce the change, or for the sake of helping the relatives primarily, it won't work, or at least it won't work as well. The paradox here is resolved, I think, by remembering that as long as you are doing it for others you would be behaving as a therapist, a role that is hard to get out of and that secretly maintains homeostasis.

The approach I have been taking, therefore, is to do these things to see what it teaches me about my family. This in turn, however, has raised some interesting and serious theoretical questions. First of all, I have been wondering recently if these five techniques do not wind up with exactly the same effectiveness rating when one is working professionally with families. This is an exciting idea, for I have never been comfortable with a style of therapy that could not also be a style of life. Thus, I have begun to ask myself if what I have most in common with those who see me professionally is that we have both been the results of similar processes and that, therefore, the more I understand about my family and my position in it the more I will understand family process in general. These are insights I can share.

From the personal point of view I should also like to make a passing comment on what I have most obviously avoided, namely, the effect on one's nuclear family if one tries to obtain change in one's extended family. To talk publicly about relationships in this area is to get too personal; on the other hand, I would not want to imply, by ignoring that area, that there are no repercussions.

It may also be worth noting that my wife received several notes of thanks. This was quite surprising since I did not involve her in one single detail, having had the entire affair catered down to the silverware, chairs and tables, and since all correspondence and phone calls to set up the party came only from me; no one had even spoken to my wife during the preparations.

Finally, I should like to enter a disclaimer. When this paper was delivered, some heard it as playing God and suggested that I should have warned my family about what I was trying to do. Let me state clearly, therefore, that I knew I could not be fully aware of the results. This is not to say I had no fears, trepidations, or fantasies. (None of my fantasies about deaths and suicides materialized—perhaps because fantasies come out of the system as it exists. If individuals are to be seen as symptoms of the family, so must their fantasies.) Things had been the way they had been for an awfully long time; members of the family were suffering now because of the irresponsibility (dependency?) of others. I decided, therefore, I would take responsibility only for my own feelings and behavior and each other member of the family would have to take responsibility for his.

In no way, therefore, do I take credit for any of the changes I have described in my family, for in no way can I prove that my new inputs produced the new outputs. But I do believe that few of the things I did would have had the same effect on the family if anyone else would have done them, and if that is true, it is not because of any special attribute, talent, or personality factor that resides within me, but because of where I am on the family diagram.

A GENERATION LATER

A generation would appear to provide an adequate yardstick for measuring change in a family, in a societal "movement," or in a thinking person's thinking. However, as may be deduced from the diagram below (Fig. 9–2), it probably takes at least six generations to decide whether any change that occurs in family process is a fundamental change or the recycling of a symptom. In all events, two decades in the course of a family is enough time for a child to be born and leave home; for a marriage to mature and dissolve; for vibrant individuals to enter senility; for close relatives to become irreconcilably distant; for kin to be almost forgotten; for unquestioned expectations to be obliterated, or for undreamed-of surprises to materialize; for improbable connections to become connected, and for the seemingly impossible not only to become possible, but to be taken for granted. Almost all of these emotional phenomena occurred in my family since "the Party."

Looking at the diagram of my mother's family of origin (Fig. 9–1), how could I have predicted that the same diagram almost twenty years later (Fig. 9–2) would have shown my daughter (57), two years old at the time, now the deep-thinking, fashion plate of her deep-South sorority; a 16-year-old son (58), four at the time, now playing with robots, repairing video arcade games, and rewiring our beach house for a

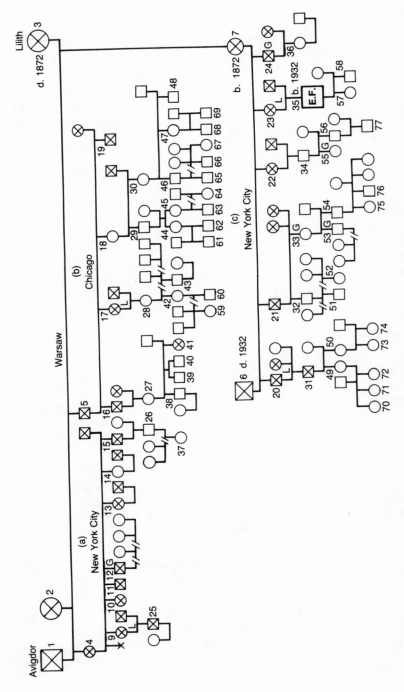

Figure 9–2. Maternal family diagram.

178

hobby; my mother's entire generation gone, save for two of her first cousins, (18) age ninety and (14) age ninety-six, who have not seen one another for sixty years, and only recently found out each still exists through my contacts with the other; all my own older first cousins still alive, save one (31), the gentle son of my mother's gentlest (and oldest) brother, who gently killed himself in his office at the close of work one day with sleeping pills and a plastic bag; my CPA "drinking" cousin's attractive, intelligent daughter (55), who was *my* daughter's present age at that time, now, at thirty-eight, the emergency room director of a major metropolitan hospital.

Or was it predictable that my unmarried, dentist, second cousin (V) in the original article, from the oldest branch, not only would finally have gotten married but also divorced (with custody of his daughter), and married again, or that *his* only first cousin (25), whom I hardly knew, a childlike, childless, outdoors enthusiast, would be killed at age fifty on a bicycle by a jackknifing "semi," thus leaving "V's" intellectual self and on-the-verge-of-punk, fifteen-year-old daughter (37) the only living branch on that part of the family tree?

I do remember, though, when they told my grandmother (7) in 1949 that my cyclist cousin's mother, her favorite, superresponsible niece (9), had killed herself upon learning she had cancer (some say glaucoma), that her own mother, my grandmother's older sister (4), had assumed responsibility for my grandmother when *their* mother (3) died two months after my grandmother's birth, leaving their widowed father (1)—my grandmother once told me—to marry a shrew (2).

Nor could I have expected that my oldest, first cousin (32), the only one in my branch who had been divorced, at twenty-five, would be divorcing again at age 67? . . . and remarrying within the year? Or that he would at that ripe old age first begin to move toward me after a generation of my pursuing him, now that he had finally left the wife with whom he had been fused for more than a generation? His father (21), incidentally, had been the only one of my mother's siblings not to come to "the Party," because he had to go with his wife "to the mountains," although, in retrospect, his failure to attend was perhaps due to the fact that he wanted to avoid questions about his other child, his expatriate daughter (33), who had cut herself off from the family around that time in order to keep secret the fact that her brilliant, oldest son (53) had been imprisoned for his own creative version of "the international drug trade." And who could have expected that a generation later she would now, along with her brother, be two of my closer kin, or that the former "jailbird" would now be the head of his own software consulting firm, no less that he would now be "in" and his brother (54), the physician, "out" because of the good doctor's marital choice; even as her father (21), "who went to the mountains," received similar treatment from our grandmother for his marital choice (her own mother) — and his choice at least was Jewish!

Looking at the family diagram (Fig. 9–2) of my mother's family of origin, it could hardly have been foreseen that my favorite aunt (22) (of the glass sliding door) would never forgive me till her dying day after she read "The Birthday Party" (even though reading it helped bring her aforementioned expatriate niece back into the fold), creating a cut-off of such intensity that neither her son (34) nor his children would ever relax with me again (until her death). The cut-off was intensi-fied — if such a thing were possible — when, in my mother's last years, they all fought all my efforts to keep my mother out of a nursing home, where they were convinced "she" would be more comfortable. (Friedman 1985, pp. 294–295.)

In some ways, if I look at the family diagram, some of this makes sense, but it is always possible to play such games of hindsight. Every family provides enough different directions for an observer to say the connections are apparent.

But are these the changes and connections that count? Is there any evidence that the next generation is better differentiated, any evidence that the physical or mental health of the family has changed, or its den-sity been significantly affected, by what happened on that Bastille Day seventy years after my mother was born? There is absolutely none. But that is not the only conclusion to be drawn, for I have continued to work at relationships in my family of origin, throughout the passing of this generation — however, for a different set of reasons and with a very different rationale (see below) than I applied in 1968. In this respect there has been change — significant change. In 1968 most of my major motivation was to "help the family." There were pockets of fusion that I saw leading to severe symptoms. My major intent was to "disequil-ibrate" things. Over the years I gave up that self-important (or really no-self) view of saving others and reached a position of making all con-tacts simply for my own benefit and for the benefit of my children. I was an "only" with only "onlys" for first cousins. I understood all too well, both from my clinical experience and my family, the pernicious potential both for my children and for myself in that sort of isolation that tends to promote cutoffs, or their similar opposite, fusion. The most cut-off branch (21 and descendents) had the severest types of dysfunction for three successive generations. In this respect, I would claim to have succeeded to some extent in helping to derail what appeared to be a multigenerational trend. It has not been easy, and it has taken most of this past generation to understand and accomplish. Here are two examples of this change in approach, one from my father's side, and one from my mother's.

CHANGE IN MY OWN THINKING SINCE "THE PARTY"

Both my mother's and father's families of origin have tended to be explosive rather than implosive. With the deaths of my uncles and aunts, almost none of their children (my first cousins on either side) have remained in touch with one another, not that there has been any outright feuding or backbiting. They all simply drifted apart and became swallowed up in their own nuclear groupings. All very nice people. If some have met with violence, none have ever expressed it. Almost all have recovered from what has ailed them. Hardly anyone has died prematurely (before 70) from illness. And each, as I told him or her about my journeys to visit the others, has been genuinely interested in my reports—including, on my mother's side, a recent, first-time-ever visit to the Chicago branch, most of whom (generation five and six) were astounded to find they had relatives in New York. My efforts on both sides have included persistent pursuit, cross-country travel to nodal events, and refusal to be "turned off" by unintentional insults and, at the beginning, suspicion and argumentative initiatives.

On my father's side, I am the next to youngest of six male first cousins, the children of two brothers and two sisters, all now dead for more than a decade (see Fig. 9–3). Their parents (our grandparents) are buried in separate cemeteries in Brooklyn and Queens, though no one

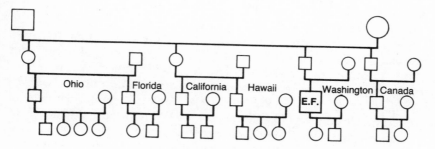

Figure 9–3. Paternal family diagram.

knows why. We live on a perimeter that is circumscribed by Hawaii, California, Ohio, Canada, Washington, D.C., and Florida. We range in age from fifty-three to seventy. I have been the only one to retain contact with each of the other five. Over the past ten years I have made sure to visit all of them as I traveled to their area, in one instance persevering carefully and patiently to rework a cut-off with the closest cousin from my youth by purposefully getting into a triangle with his reclusive mother, and having our children "jet-set" visit. With regard to another "distant" cousin, I once rearranged a speaking engagement so that I could travel cross-country to his son's wedding, making sure to bear good wishes from the others (I called them all beforehand) and bearing back similar greetings when I told them all about the "lovely affair" upon my return. Six months later, he worked out a similar way of attending my son's Bar Mitzvah. And, on that occasion, *for the first time in the family's history*, a representative of each of my father's siblings (four of the six offspring) gathered in the same place at the same time! And I did not have to point that fact out to the others, who all suddenly turned photographer. Some had not seen each other in more than thirty years. Not only that, soon after, they planned what amounted to an international cousins' reunion saying, "Isn't it a shame that the next generation has never met?" It took place in Florida, after a year of negotiation about the site, and all six first cousins came. We had never been all together before, though some of our children were unable to make it. I prepared a six-generation family diagram, similar to the one of my mother's family, for distribution before the event. They are now planning a second reunion on the west coast so that the next generation who could not afford the trip east could meet.

On my mother's side, the greatest cutoff, as I said, had been with my aunt (22), and her son, and his children—in many ways most painful. This is the part of the family with whom I had been closest from earliest childhood. My aunt had been a second mother to me since her mother lived with us, and she often came to visit. I had officiated at the funeral of her husband (1963) (my favorite uncle) and had delivered the talk at her grandson's Bar Mitzvah, and I had always liked his older sister (the emergency room physician). However, no effort, from nonchalant surprise telephone calls to genuine letters, or reports about the doings of other family members, brought any change in their view of me as cruel for the way I kept my mother (23) out of a nursing home. In fact, they could not tolerate being in the same room with me, all pointedly avoiding my daughter's Bas Mitzvah the year after my mother died. Finally, I just gave up, but did not reciprocate the cutoff; cutoffs take *two*. I stopped trying but was able emotionally to keep the door open, and said to others, "I will just have to wait till she dies." (She told me in one, exceptional, friendly moment after my mother died that her father (6) had said, on his deathbed, "Always take care of Lillie.") When my aunt did die, my cousin, now having experienced for a year what I had experienced with his aunt's death, and finding himself aping my determination to keep her out of a nursing home, called me immediately; and with a soft, familiar, loving voice I had not heard in twenty years, asked if I would do the funeral. I jumped at the chance, and when he and his children begged out of my suggestion that they do the eulogy, delivered my own, anecdotal and with warm humor, praising her foibles and her overfunctioning. I had been sure, to bring my whole family with me. My son (58), now almost thirteen, was practically the same age that my cousin's son (56) had been the last time we had been friends, at "the Party," twenty years ago. As this former Fullbright Scholar in stage design drove us to the airport, he engaged my son, seated next to him (I had carefully taken a back seat) in the same kind of elder–mentor relationship I had had with him when he had come of age. They all came to his Bar Mitzvah two months later.

One last event is particularly worth noting. Three years ago, I spent a day visiting two cemeteries, one in New Jersey, where my parents were buried, one "across the bridge," in Queens, where my mother's parents have lain, unvisited, for more than thirty years. It was the first time since my grandmother's funeral that I had visited, even though she had been my roommate for the first fourteen years of my life. She had moved in when I was a newborn, since her husband, my grandfather (6), had died seven months after I was born. I had always assumed that my position in the family's triangle was due to that "transference." It had never occurred to me that if that was the significant replacement in my prepartum past, it did not explain why I also felt so close to my grandmother's sister's children, or those from my grandmother's brother's branch. They, after all, were only my grandfather's in-laws! At the cemetery that day I read my grandmother's father's name, Avigdor (1), for the first time (though I once used it in a short story, not knowing where I had gotten it). As I stood looking down, some long-unthought-of associations returning to my consciousness, I suddenly realized that it was he, my great-grandfather (number 1), whom I had replaced in my anointing grandmother's life; he had been the *scholar*, my grandfather only a *tailor*; it was this widower, who had lost his own wife in the birth of his youngest daughter, my grandmother, who with her siblings fled *not* the pogroms but the shrew. When I told the tale to Murray Bowen (it was then eighteen years since he "coached" me about "The Party"), he said, "Ed, it's been a long time coming."

Four years later, I am now beginning to realize, it was really only the beginning.

Both the power of multigenerational transmission as well as its ability to disguise itself will now be documented in a scientific manner. Only after I wrote all this, and observed the family diagram for the hundreth time, did the following facts become clear to me.

Three characteristics of multigenerational transmission process stand out in the family diagram of the maternal side of the family (Fig. 9–2). Most striking is the descending order of dysfunction from branches a–c. A is dying out and has only one female member, age fourteen, in the fifth generation (her parents are divorced and she is troubled). B and c, quite on the contrary, are flourishing, increasingly, with two exceptions. In branch b, the four grandchildren of #16, who is next in line after branch a also, are not reproducing, and until 1985 only one had married; she was divorced and then was murdered in her thirties. The descending order of dysfunction, from a to c, is thus kept intact down to the fifth generation. Members of c, on the other hand, with only one exception, are not only all reproducing "from generation to generation," but have all also tended to do very well professionally. Only one member of that branch (c) has failed to reproduce (#36), although one in the next generation is unmarried at thirty-eight. The major event in the family history that may have promoted this pattern is the aforementioned death in the first generation of #3 shortly after the birth of #6 (grandmother of the author, #35). As stated earlier, family oral history has it that the widower at first farmed them all out, then took them back after marrying a shrew. It is generally a good rule of thumb when studying family diagrams that if the younger siblings are doing better in life than their older sisters and brothers, the dysfunction came into the system early and was as if "absorbed" by the older children. The child who loses her mother in childbirth will not suffer the same trauma as her older siblings who have already established a bond. The most significant fact, however, is not that this occurred in the 1870s, but that its residue seems to be around in the 1980s.

A second significant characteristic of the family is its tendency to stay together as well as an apparent correlation between infertility and moving away from a family center. One effect of the centripetal or gravitational forces may be evidenced in that almost all of c settled in Manhattan and environs, with few moving away even in following generations. A and b moved to California and then back to New York and Chicago, where both have tended to centralize. As mentioned in the original article, two sisters from each set (and in *b*'s case a pair of brothers also) stayed in close touch (into their eighties) and, in *b* and *c*, came together again in the same apartment house. The correlation between geographical distancing from the family and failure to reproduce can be seen in generations 3, 4, and 5 (12, 24, 36, 53, 55). The author (35), who also moved away, did not become a parent until age thirty-four (after completing five years of psychoanalysis!). He is almost the only member of any branch who keeps in touch with members of the other branches. This may be related to his position, as described in the text, as the emotional replacement for #1 (and incidentally, may help explain his emphasis within the family movement on the importance of nodal events).

A possible third characteristic of the multigenerational transmission process has to do with untimely death and the names of family members beginning with "L." Number 3, the author's great-grandmother (first generation), who died in childbirth, was named Lilith, and each of her children gave at least one of their children a name that began with "L." In 1980 (a century after the death of their great-grandmother), within a six-month period two of the children of those so "honored" died, and a third came very close, although none of the three had any knowledge of the misfortune of the others. One (25), age fifty-two, by accident, and the second (3), age fifty-five, by suicide; the third was the author (35), age forty-eight, who needed immediate bypass surgery after discovering that his right coronary artery was totally occluded and his left main 99 percent so. What makes the above pattern so unusual is that in all three branches of the family (*a*, *b*, and *c*) and throughout all six generations (80 people), untimely death is extremely rare. With the exception of the murder of (4) and the suicide of (9) — one of the "L's" — the only family members to die naturally before their seventies were three of the young children born to (4), and (24), who left the family center and died at sixty-eight. It is, of course, too far-fetched to assume that such family emotional history helps explain the author's habitual use of the term *dybbuk*, and *demon*, in his teaching over the years when referring to the uncanny persistence of families in resisting change.

OTHER CHANGES IN MY THINKING

The following are some conclusions I have reached about family of origin work based on my continued experience with my own family, my coaching of clients with their families, and my supervision of other therapists during the generation since "the party."

1. The primary purpose for all work in one's family of origin has to be for one's self, and it cannot be just in the service of self-differentiation—one has to get a kick out of it.
2. Families can come together again even after a generation of distance, and sometimes only after a generation has passed or has "passed away."
3. For the distance in that time–space continuum to be bridged, however, there must be a catalytic family member prepared to take advantage of catalytic family moments. Such a "family leader" must love his family, have a genuine desire to be with (at least some of) them, and possess a sense of responsibility that enables him or her to resist resistance. Yet that sense of responsibility cannot be borne so seriously that it destroys his or her ability to introduce the playful and sometimes downright ludicrous initiatives that are necessary for maintaining a nonanxious presence.
4. Accomplishing this task takes years. Processes must be allowed to develop so that the watchful eye can take advantage of the crises and turn them into opportunities. The task cannot be willed, though serendipity will help. In short, the involvement must be relegated to the "back burner" of a lifetime project, rather than being given the priority of something to be accomplished in the near future.
5. The importance of nodal events, family reunions of any type, and rites of passage cannot be underestimated. They were our species' own natural device for dealing with change and separation, the two major goals of all activity that has come to be called "therapy." They are, in fact, the original form of all therapy, and began, indeed, as family therapy (Friedman 1980, 1985).
6. The effort as described above will have major effects on the intellectual and professional development of the "leader," whether or not he or she is a "therapist." Chief among them will be increased clarity on all issues of life; second is a broadened capacity to deal with anxiety, anxious situations, and anxious people not obtainable through any other human endeavor; and third is an ability to think process and disdain technique that makes all other forms of training and supervision appear superficial.
7. The power of family process is awesome. Its capacity to resist efforts to mold it into other forms, change its direction, or stop it in its

tracks is all but beyond human potential. It is also a wily cat that cannot be fooled and, indeed, will put to its own service all efforts to lead it astray. It can, however, be skinned in another direction—

8. That other direction develops when the family member with the most motivation to help his or her family change (whether they come by this because of their family position or because of their understanding of family process) works primarily to keep himself or herself from being zapped by the family emotional system, while remaining in touch. It is success in that direction that can have a ripple effect, sometimes leading to change—but *not* if you even try to keep that potential benefit in mind.

9. To the extent all of the above is correct, then what Murray Bowen has been trying to teach this past generation differs so from what the rest of the world of family therapy, if not psychotherapy, appears to be aiming for, it should be given another name completely.

CONCLUSION

The totally unexpected nature of the changes in my family and my thinking during the past generation has also led me to some thoughts about future changes regarding Bowen theory and the family movement itself. When I entered the field in 1968, in order to catch up, I immediately purchased all the back copies of *Family Process* (for almost $24), and for another $75 secured all the well-known books thus far published—but I will never be able to catch up again. Today the Bowen approach is only one among many ways to understand families, and though it may still be the only coherent system of family-systems thinking yet developed, it is little known, greatly misunderstood, often misquoted, or referenced with terms long since discarded by its founder (e.g., ego-mass). On the other hand, family of origin concepts are being applied in inconceivably new directions, from cancer rehabilitation to organizational management by people who were never trained at Georgetown, know of Murray Bowen only as some prophet or folk hero, and with no sense of his theory's biological and evolutionary imperative, employ the word *differentiation* synonymously with *individuation* or *autonomy*. It well may be that the future significance of such concepts as *multigenerational transmission, emotional system,* and *differentiation,* if not all of Bowen Theory—as well as any major contributions to the evolution of these seminal ideas—will show up in political theory, international relations, sports, or economics—or even astronomy! Fantasy: In the year 2150, one intergalactic research associate turns to another and says, "You know, the other day I came across something on the origins of our par-sec methods for spatial dichotomy, and according to the notes, they were originally conceived in a field called *family therapy*."

REFERENCES

Friedman, E. H. (1971). The birthday party: an experiment in obtaining change in one's own family. *Family Process* 10: 345–359.

Friedman, E. H. (1980). Systems and ceremonies. In *The Family Lifecycle*, ed. E. Carter and M. McGoldrick. New York: Gardner Press.

Friedman, E. H. (1985). *Generation to Generation: Family Process in Church and Synagogue*. New York: Guilford Publications.

Toman, W. (1967). *Family Constellation*. New York: Springer.

Part III
Bridging Emotional Cut-Offs

Chapter 10

STRATEGIES TO EXPLORE CUT-OFFS

Ellen G. Benswanger, Ph.D.

The phenomenon known as *cut-off* is a condition of estrangement between family members that prevents them from confronting, or resolving, conflicts. The concept occupies a central position in Bowen theory and is used to clarify the "process of separation, isolation, withdrawal, running away or denying the importance of the parental family" (Bowen 1978, p. 382). The more intense the cut-off from one's parents, the more likely it is that dysfunctional patterns will be repeated in other relationships. Bowen has emphasized that a cut-off may be achieved by internal mechanisms, physical distancing, or a combination of the two (Bowen 1978). The type of mechanism used to sustain a cut-off is not an indication of the intensity or degree of the unresolved emotional conflict.

Cut-offs can occur between family members who live in the same house, as well as between people who live a continent apart. They may be characterized by every hue of the emotional rainbow, from bitter rage to lingering sadness, from abrupt rejection to imperceptible distancing, from vivid intensity to apparent indifference. The process of cutting-off may be accomplished by ostracizing family members, maintaining silence in their presence, or engaging in intermittent bursts of anger interspersed with coolness. A cut-off may be experienced as an intentional, tangible act or as an unconscious, latent proc-

Appreciation is expressed to Paulina McCullough, Cynthia Larkby, Dan Papero, and participants in the Advanced Pittsburgh Family Systems Group for their guidance and support.

ess. The essential feature is the avoidance of effective communication and the maintenance of rigid, repetitive patterns of thinking and feeling.

Virtually every type and intensity of cut-off has been depicted in the literature. The phenomenon has been discussed in relation to emigration (Bunting 1982; Rutenberg 1982), intermarriage (L. Lampiris 1979), and psychosomatic illness (B. Lampiris 1978). Case studies and videotapes of family therapy sessions document specific examples of cut-offs (Bowen and Yanks 1980, McCullough 1979). Vivid descriptions also appear in fiction and drama. The prototypes of all cut-offs are portrayed in the Old Testament. The murder of Abel by his brother, Cain, Abraham's banishment of Hagar and Ishmael, and the estrangement between Jacob and Esau exemplify the most fundamental human responses to perceived wrong-doing, stolen legacy, or conflict of values. Obviously, the cut-off constitutes a universal response to certain life situations.

The most basic type of cut-off occurs in relation to one's own parents, as an ostensible effort to achieve independence and separation from parental constraints. However, cut-offs can, and do, occur at every level of the family system, in vertical and in horizontal configurations—that is, between members of the same generation as well as between generations. The phenomenon appears in many guises and forms. In some families, cut-offs occur periodically as the means for defining boundaries and achieving separation. In other families, they occur rarely, but their impact may be widespread and enduring. A family with distant, formal patterns of interaction will be likely to generate forms of cut-off different from those in a family with high intensity and close involvement. For some family members, provoking a cut-off is the only way to separate from the past and move on to create a life in the present generation. Whatever the reasons, intention, or method, in any family where a cut-off has occurred the entire system is affected.

ESSENTIAL FEATURES

Connections between family members can be identified according to three main foci, or areas of concern: social/emotional, financial/material, and functional (Meyer 1980). The ostensible "cause" of a cut-off can generally be traced to one or more of these areas, as illustrated by the following classification:

1. *Social/emotional:*   Disloyalty to a family member
                          Rejection of values or beliefs perceived as
                          necessary to family unity or survival
                          Opposition to individual or family life styles
                          Refusal to participate in family rituals,
                          ceremonies
                          Rejection of religious or ethnic affiliations
                          Divorce, separation, or intermarriage

2. *Financial/material:* Deprivation of inheritance
                          Withholding of possessions
                          Refusal to provide support for education or
                          preparation for work role
                          Inadequate provision of a dowry

3. *Functional:*   Rejection of an assigned role, i.e., caretaker,
                          breadwinner, homemaker
                          Relinquishment of responsibility for ill, de-
                          pendent, needy, or aged members

Ultimately, every cut-off is a reaction to the articulated or implied conviction that "you killed my god," whether the "god" is defined as material possessions, adequate care, or respect for a significant person, value, or belief. The cut-off serves to dichotomize good and evil, so that all family members are compelled to take sides and to identify other members as either "friend" or "enemy." When a single member or one side of the family is the focus of the cut-off, the "badness" in the family can be projected onto that person or branch, with subsequent efforts directed to justifying the rejection and persuading others to participate.

A cut-off prevents the working-through and resolution of anger. It puts the emotional elements on "hold" and allows family members to deny the problems and avoid constructive confrontations. The essence of the conflict is transposed from one problem area to another, somewhat like the inner voices of a fugue. When the cut-off is long-lasting, family members in succeeding generations may inherit the attitudes, tensions, and inhibitions that were initially associated with the cut-off without recognizing their origins or achieving effective resolutions of conflicts.

Cutting off a relationship by physical or emotional distance does not end the emotional process; in fact it intensifies it. If one cuts off

his relationship with his parents or siblings, the emotional sensi-
tivities and yearnings from these relationships tend to push into
new relationships, with a spouse or with children, seeking all the
more urgently for resolution. The new relationships will tend to
become problematic under this pressure and lead to further distancing and cut-offs. [Carter and Orfanidis 1976, p. 198]

According to Bowen theory, differentiation of self is defined according to the degree of emotional objectivity a person can maintain
while relating actively to key people in the family of origin (Bowen
1978). In a family in which a cut-off has been sustained, there is likely
to be a high degree of unresolved emotional attachment and strong resistance to change. Because the cut-off represents the core of the resistance, it also provides the most promising opportunities for initiating
change and achieving a higher level of differentiation.

The task of exploring and reinterpreting a cut-off requires three
fundamental shifts in perspective: (1) from a predominantly instinc-
tive or emotional response to a predominantly cognitive, rational position; (2) from cause-and-effect to process thinking; and (3) from considering the self as the focus of attention to seeing the family or the
system as the context of experience. These are radical changes in perspective. They signify a willingness to suspend habitual assumptions,
to avoid making causal connections between events, and to consider
alternative meanings. They also require the abandonment of such
emotion-laden dichotomies as perpetrator and victim, winner and
loser, rejector and rejectee, guilty and innocent.

I shall describe an effort that was undertaken to explore, reinterpret, and resolve a cut-off in my own family of origin. It is intended to
provide a working model for the exploration and reinterpretation of
any phenomenon in the family system that has inhibited change and
contributed to the maintenance of automatic and rigid patterns of
response.

FACTUAL REVIEW OF THE CUT-OFF

I was born in 1931, when my mother was forty-three and my father
fifty-three years old. My father's first wife had died of a brain tumor
three years before, leaving him with two daughters, ages twenty-four
and eighteen, and a thirteen-year-old son. My mother had not been
previously married and I was her only child. My father's son and

daughters perceived his new wife—my mother—as angry, rejecting of them, and possessive of him. Several events confirmed their conviction that this was an unfortunate marriage, and convinced them to reject my mother and become increasingly alienated from their father. They became more closely attached to the relatives on their mother's side of the family, who joined in their rejection of my parents and me. When I was ten, my father suddenly became ill and died. The cut-off was further exacerbated because he left no will, and his children incorrectly surmised that they had been deprived of a large inheritance. During my childhood, I had a vague sense of sisters and brother, but no real understanding of their behavior and almost no contact with them. For more than forty years, I experienced only negative feelings about that entire segment of the family, identified them as the "enemy camp" and never intended to initiate any contact with them.

During a three-year training sequence in family therapy, I participated in a family systems group that was conducted according to Bowen principles. With the support of the group, I began to consider the implications of the fifty-year period of estrangement in my own family. Eventually I was able to map out a plan to modify my perceptions of the "enemy camp" and achieve some new understandings of the cut-off.

STAGES IN RECONNECTING

The process of reconnecting consisted of four distinct stages: (1) a preparation phase, (2) a sequence of strategies designed to reinterpret the cut-off, (3) the actual implementation of the reconnection, and (4) the aftermath. The following sections summarize the essential elements in each of the four stages and explain the factors that facilitated change.

Preparation

The first stage evolved from discussions in the family systems group. Listening to other participants' descriptions of family conflicts and cut-offs, I sensed tension, which eventually became unwillingness to continue with the status quo and then readiness to risk the opening of a potential Pandora's box. The early awareness of the possibility of change was followed by a swift (but temporary) return to a more familiar, rigid perspective: What am I getting into? Why should I submit myself to this ordeal? Without the support of the group and the guidance of a skilled coach, that could have been the end of the effort. But with the group's encouragement, I began to review the past and present implications of the cut-off, and to wonder how it had continued to influence my perceptions, feelings, and relationships. I began to pay attention to the impulse to cut myself off from unresolved conflicts and reject people who threaten or challenge my position. In what manner, then, does the cut-off still operate, and how are the old patterns repeated?

During one group session, a visiting consultant contributed an important insight when he pointed out that the other side of estrangement is often intensity of attachment. He emphasized the value of examining patterns of attachment as counterparts of the cut-off. Those who perceive themselves as victims of a cut-off will be likely to seek close, dependent relationships that provide a contrast or antidote to the cut-off. It would be worthwhile to consider how such expectations had been operating in my own relationships.

I was also encouraged to review the history of my family, to clarify when and where the cut-off occurred, and to reconstruct the events in more precise detail, without emotional overtones or causal explanations. I attempted to revise the family diagram to include the estranged parts of the family, leaving gaps and empty branches that would eventually need to be filled in (Fig. 10-1).

Having posed some relevant questions and achieved a slightly more objective attitude toward the cut-off, I was ready to embark on the second stage, a series of strategies intended to achieve face-to-face contact with the estranged members of the family.

Strategies

INSIGHTS FROM PARALLEL DISCIPLINES: DAMPENING THE EMOTIONAL INTENSITY WITH A COGNITIVE ADDITIVE

The first strategy was intended to reinforce my intellectual objectivity with some new insights. I decided to study specific aspects of family process from the point of view of a researcher or student. To focus on particular issues, I consulted portions of the literature from parallel disciplines, specifically social evolution and cultural anthropology. For example, I explored such questions as the significance of lineage and the patterns of inheritance in family systems. I learned that all human societies have rules of descent to govern the recognition and dominance of one line of descent over the others. Kinship systems are based

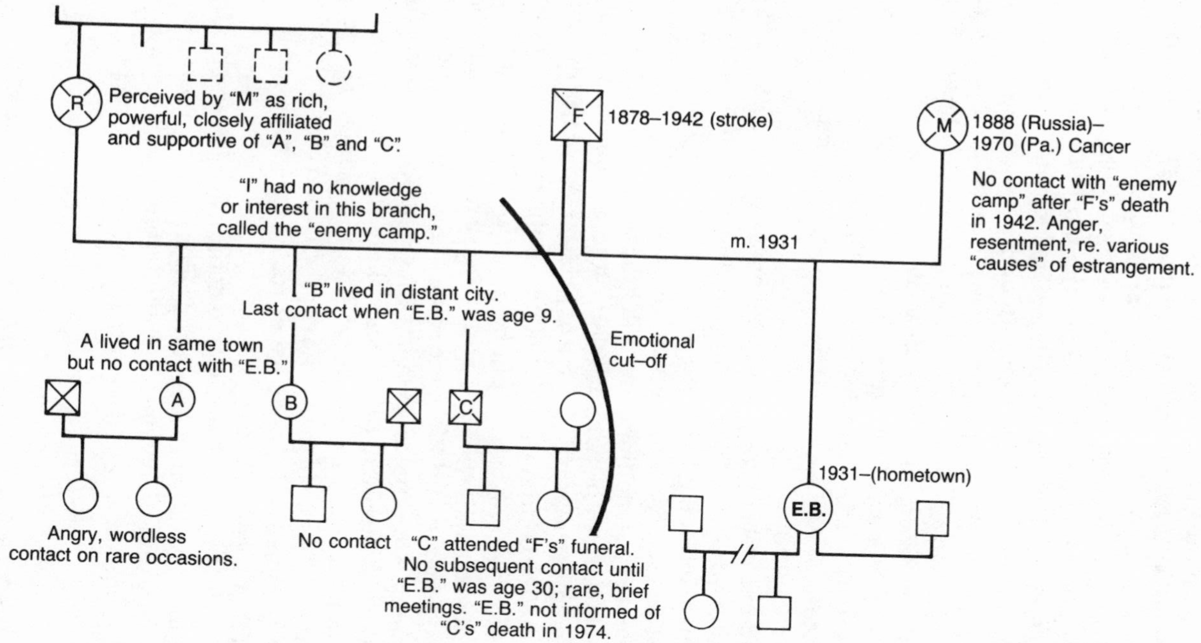
R
Perceived by "M" as rich, powerful, closely affiliated and supportive of "A", "B" and "C".
F
1878–1942 (stroke)
M
1888 (Russia)–
1970 (Pa.) Cancer
No contact with "enemy camp" after "F's" death in 1942. Anger, resentment, re. various "causes" of estrangement.
"I" had no knowledge or interest in this branch, called the "enemy camp."
m. 1931
"B" lived in distant city.
Last contact when "E.B." was age 9.
A lived in same town but no contact with "E.B."
Emotional cut–off
A
B
C
1931–(hometown)
E.B.
Angry, wordless contact on rare occasions.
No contact
"C" attended "F's" funeral. No subsequent contact until "E.B." was age 30; rare, brief meetings. "E.B." not informed of "C's" death in 1974.

Figure 10–1. Perceptions of the family *before* the reconnection.

on these rules and preferences, and family members usually favor certain relatives over others. There are three main patterns of descent: *bilateral*, which places equal emphasis on all lines, *double*, which recognizes only the male line of the father and the female line of the mother, and *unilateral*, which emphasizes either the mother's lineage (matrilineal) or the father's (patrilineal) to the exclusion of the other (van den Berghe 1979). Applied to my exploration of the cut-off, these concepts helped to clarify the kinship patterns in my own family, the weight of prominence given to one line over another, and the implicit preference of some relatives for others. These ideas also made me more aware of the emphasis I had unwittingly given to certain parts of the system, the connections, boundaries, and hierarchies I had unconsciously constructed, and the ways I had acted on my own interpretations of these patterns.

A second example of the use of insights from a parallel discipline may be illustrated by the Darwinian concept of *natural selection*. Natural selection refers to the process of evolutionary change in which those traits that contribute to the survival of the species are preserved, while other traits are modified and still others disappear (Mayr 1978). Applying the concept of natural selection to the family system, one might ask, what is the survival value of a cut-off? How has this maneuver supported the continuity of the family or the survival of individual members? A better question might be, how has the cut-off facilitated (as well as hindered) the family's evolutionary process during the past two or three generations? What are some of the *positive* aspects of cut-offs? For example, we might speculate that distancing or becoming estranged from the family of origin may allow some members to form closer relationships with persons outside the family. The resulting shifts in family relationships may have positive survival value through generating personal independence or fostering accommodation to a new cultural or social milieu.

These speculations may not lead to definitive answers, but they do facilitate a shift to a different level of thinking. By transposing the emotional intensity and involvement to intellectual inquiry, I was able to observe the phenomenon of cut-off from a more detached, neutral point of view.

IMAGINATIVE VARIATIONS: SCRAMBLING THE ELEMENTS TO FACILITATE A DIFFERENT PERSPECTIVE

The process of playing with ideas at a general or theoretical level suggested the next strategy, which involved playing with ideas at an imaginative or hypothetical level. Now, I used a playful approach to scramble the elements and lighten the intensity. I began to ask myself audacious questions, and to try out new roles, sequences, and scenarios. What if my sisters had been brothers? What if my father had been divorced instead of widowed? (Things could have been much worse!) How would I have felt in my sisters' place? Why was my mother so eager to assume the role of wicked stepmother?

This play of ideas served to break through a shell of rigid assumptions and open up a broad range of new possibilities. I became aware of the gaps in my knowledge and the narrowness of my perspective. I began to conjure up alternative hypotheses, weighing them against the facts and recognizing the need for more information. Why had I never wondered about the relationship between my father and his first wife? Why had I so assiduously avoided discussing the cut-off with my mother? After so many years, several of the key participants had died. Who was left to connect with, and where were the remaining sources of information? These questions led me to the third strategy.

INDIRECT COMMUNICATION: TESTING THE TEMPERATURE OF THE SYSTEM FROM A SAFE DISTANCE

The play of ideas had succeeded enough in opening up new possibilities and decreasing my level of anxiety so that I could try some indirect communication. I composed a brief letter expressing my interest in knowing about people in the family, especially those I had not heard from in a long time. The letter contained no direct reference to any conflict or alienation, only a wish to "be in touch." I sent this letter to the forty-five-year-old daughter of my eldest sister. I did not receive an answer.

During the next few months, I reviewed additional portions of the literature and continued to play with ideas. Then I attempted a somewhat indirect approach, by requesting a meeting with one member of the so-called enemy camp, a niece of my father's first wife. I had never met her, and her suspicions about my intentions were revealed in her first question: "Do you intend to harm anyone in the family?" After several reassurances—and a series of intermediaries, letters, and telephone calls—the meeting was arranged. I had planned my questions carefully and determined to assume the role of the curious observer, not casting blame or seeking sympathy, but merely wanting to know what she remembered about the family and how she had perceived the situation. Her descriptions were punctuated with vivid references to evil deeds and misplaced loyalties. It was difficult to listen calmly to her stories and to find that even after fifty years, the intensity of the cut-off was potent and essentially unchanged. Our conversation ended with her insistence that my sisters would never be willing to see me. The meeting was extremely fruitful in providing me with new information, expanding the context of inquiry, and intensifying my determination to reconnect. Pandora's box had been opened: the demons were alive and well—and at least partially under my control.

ATYPICAL BEHAVIOR: REPLACING A HABITUAL PATTERN WITH A NOVEL RESPONSE

During the following weeks, I reviewed my progress and planned my next move. The previous strategies had succeeded in defusing a great deal of the emotional intensity and arousing my curiosity about particular events. I began actually to feel like an interested observer, no longer caught in the current but now able to navigate my own course and even ready to try a radically different direction.

In the course of a visit to my home town, I went to the cemetery where my parents are buried and placed a pot of flowers on the grave of my father's first wife. This act had great symbolic significance, even though no one in the family was there to observe it. For me, it marked the beginning of a new level of understanding. By replacing my habitual pattern of denial, hostility, and blame with a response that acknowledged the reality of her life and death as distinct and separate from me, I was able to shift my focus from self as victim to a perception of the system: self-with-others. For the first time, I was able to think dispassionately about the family's situation at the time of her death, realize how much tension my parents' marriage must have generated in the system, and wonder what my sisters could tell me about that period in the history of the family.

DIRECT COMMUNICATION

The time was ripe to attempt a direct contact. Ongoing support from the family systems group had reassured me that the effort itself was worthwhile and that a failure to connect would not be disastrous. Circumstances in my own life, especially my impending marriage, had provided me with a new measure of support for my efforts. From information gathered from all sources, it seemed that the younger of my two sisters (then aged seventy-two) would be more likely to respond. After several false starts, I composed the following letter:

Dear A– –,

It's been a long time since I've had any news of you or L– –. Recently I've been thinking about the family and wondering how you are. I'm planning to be married soon, and I guess such important milestones stir up thoughts of family. Last month, G– – (my future husband) and I spent a weekend in Home Town so he could meet some of the cousins. It was interesting to reminisce about the old days, and to see how various parts of the family have aged and changed. G– – and I also visited the cemetery because I wanted him to see my parents' graves. You are all so far away, and you probably don't get back to Home Town very often. I thought you might like to know that I left a plant of yellow mums on your mother's grave.

I hope all is well with you and your family.

A few weeks later I received a reply from my sister, expressing her appreciation for my gesture at the cemetery and indicating her willingness to be in touch. After an exchange of letters, we decided to meet. When I flew to New Mexico for the first visit, I had not had any direct communication with her in more than forty years. Needless to say, my anxiety level was exceedingly high.

Implementing the Reconnection

It is during this stage that the actual work of reconnecting is undertaken. Now, the task is to develop an authentic face-to-face relationship with those family members who had been alienated. According to Guerin (1972) this is the "pot of gold" at the end of the rainbow in the project of working on one's own family. In my case, the task was complicated by the fact that my brother and other key members had died and my sisters had moved to a distant city. Despite these obstacles, the process was set in motion. Several different mechanisms were used, including letters, symbolic gestures, gifts, planned visits, and participation in family events.

The general methods for implementing the reconnection have been described by Meyer (1976), and correspond to my own efforts. They consist of at least three distinct modes of interaction, each of which promotes a different facet of the face-to-face relationship.

The first mode is contact for its own sake. This refers to the times when communication occurs without any attempt to deal with emotionally charged issues. At these times the focus is on just getting to know one another by observing, visiting, or simply being at home with the family. This mode provides the essential preparation for the eventual discussion of the critical issues relating to the cut-off.

In the initial meetings with my sisters and their families, I tried to maintain a position of curious detachment. I asked questions about their children, grandchildren, family milestones, and moves. I observed how they related to each other, what made them laugh, and what kinds of ideas and experiences interested them. I noted the warmth and ease with which one sister greeted me and the coolness and apparent suspicion in the other. I tried not to react emotionally or form premature conclusions about either response. I was aware of feeling alternately anxious and euphoric during those first meetings. These feelings were followed by a sense of relief and utter exhaustion when they concluded. It was important that I keep the first visits brief and escape with my husband to a neutral place where I could review the experience and consider my own impressions. Each subsequent meeting has contained elements of the earlier ones, but the peaks of feeling have gradually subsided as the face-to-face relationships have begun to take on more form and substance.

The second mode of interaction involves the discussion of emotionally charged issues with key family members. In this mode, one is most vulnerable to reacting emotionally and to reverting to habitual patterns of relating. The outcome of this difficult phase depends to a large extent on the preparations that have preceded it as well as one's ability to remain in the role of curious observer.

When my sisters and I began to confront the issues related to the cut-off, I was amazed at the vividness of their recollections, the verbatim reports of angry encounters, and the emotional intensity of their descriptions. It was as if those memories had been bottled up for more than fifty years, waiting to be expressed, heard, felt, and reconsidered. I noted the saintly role they ascribed to their mother and the wholly negative images they used to describe mine. I found it was not useful to correct their misperceptions (for example, the extent of my father's imagined "fortune") or to respond defensively to their accusations about my mother. Instead, I took notes to preserve distance and to reinforce my role as fact finder. ("What you are saying is important and I don't want to forget anything.") I also needed to return periodically to casual chatter and neutral topics, which helped to relieve the tension and restore equilibrium.

I had brought a collection of family pictures, some dating back before the cut-off had occurred. The photographs evoked a range of reactions from my sisters, from nostalgic reminiscences to angry questions

("What happened to our mother's dishes? Who took the figurines that used to sit on the mantel?"). They also led to detailed descriptions of parallel events, disappointments, and frustrated ambitions. For the first time, I was able to empathize with their sense of grief and loss and I began to see some portions of family history from their point of view. In subsequent conversations, additional elements were added to the story, expanding the context and clarifying some of the details. The task of confronting these issues is ongoing, and the history will never be complete.

The third mode of face-to-face interaction occurs through participation in family events and observances, those "moments in life which hold special meaning for the family" (Meyer 1976, p. 3). These events offer exceptionally good opportunities to be with the family when emotions are most exposed and intense. At a wedding or other life-cycle event, it is likely that recollections of past events will be evoked and habitual patterns of behavior will be reenacted. The mourning rituals that are observed at a funeral or the anniversary of a death can enable family members to grieve together and, at the same time, confront the reality of past grievances. For a member who was previously alienated, attendance at such an event can signify reentry into the family.

My participation in family events has exposed some of my own vulnerabilities as well as some of the raw nerves in the family system. At the wedding of my sister's granddaughter, I was greeted with a variety of reactions ranging from suspicion and shocked disbelief to enthusiastic welcome. Encountering these people for the first time, I realized that they had all heard about the cut-off and had formed their own versions of the story. Those versions had been incorporated into the family mythology and preserved for decades with little or no change. My presence at the wedding seemed to signify a shift in perspective, as one family member after another approached me with fragments of recollections they wanted to share, question, and clarify.

Recently, an ambiguous invitation to another wedding aroused such a constellation of conflicting feelings in me that I vacillated for weeks and eventually decided not to go. I attributed my response to a lack of experience in interpreting cues and messages from my sister's branch of the family. In retrospect, however, my avoidance of the event seems to represent a regression to an earlier, more emotional and self-focused position. It is useful to pay attention to the circumstances in which the family work proceeds smoothly as well as those that retard or obstruct the process. The nature of one's participation in (or avoidance of) family events provides a reasonably accurate indication of progress.

Aftermath

In the aftermath of reconnecting, there are new opportunities to expand the process and countless dimensions to explore. I am learning to ask more appropriate questions and to direct my curiosity to other events and people in the extended family. I have constructed a more complete family diagram, which includes previous and present generations (Fig. 10–2). In the course of filling in the gaps, I have gleaned information that contradicts many of the previous assumptions about the family. Gradually, I have begun to see the estrangement as one event among many in a complex family history.

It is inevitable that a pervasive, long-lasting cut-off will solidify certain behavior patterns and color one's expectations of other people. The process of reconnecting has generated some vivid insights and clarified certain patterns in my personal as well as professional relationships. I have been made aware of my tendency to dichotomize "good" and "bad" qualities in others, my readiness to assume the role of rejected child, and my chronic ambivalence about expressing anger. In my professional role as consultant and family therapist, I have noted parallel patterns emerging in response to clients and colleagues; for example, exaggerated emphasis on clients' resistance to treatment, a sense of anxiety when anger is expressed in the work setting, and the tendency to assume that cut-offs are the hidden agenda in every system.

Insights about myself and new knowledge about the family seem to emerge in a contrapuntal sequence, each one complementing and reinforcing the other. Once the process is set in motion, the sense of discovery serves as a powerful motivating factor and there is a compelling need to continue the effort. Considerable progress has been achieved: the enemy camp has been transformed, my perception of self has been refocused, and my understanding of the family has been revised and substantially expanded. The next sequence of family work will build on these achievements and move on to issues yet to be identified.

CONCLUSION

This chapter has described the essential features of a cut-off in the family system and has traced my efforts to explore and rework a long-standing estrangement in my own family. A sequence of strategies

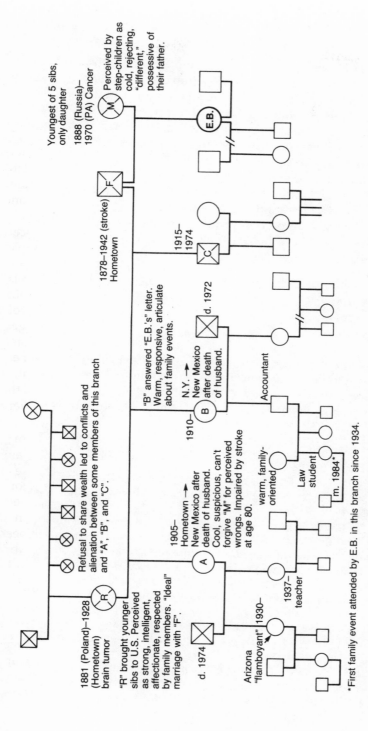

Youngest of 5 sibs,
only daughter

1888 (Russia)–
1970 (PA) Cancer

Perceived by
step-children as
cold, rejecting,
"different,"
possessive of
their father.

E.B.

1878–1942 (stroke)
Hometown

1915–
1974

d. 1972

1881 (Poland)–1928
(Hometown)
brain tumor

Refusal to share wealth led to conflicts and
alienation between some members of this branch
and "A", "B", and "C".

"R" brought younger
sibs to U.S. Perceived
as strong, intelligent,
affectionate, respected
by family members. "Ideal"
marriage with "F".

"B" answered "E.B.'s" letter.
Warm, responsive, articulate
about family events.

N.Y. →
New Mexico
after death
of husband.

1910

Accountant

1905–
Hometown →
New Mexico after
death of husband.
Cool, suspicious, can't
forgive "M" for perceived
wrongs. Impaired by stroke
at age 80.

warm, family-
oriented

Law
student

m. 1984*

d. 1974

Arizona
"flamboyant" 1930–

1937–
teacher

*First family event attended by E.B. in this branch since 1934.

Figure 10–2. Perceptions of the family *after* the reconnection.

205

was used to bring about three major shifts in perspective: a shift from an emotional to a cognitive position, from cause-and-effect to process thinking, and from a focus on self to a systems orientation.

Major changes in one's point of view are difficult to achieve and even more difficult to sustain. The family system, with its multiple attachments, tensions, and demands, is a vehicle par excellence for maintaining habitual patterns and avoiding change. Reworking a cutoff provides the opportunity to experience major shifts in perspective. It gives impetus to other family members to rethink their own roles and develop more effective modes of communicating. The understandings achieved through the process of reconnecting can also be applied to other life situations to facilitate beneficial change and bring about more flexible patterns of response.

REFERENCES

Bowen, M. (1978). *Family Therapy in Clinical Practice.* New York: Jason Aronson.

Bunting, A. (1982). *Emigration as cut-off.* Paper presented at the Fifth Pittsburgh Family Systems Symposium, The Family Institute of Pittsburgh, Western Psychiatric Institute and Clinic, University of Pittsburgh.

Carter, E. A., and Orfanidis, M. M. (1976). Family therapy with one person and the family therapist's own family. In *Family Therapy,* ed. P. J. Guerin, pp. 193–218. New York: Gardner Press.

Guerin, P. (1972). The family therapist's own family. Part I. *International Journal of Psychiatry* 10(1):6–22.

Lampiris, B. S. (1978). Cut-offs and illness. In *Pittsburgh Family Systems Symposium,* ed. P. G. McCullough, J. Carolin, S. K. Rutenberg, and P. Titelman, pp. 151–165.

Lampiris, L. (1979). From a Greek tragedy to a Greek drama. In *Pittsburgh Family Systems Symposia,* ed P. G. McCullough and J. Carolin, pp. 112–137. Pittsburgh: Western Psychiatric Institute and Clinic.

Mayr, E. (1978). Introduction to evolution. *Scientific American* 239(3):47–55.

Meyer, P. (1976). Patterns and processes in working with one's family. Paper presented at the Georgetown University Symposium on Family Psychotherapy, Washington, D.C.

Meyer, P. (1980). Between families: the unattached young adult. In *The Family Life Cycle: A Framework for Family Therapy,* ed. E. Carter and M. McGoldrick, pp. 71–91. New York: Gardner Press.

Rutenberg, S. K. (1982). Bridging cut-offs: an exploration of the function of genealogical research in extended family work. Paper presented at the Fifth Pittsburgh Family Systems Symposium. The Family Institute of Pitts-

burgh, Western Psychiatric Institute and Clinic, University of Pittsburgh.
Van den Berghe, P. (1979). *Human Family Systems: An Evolutionary View*. New York: Elsevier.

Videotapes

Bowen, M., and Yanks, K. (1980). The emotional cut-off—a clinical example. Washington, D.C.: Georgetown Family Center.
McCullough, P. (1979). Family cut-offs and psychosomatic response: A study of reconnecting with one's own family. Pittsburgh: Western Psychiatric Institute and Clinic.

Chapter 11

EFFORTS TO DIFFERENTIATE A SELF IN MY FAMILY OF ORIGIN

C. Margaret Hall, Ph.D.

The efforts to differentiate a self in my family of origin that I will describe here are selected from efforts made over a period of eighteen months, during which time I had six different contacts with my families of origin. For five of the visits, I went to my parental home in England, and for one, my mother came to the United States—her first visit here, even though I have lived here for a number of years.

I shall present in some detail a description of my family of origin before my systematic efforts to differentiate a self, including a focus on location, primary triangles, and multigenerational process. I shall also describe the chronology and precipitating events which led to the six visits with my family of origin, from May 1971 to August 1972. Included in the description of these visits will be a report of some changes in self and in my family of origin over the period. I shall finish with conclusions and tentative theoretical propositions that relate to these efforts.

Although it is now five years since I first attempted to apply family systems concepts in my own family of origin, this chapter highlights some of my more *effective* efforts to differentiate a self during the last eighteen months. This research on differentiating a self in my family of origin is also an attempt to apply to my own family the pioneering research of Dr. Murray Bowen, reported in "Toward the Differentiation of a Self in One's Own Family," a paper delivered at the Eastern Pennsylvania Psychiatric Institute in Philadelphia in March 1967, and published in Dr. Framo's *Family Interaction* in 1972. I was motivated to make organized efforts to free self in my own family emotional system throughout the eighteen-month period for both personal and research purposes.

Before describing the sequence of six visits with my family of origin, I shall enumerate some of the methodological considerations of the operations I used in my efforts to differentiate a self, first, the formation of two basic hypotheses: (1) a self can be more effectively differentiated in a family system at a time of slight unrest in that system, and (2) after a self makes differentiating moves in one part of the system, there will be automatic, and related, changes in self and other parts of the system, provided that the one who is differentiating within the system maintains emotional contact with that system.

A second methodological consideration is the selection of specific family systems concepts and strategies that seemed to be most appropriate for utilization in my efforts. These included (1) the identification of primary triangles and multigenerational transmission processes in my family of origin, (2) devising plans before each visit (where the creation of a "tempest in a teapot" was indicated by an emotional impasse in my family of origin, the blueprints would include the composition and sending of letters containing contradictory or "unexpected" messages), and (3) specification of the process of detriangling, including multigenerational detriangling, and the creative use of reversals in this process.

An organizing principle throughout this research has been the premise that the outcome and effectiveness of my efforts to differentiate a self in my family of origin are largely determined by the accuracy and comprehensiveness of the specific "operational blueprints," based on family systems concepts, that were drawn up before and during the different visits with my family of origin.

DESCRIPTION OF FAMILY OF ORIGIN BEFORE MY SYSTEMATIC EFFORTS TO DIFFERENTIATE A SELF

Location

For several generations, both my father's and my mother's families have lived in the same small industrial town in the north of England. I left England after my marriage, in 1959, and have lived in the United States since 1962. The practical considerations and dramatic implications of this degree of geographical separation are significant. Each visit to England involves financial sacrifices and becomes more traumatic (from the point of view of members of my family of origin), as an accompaniment of my investment of effort in the journey and the necessary infrequency of my visits. On the more positive side, my presence is usually welcome in my family—because of the infrequency of my visits—and I am also generally given immediate attention when I want to make contact.

Primary Triangles

Before my systematic efforts to differentiate a self in my family of origin, both my father and grandfather were living. Figure 11–1 shows the members of the primary triangles in my family system at that time. I am the only child of a father who was an only son and middle child of three children, and a mother who is the younger sister of one brother. My father ran a family business, which was started by his paternal grandfather and continued by his father. He had been very deaf since adolescence.

Since the death of my mother's mother in 1963, and the death of my mother's brother in 1968, my maternal grandfather had become an increasingly significant person in my family of origin. Although he did not live with my parents, my mother or my father visited his home daily with food, laundry, and other personal items. My mother idealized her relationship with her father—which she herself described in terms of "Romeo" and "Juliet." Figure 11–2 illustrates the emotional system operating in these primary triangles.

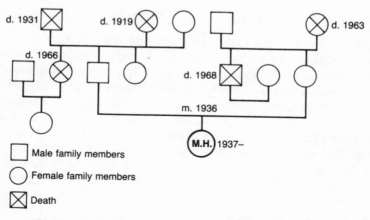

Figure 11–1. Primary triangles in family of origin.

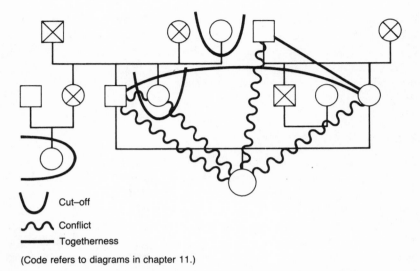

Cut–off

Conflict

Togetherness

(Code refers to diagrams in chapter 11.)

Figure 11–2. Emotional system of primary triangle of family of origin.

Although several primary triangles can be identified in my family of origin – including the siblings of my parents, their spouses, and my cousin – I chose to focus on the two basic primary triangles of which I am a member, and where I was the outsider of an intense two-some. These are the triangles with my father and mother and with my mother and grandfather.

Multigenerational Transmission Process

Figure 11–3 shows the extended system of my father's family. The graphic presentation of five generations of my father's and mother's family systems illustrates a prevailing tendency, in both systems, for there to be a "dying-out" of the family line through less frequent marriage, less reproduction, and more deaths, including accidental deaths and suicides. I have only one cousin, who is on my father's side of the family, and I was the only grandchild of my maternal grandparents. Figure 11–4 sows the extended system of my mother's family.

From 1963 to 1969 there were at least eight deaths in these extended systems, and only three births I know about. In each family there are at least three cut-offs between "close" relatives in the family system. Taken together these characteristics of the emotional systems of my family of origin portray a system that tends to be rigid and relatively closed.

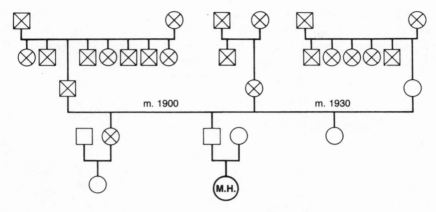

Figure 11-3. Paternal extended family system.

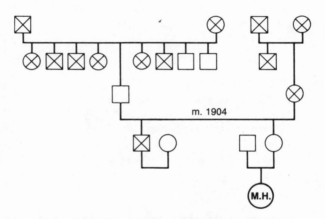

Figure 11-4. Maternal extended family system.

CHRONOLOGY AND PRECIPITATING EVENTS FOR EACH OF SIX VISITS WITH MY FAMILY OF ORIGIN

VISIT 1: MAY-JUNE 1971 (NINE DAYS, WITH ALL THREE DAUGHTERS) — "GETTING REACQUAINTED"

I had not been to my home in England prior to this visit. Although I had remained in communication with my family by letter throughout the period, relationships had been considerably strained. This tension was due in part to waves of anxiety following three significant deaths in my family of origin—(1) mother's mother, (2) father's sister, and (3) mother's brother—and also to tensions in my own nuclear family emotional system. Furthermore, I wanted to follow up a visit my cousin had made to me in the United States one year before this visit, after I had reestablished contact with her by letter.

VISIT 2: JANUARY 1972 (FIVE DAYS, ALONE)—"A BREAKTHROUGH VISIT"

I had reached what I thought was an emotional impasse in the work I was doing by letter in my family of origin. I also wanted to use this visit to England as an introduction to a first visit to my "cut-off" maternal grandfather's brother and his son, who live in Massachusetts. This great-uncle had left England in 1911, but I had only learned about his presence in the United States, at the time of my cousin's visit, owing to the estrangement between him and my grandfather over the past sixty years.

VISIT 3: APRIL 1972 (FIVE DAYS, WITH MY OLDEST AND YOUNGEST DAUGHTERS)—"MAINTAINING AN I-POSITION"

After a second visit to my great-uncle in Massachusetts, I wanted to consolidate what I thought were differentiating moves of self in my earlier January visit to England. I wanted to substantiate, in action, my decision not to "two-step" again in my family of origin.

VISIT 4: JULY 1972 (TWO WEEKS, WITH ALL THREE DAUGHTERS)—"MY FATHER'S FUNERAL"

My father died suddenly, of a heart attack, on July 3 at his place of business.

VISIT 5: JULY 1972 (TWO WEEKS, ALONE)—"MY GRANDFATHER'S FUNERAL"

My grandfather fell and was later hospitalized on the day that my father's ashes were interred. He died from this fall sixteen days after my father's death.

VISIT 6: AUGUST 1972 (FOUR WEEKS, MY MOTHER STAYING WITH MYSELF AND MY HUSBAND AND THREE DAUGHTERS) – "MY MOTHER IN THE UNITED STATES"

Neither of my parents had visited me in the United States during the ten-and-a-half years that I had lived here. I wanted to continue work on my person-to-person relationship with my mother and to introduce her to her uncle and her cousin in Massachusetts, neither of whom she had ever met.

DESCRIPTION OF THE SIX VISITS

Visits 1–3

Although visits 1 and 3 were necessary initiating and consolidating stages of my more specific efforts to differentiate a self in visit 2, in retrospect they owe their uniqueness to the changes made in my relationship with my only cousin. Before her trip to the United States in 1970, I had not seen her for twelve years. I met her two children, now aged twenty-two and twenty, for the first time in January 1972.

I tried to create a "tempest in a teapot" by letters before visit 2. My messages included an externalization of my anxieties about my own nuclear family emotional system; observations about the health of different family members, together with "reversal" suggestions about how different members might be cared for; and remarks on what I had thought was a "suspiciously" intimate relationship, over the years, between my father's sister's husband and my mother.

To show more graphically how a working knowledge of triangles in an emotional system becomes a basis for detriangling efforts, I have illustrated the usual emotional forces operating in the triangles of myself, mother, and father and myself, mother, and grandfather (Fig. 11–5). To see more nuances in these two basic, primary triangles, I have shown the emotional system in the related triangle between my father, mother, and grandfather (Fig. 11–6).

I made visit 2 to my parent's home alone – my first visit alone with my parents in fourteen years. For the first two hours of the visit my parents voiced their "united" disapproval of my recent letters and ideas. Neither of my parents had wanted me to visit at this particular time, and so my very presence was a theme for argument. Both of them focused on their distress at the "changes" in me, my mother accusing me of taking drugs and my father telling me that I was "crazy" like his

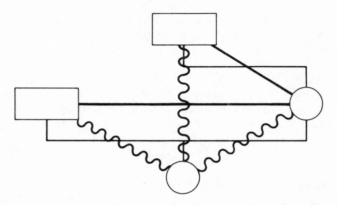

Figure 11-5. Emotional forces in two primary triangles.

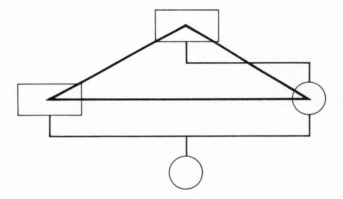

Figure 11-6. Emotional forces in one primary triangle.

younger sister! The changes that occurred in the emotional system of
the two primary triangles following the conflict that had developed
more acutely between my mother and me are represented in Figure
11-7. After conscious efforts to reverse the usual patterns of communication in these two primary triangles, the system became calmer and
more "respectful" to my changed I-position. Figures 11-8 and 11-9
show how these patterns of communication were changed. My father
and I developed a more personal relationship than we had had in
many years—perhaps in a lifetime—and I visited his parents' grave
with him at the end of this visit.

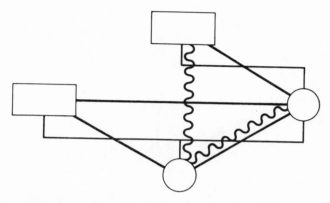

Figure 11-7. Changes in two primary triangles.

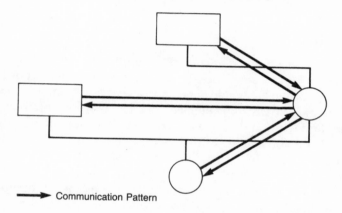

Figure 11-8. Usual communication pattern in two primary triangles.

As well as the differentiating moves already described, I also made new contacts in the extended families of my parents throughout these visits. Each parent reacted emotionally to a new contact made in his or her extended system, triangles between myself, mother or father and the person being contacted. These moves contributed to my attempts to detriangle myself from the relationship with the parent now involved in the new triangle by diffusing the feeling that had heretofore been invested in me. I was able to free self by creating a situation in which a parent could react emotionally to a significant other person in his or her family system.

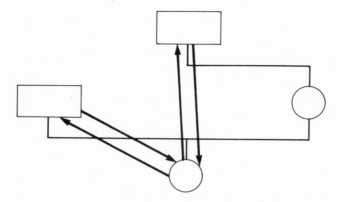

Figure 11-9. Changed communication pattern in two primary triangles.

Visits 4-6

Contrary to the expressed wishes of my mother, I took all three of my daughters to my father's funeral. From a more detriangled position in my family of origin I was able not only to attend the funeral ceremonies but also to participate in the details of related activities, often with my children, and without denying the reality of the death of my father or evading this involvement. I think this quality of participation would have been impossible if I had merely maintained—if that had been possible—my former position in this family. Although my father's only living sister would not come to my father's funeral, the fact of the death of my father and the increased participation and contacts of system members upon his death expanded my relationship with his family system considerably.

Visit 5 followed upon learning that my grandfather had died as I left England after visit 4. My children and I were the last people to see my grandfather alive, my grandfather having died as our plane left England. There were just two days between visits 4 and 5. (I had returned to the United States and left my children before returning to England two days later.)

It was now the turn of my relationship with my mother's family system to be opened by the death of my grandfather. I met many members of this system whom I had not known before my grandfather's death. Within sixteen days, my mother had lost her husband and her father, both of whom had been the focus of her life since I left my parental home in 1955, and it was largely this "gap" she felt in her life that moved her to accompany me back to the United States for her first visit to this country and, in fact, to my home in twelve years.

Not one of visits 4, 5, or 6 was conflict-free, especially in terms of my relationship with my mother. In fact, it was these conflictual situations that would afford opportunities to establish a more solid I-position in relation to my mother and in relation to my family of origin. And during visit 6, my mother met her uncle and her cousin in Massachusetts for the first time.

Throughout visit 6 there were great opportunities to relate to my mother as an adult—and sometimes I was able to do so. Currently she invests much feeling in her three granddaughters, especially the youngest one. For the first time I allowed myself to feel emotional attachment to my mother, and for the first time the relationship between my mother and my daughters "came alive." Although these indicators may relate to some progress in terms of my position in this relationship system, at present I am aware most of all of how much work there is yet to do in my effort to differentiate a self in my family of origin.

CHANGES IN SELF AND MY FAMILY OF ORIGIN OVER THIS 18-MONTH PERIOD

I think a precondition for change has been the maintenance of continuous emotional contact between myself and the rest of my family system. Figure 11–10 illustrates some of the wider system changes.

Apart from the obvious structural changes in my family of origin resulting from the deaths of my father and my grandfather, the quality of emotional relationships in this system has changed considerably. By increasing the number of personal contacts in the system, the relationship of myself to the rest of the system has become more fluid and diffuse. The level of anxiety in self is much reduced and, correspondingly, the emotional systems of both my family of origin and nuclear family are more flexible.

During the year before my father died, comments had been made by extended system and community members as to how much improved his health appeared to be and how much less anxious and worried he seemed. There had also been marked improvement in the health of some other system members.

Another example of the increased flexibility of my family of origin is a tendency for more humor and less seriousness amongst them. During my visit in April of this year (visit 3), my mother commented that

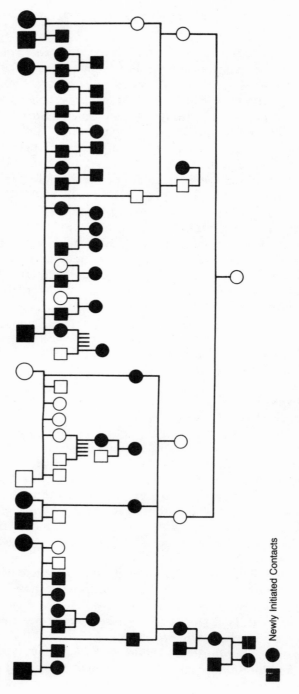

Figure 11–10. Increased number of contacts with wider systems.

Newly Initiated Contacts

she could not remember a time that she and father had enjoyed so much as this visit with myself and two of my daughters.

Over this same period there have also been some changes in more extended parts of the system. For example, my cousin's husband and children have all been able to make career decisions that had hitherto proved too difficult.

CONCLUSIONS AND TENTATIVE THEORETICAL PROPOSITIONS

These six visits with my family of origin provide some factual data to support the hypotheses that a self can be more effectively differentiated in a family system at a time of slight unrest in that system; and that after a self makes differentiating moves in one part of the system, there will be automatic and related changes in self and other parts of the system provided that the one who is differentiating within the system maintains emotional contact with it. A series of related propositions stemming from these efforts to differentiate a self might also be formulated:

1. The effectiveness of differentiating moves is dependent on an adequate working knowledge of family systems concepts and the degree to which moves could be planned and predicted before actual encounters with family members.
2. Detriangling self, that is, achieving an I-position relatively outside the automatic emotional family system, is a means to
   a. attain a comparatively calm level of self;
   b. reach a level of relative objectivity;
   c. become a more responsible "I."
3. Gathering information on the extended family system serves to
   a. create a personal relationship with the person giving the information;
   b. check perceptions of different family members, thereby increasing the objectivity of the observations.
4. Family members relatively cut off from the rest of the system supply noticeably more (and different) information than those members comparatively "in" the system.
5. The marked similarities in the thought patterns of those "in" and those "out" of the system indicate that geographical and physical separation from the family system is not synonymous with emotional separation from the system.

6. Repetition of efforts to differentiate a self is a means of giving objectivity to one's perception of self and one's family system. Levels of anxiety in the responses of family members to differentiating moves on the part of self become increasingly predictable.
7. In the aftermath of some degree of conflict and tension surrounding efforts to differentiate in the family system there are indicators of the "respect" and "appreciation" of family members for these differentiating actions of self.

I would like to add that these efforts in large part appear to endorse others' findings on factors contributing to and the effects of differentiating moves in one's family of origin.

Chapter 12

A VOYAGE INTO AN ITALIAN FAMILY

Joseph M. DiCarlo, M.S.W.

Since the time I was a teenager, I have been conscious of playing the role of bridgebuilder in life situations, especially in my family. I felt increased isolation from my family as I grew older. Considerable guilt has motivated my efforts to relate to family members, either to prevent distancing or to repair cut-offs. Since the age of thirty, I have made efforts to bridge the gap between myself and family members, i.e., father, mother, siblings, and my parents' families in Italy.

This chapter displays significant events in my life against a sketched-in background of family history, in order to set into relief the patterns of distancing and the feelings of guilt. I shall attempt to describe the major family patterns at work by drawing attention to (1) the primary triangle, mother–father–children, and (2) interlocking triangles of my parents, siblings, and me as well as my parents, their families of origin, and me.

The study of my parents' families occurred as a result of two trips to Italy in the last two years; the first was made by my nuclear family and me, and the second was made by my mother and me. Throughout the description of events, I shall comment on my efforts to act differently than the emotional patterns would have me act. And then I shall draw some conclusions based on the material presented to clarify how I got into the family role of bridgebuilder and what has happened to my family and me through my consciously assuming that role.

MY PARENTS' BACKGROUND

Father

My father, a middle child, was the fifth of nine children. He came to the United States from Italy at the age of seventeen in 1908, in order to find work. At age twenty-eight in 1919 he married a woman who came here from a village neighboring his own in Italy. His parents disapproved of this marriage because she was considered a "stranger"; i.e., she came from a different village, and her family were laborers, not landowners like my paternal grandparents. My paternal grandmother is said to have "cursed" the woman and to have "got down on her knees to thank God" when she heard that her son's wife had died of pneumonia a few days after the wedding. Everyone that I have spoken to who knew my grandmother has indicated that she was an unusual woman.

My father returned to Italy that same year, and conflict erupted between him and his parents when he demanded the money he had been sending them for safekeeping. His parents claimed the money as his contribution to the family, since his brothers and sisters labored in the fields at home for the sake of the family. The conflict resulted in my father's leaving his paternal home to live with a younger brother. He began courting my mother and gravitating toward her family, especially her father. In 1921, at age thirty, he married my mother. Again his parents objected—her family owned land but not animals! My parents' wedding reception took place at the home of my father's older brother, although his mother and some siblings did not attend. For five years after his marriage my father fruitlessly farmed the land. His father-in-law helped him extract rocks from the earth to build a house. Discouraged by hard work without results, from farming, he took the opportunity to return to the United States in 1927, when immigration reopened. He left his wife and three children in Italy until they were able to rejoin him here.

Shortly after his father died, my mother reports, my father's response to his father's death was not very noticeable. However, my mother was still in Italy when my father heard the news of his father's death, and furthermore, my father seldom showed his feelings. His mother died in 1952, after his only return visit to Italy. I do not recall any significant emotional reaction from *either* parent then.

Mother

My mother is the second of five children. She was very fond of her only brother, the eldest. He died at age nineteen of an apparent heart attack while in the Italian army. Two years later, at age nineteen, my mother married my father. She and their three children rejoined my father in the United States in 1931. Her mother died in 1950 at age seventy-five. Her sister died of heart disease in 1952, at age forty-two, and her father died at age ninety in 1965. My mother cried very much over these deaths.

I was born in the United States, in 1935; my sister was born in 1941. Of her birth, my father remarked to my mother that she would take care of them in their old age. When my father died, my sister was eleven, and my mother has remained with her and her family till this day. I was frequently kidded that I belonged to the garbage man.

The paternal and maternal family diagrams are shown in Figures 12–1 and 12–2.

CHILDHOOD RECOLLECTIONS

Childhood impressions of my parents' attitude about their heritage was that they were proud to be Italian. It was expressed defensively, though. I recall their negative attitude toward both the rich and the Americans, i.e., those who spoke English. My own feelings were of embarrassment. I refused to speak Italian, even though my parents spoke only in Italian to me. Through the years I viewed Italians as argumentative, crude, and loud. My mother often spoke of her family, and she communicated with them by letter and regularly sent them money as well as packages of food and clothing. My father did not communicate directly with his family, but my mother and her family acted as channels for communication with his family. However, I recall very little of what was said.

I remember from my teenage years the emotions of my parents in response to information from Italy: anger—over money, or the way one person treated another—and sadness when a death occurred stand out; my mother's singing while doing housework reflected happier news.

In 1950, my father visited Italy. It was his only visit since his departure in 1927. The trip resulted in some business transactions involving land, in which both his brother and my mother's father were involved. There was also an explosive misunderstanding with another brother over my father's loss of his wallet. Both events left relatives in Italy, on both my mother's and father's side of the family, and my parents angry and hurt, and probably contributed to the cut-offs that became more pronounced after my father's death in 1954. After that visit, my father's

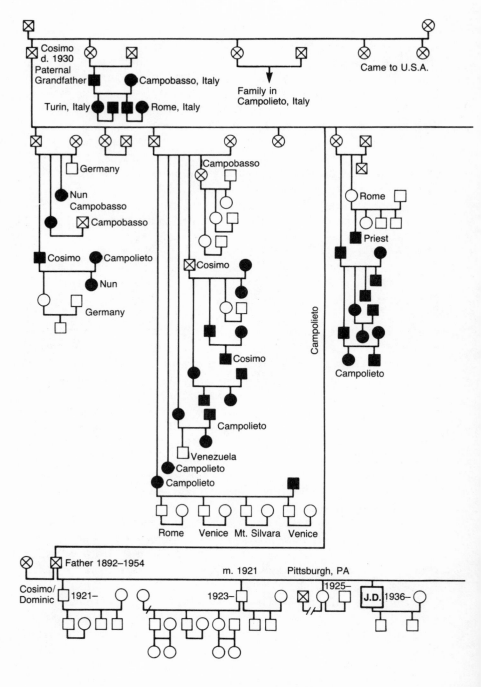

Figure 12-1. Paternal family diagram.

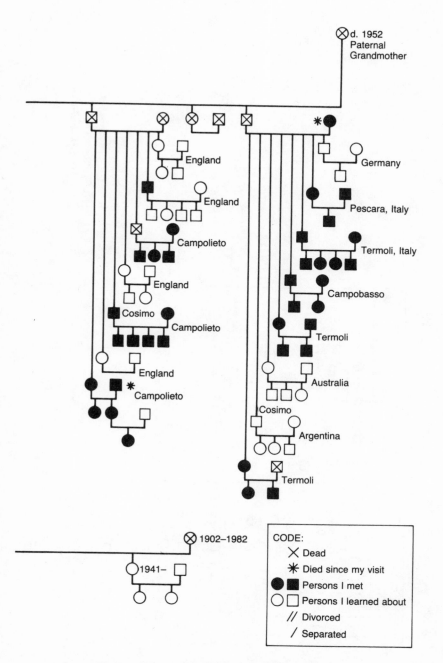

Figure 12-1. Paternal family diagram *(cont.).*

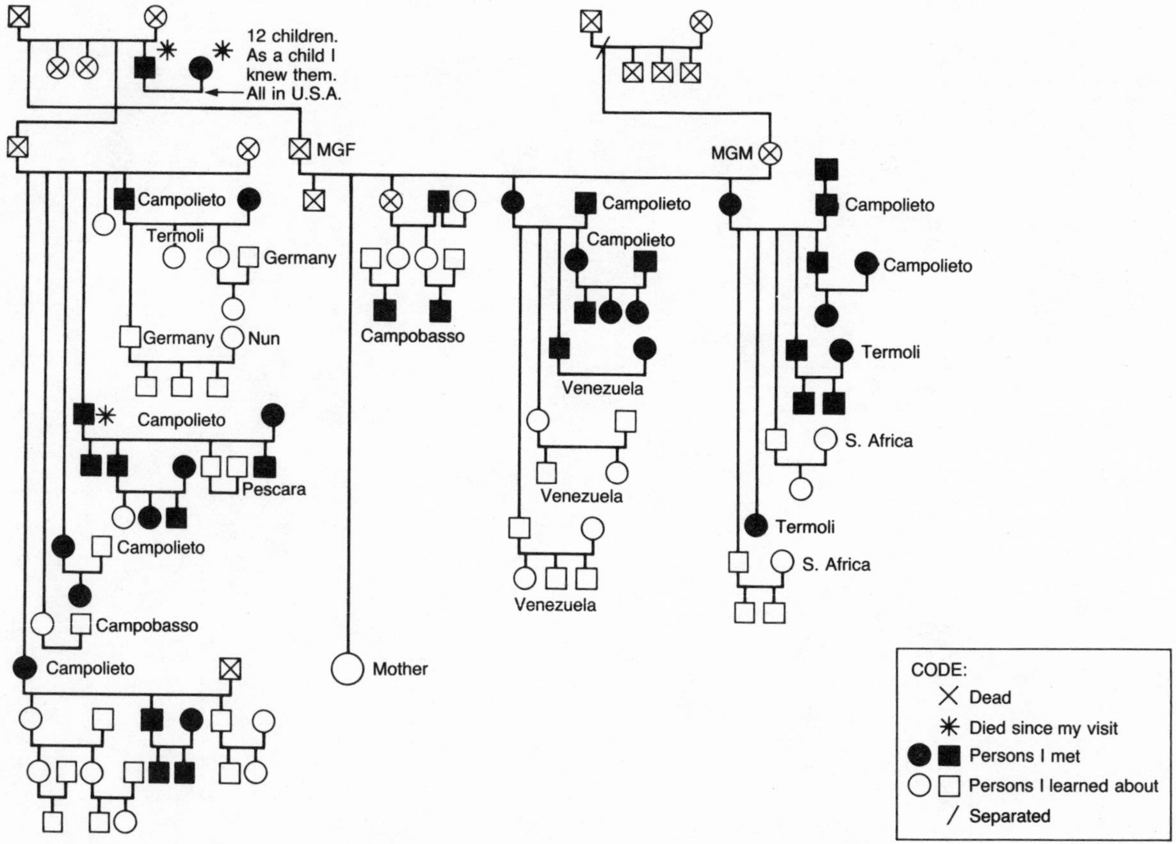

Figure 12-2. Maternal family diagram.

CODE:
X Dead
✳ Died since my visit
■ Persons I met
□ Persons I learned about
/ Separated

228

mother and brother—with whom he had had the misunderstanding—died, as did my mother's mother and sister. All five died within four years.

I remember as a child that Sundays at our house were occasions for feasts with relatives and my parents' friends, and that on weekday evenings my parents played card games or listened to radio programs with their children. My father's generosity to friend and stranger alike was evident to everyone, as were his dedication to hard work and strictness in the matter of parental authority. My mother "bent the rules" more, while remaining faithful to her role as homemaker, wife, and mother. When she cried in later years as a result of conflict with her husband and deaths in her family, it upset me deeply. I did not interact much with my older siblings (fifteen years separated me from the oldest, ten years from the youngest), but I clearly remember the major emotional patterns that developed with them and my parents. During their later teenage years, they ran head on into my father's strict paternal authority. Since my mother was more flexible, the result was that mother and child were close while conflict emerged between mother and father and between father and children.

PERSONAL HISTORY

My own turn came when I became a teenager. I recall the New Year's Eve at age thirteen when I returned home from a downtown movie with friends at 1 A.M. and was greeted by angry parents. That night I promised God that I would reform my behavior so that my parents would be free of grief. From that day on I attended Mass and took Communion daily until age thirty. The pattern that developed found me increasingly on my mother's side against my father—the typical family pattern.

Shortly before his last trip to Italy, my father suffered a head injury which, during the next four years, led to a steady decline in his control of aggressive impulses. More and more he responded with anger and violence to provocation. He eventually died of a cerebral thrombosis, in 1954, when I was seventeen years old. My reaction to his aggression toward my mother was to protect her. He and I came to blows at one point, when he had already removed me from his will. We had a death-bed reconciliation, but years of guilt were to follow for me.

I remember thinking often of my father in the first two years after his death and having feelings of guilt; but then my attention turned away from my father to issues of justice and morality. Through the influence of new associates I became more concerned about the poor and disadvantaged. Doing good for others, prayer, and the ascetic life became very important to me. In 1956 I entered the Catholic seminary, and seven years later I was ordained a diocesan parish priest.

I do not know for certain whether going into the priesthood was related to the guilt I felt over my father's death, since I cannot recall any conscious connections made during that time. However, my life had become one of such total concentration on the penitential life and the rigors of spirituality that, it seems to me, I was trying to make up for some wrong I had committed. I thought I would become a Trappist monk, but was dissuaded from this by the author-monk Thomas Merton. My theology dissertation was a biblical study of the Suffering Servant of Yahweh; and on the retreat before ordination, a classmate friend of mine seriously predicted I would be a martyr saint!

In my family I became the unwanted, but tolerated, family conscience. I preached morality, justice, and love, but was not able to be personal and understanding. I could forgive, but I was always judgmental. I had become something of a psychological isolate.

My family position shifted to the No. 1 spot in my mother's eyes, in competition with my oldest brother, who had always held that spot. But I had become a distant member of the family, whose other members, since my father's death, had distanced a great deal from each other as well. Contacts were very infrequent and formal. The same thing happened with my mother and the families in Italy. Contacts with them diminished after my father's death and almost ceased after the death of my mother's father, in 1965.

In the final years of seminary a process of psychological "opening up" to people had begun in my life, and by 1967 I had fallen in love with a woman. Everything inside me told me this was right, because it was consistent with what had been happening to me for the last four to five years. But everything outside me said it was wrong. Nevertheless, I attempted to leave the priesthood to marry her.

This move occurred amidst the most severe emotional turmoil I had ever experienced. I experienced pressure not to leave the priesthood, from multiple sources, the most intense pressure coming from my mother, who indicated that she could not survive this action, socially, psychologically and, perhaps, physically. I was pulled in all directions: by members of the church, to remain faithful to my vow of celibacy; by my fiancée's family, to avoid the scandal; by my mother, to not expose her to shame, and by my own sense of responsibility to my future wife and to myself. Because I could not tolerate the emotional tug-of-war, I made efforts to quit the priesthood by leaving town to be with my future wife. After two unsuccessful attempts, I finally broke away, and joined her in Chicago, where we were married.

I had received some support from my younger sister. My other siblings did not stand in the way, but disagreed with my move. All my siblings were concerned about my mother. I knew that she had survived many personal disappointments with her children. Knowing the deep pain I had caused, but confident that she would not reject me, I immediately began to rebuild bridges with my mother once we got to Chicago. My mother came to visit us within four months, and again two years later. We returned to Pittsburgh for two visits during our two-and-one-half-year stay in Chicago. I named my son after my mother.

While my relationship with my mother slowly improved, the cutoff of my mother from her family in Italy solidified. She had told them that I was ordained a priest, but she would not let them know I had left the priesthood. My mother had always kept bad news from them, and this news was so bad that she practically ceased to communicate with them.

As I mentally organize these emotional events, it appears that the guilt for which I had been doing penance was compounded by my repeated pattern of hurting and withdrawing, this time with my mother. To expiate this guilt, I embarked on a task of bridgebuilding with my mother and siblings. Fortunately the process gradually became more conscious as the years passed. My first task was to resurrect the relationship of my father and mother; the second was to improve relationships with my siblings, and the third took me to Italy twice, once with my nuclear family and once with my mother.

The experience of resigning from the priesthood and entering marriage meant that I had to face the responsibility for my life entirely on my own. I began to see that I was responsible for what happened to me rather than something outside myself telling me what I should do. In my new profession of social worker I counseled children who were disconnected from their own families. I was fortunate to have had the consultation of Dr. Charles Kramer, a pioneer family therapist in Chicago. As I analyzed my life and tried to apply what I was learning, I found myself withdrawing from social causes and focusing more on relationships, especially in my nuclear and extended families.

In 1969 I returned to Pittsburgh to pursue a doctoral degree in religion. I know now that I was working on the unfinished business of leaving the priesthood and reestablishing contacts with family, friends, and associates. After six months, I left the Ph.D. program and returned to social work. Shortly afterward, I obtained an M.S.W., was steeped in learning family therapy, and practiced as a family therapist in a mental health clinic. All the while I was gradually reentering my family and reestablishing relationships in my nuclear family, extended family, and work and social systems.

During this time I received a great deal of emotional support from my wife; but as I became better able to reenter my family system alone, with the help of extended family coaching, the inevitable strain on the marriage relationship developed. Fortunately, we have been able to weather the storm.

MAJOR FAMILY PATTERNS

I have learned of many family patterns in my efforts to study my family. Two major ones are (1) withdrawal in the face of conflict and (2) the need for siblings to get close to mother.

Withdrawal in the Face of Conflict

This is what my father did when he returned to Italy in 1921. Rather than face the conflict with his parents he withdrew into marriage (with my mother), associating himself with her family and eventually removing himself to the United States.

My older siblings each had conflict with my father, especially the second and third. For two years my father and my sister did not speak to one another, and for seven years the same happened between my brother next to me in age and my father, although they lived in the same city and were frequently in the parental home together.

My oldest brother, the first born, exhibited to a greater extent the aspect of the pattern in which there is an attachment to the family of the spouse. After his marriage, he rented rooms in the home of his in-laws after refusing the same offer from my father, and after agreeing to my father's request that he and his wife live in a "neutral" place. This was the only time he ran into serious conflict with my father.

I also exhibit this pattern of withdrawal in the face of conflict. I did it with my father, I have done it at work and in my marriage: I can remain physically close to another but emotionally distant. For years I seemed to have no control over it, and anger, depression, and guilt were always associated with the problem.

Need for Siblings to Get Close to Mother

This pattern was evident in my siblings and in my practice of siding with mother and distancing from father. Since my father's death, it has continued in the siblings' relationship with mother. Each child is expected to demonstrate his or her concern for mother to the appropriate degree established by her and the child or risk the loss of closeness. However, one cannot replace another in rank or closeness by doing more for mother. Examples are numerous. My older sister, who telephones my mother daily, has more to lose in closeness by failing to call for a period of time than an older brother, who almost never calls. In my competition with oldest brother for No. 1 position, I have found it fruitless to invite my mother to my house during a holiday, because she will always refuse my invitation so that she can be at home in case her first son visits her. The major penalty for not doing what was necessary to remain close to mother was guilt in the child and anger and hurt in mother.

EARLY EFFORTS TO DIFFERENTIATE

When I began to study family systems, I discovered that the above two patterns were also operating in my nuclear family. I was distancing emotionally from my wife and children while the children gravitated toward their mother. I was so strongly reminded of my father's position in my family of origin that I decided to resurrect him in order to discover other aspects of his life and relationship with my mother, hoping that this would help me control the patterns over which I was feeling powerless. I concentrated on the primary triangle of father, mother, and self. I found a photograph of my father and had it blown up to 8½ × 11 and framed, and presented a copy to my mother and each sibling. I then began talking to my mother about my father and about their relationship. From this effort, the positive aspects of his personality and my parents' relationship were revived in my consciousness, as well as the role his illness played in his later years. Although the focus was on the primary triangle, I gradually included discussion with each sibling about the pattern in which he or she was caught in the triangle with my mother and father. The pattern became clearer to me, as did the caring, generous, and dedicated side of my father, which I learned from my mother and siblings who had a more rounded perception of him than I had.

After about two years of this work my feelings toward my father had changed a great deal. The hostility was gone. At the same time the guilt issue with mother (about being close to her) became focal. The new kind of interaction with mother (discussions concerning my father) led me to seek her out in situations where we were alone so that an expanded basis for our relationship could form. Gradually it became possible to let go of the guilt for not meeting mother's expectations, because there was another area in which the relationship could develop with greater mutual satisfaction. She also has given up most of the guilt mechanism toward me. I learned to control the anger stirred up in me when she refused my efforts of closeness and, instead, I presented her with the opportunity for personal visits about which she could make choices. Without pressure from me to be close, but with an invitation for personal interaction, she became freer to accept some of my offers. Today there is much more freedom in our relationship, and also an increasing amount in her relationship with her other children.

EXTENDED FAMILY STUDY GROUP PERIOD

By the time I entered an extended family study group, in 1975, my work on the primary triangle and the two basic family patterns was well on its way. The goal I set for myself in the extended family study group was to improve my relationship with my siblings and to look into my father's extended family.

Work with Siblings

I began this work by resurrecting the triangles of father–mother and each of my siblings. In discussions with each sibling privately (arranging to meet them alone without their spouses was extremely difficult) I was told of the same patterns that I knew about, but was surprised by the absence of anger and the focus on the positive side of my father, which they had known and experienced more than I. My older brother told me of the enjoyable side of his relationship with my father that took place when they listened to baseball games together. Recently, I learned that none of my older siblings experienced guilt when my father died. At family gatherings during that year I always talked about my father and the triangle that each sibling has been in with father and mother came up. Criticism of my mother always emerged and she ended up attacking me. My siblings began referring to me as "trouble-maker," but my refusal to be put off by the attacks and my taking them lightly—in addition to the overwhelming good feeling between mother and each child, and siblings with each other—kept the gatherings from becoming explosive. My father became more and more present at family gatherings, whereas I do not remember any sense of his presence among family members since his death. The family also gathers more easily now, and I perceive clear signs of willingness to discuss family issues and feelings of emotional warmth.

A highlight occurred in October of 1975, my thirty-ninth birthday. I was deeply depressed—half my life was over and I had accomplished so little. The extended family study group advised me to share my feelings with the rest of the family. I was learning how to gather my siblings through their spouses (who always felt left out of the family) and invited them and our mother to my house for a birthday party for me. In the days before the party I told my siblings about my depression, as well as my fear that they would not come to the party. They not only came, but also brought gifts, and we had a very enjoyable time talking about my father, my mother, and each other.

Working on Cut-offs

In the first extended family study group meeting I became aware of the void in the family tree on my father's side. I was encouraged and challenged to get information. After about six months in the study group I wrote a letter describing myself and significant life events and sent it to my three aunts (my mother's two sisters and my father's youngest brother's widowed wife). I vividly recall the physical pain I experienced in my arm and hand as I composed the first draft of that letter in English. Months later it was translated into Italian and sent along with photographs of myself and my nuclear family. I was surprised to hear myself saying in the winter of 1975 that I was thinking about visiting Italy sometime in the future (meaning about five years from then) when, in fact, early in 1976 I decided to go to Italy that May.

As I worked on my relationships with my siblings and began some effort to learn about my father's family in Italy, I pondered the connection between cut-offs and depression.

Preparation for a Trip to Italy

As I prepared to go, I once again looked at family photographs, this time, pictures of the family in Italy, and began discussions with my mother and siblings. Of special interest were the talks with my oldest brother, who, during World War II, had visited the community in which he and my parents were born and taken pictures of relatives. I went back to siblings for information they recalled about our father's and mother's families from growing up with our parents. They did not yield much information (which in itself was informative), but it was another opportunity to work on my relationship with my siblings. In early 1976 I received letters from my three aunts (two maternal and one paternal), which contained family information I had requested in my letter. Immediately, I shared this information with my family. It was well received, especially by my mother. By April 1976, my mother placed a telephone call to her sisters in Italy. This was an Easter gift to my mother from my two sisters and me. It was the first time in forty-five years that my mother had spoken to her sisters, and the first time that anyone had even thought of placing a telephone call to Italy.

The most significant preparation for my trip came in the form of interviews on audio tape of my mother and siblings which I conducted in Italian for the purpose of transporting their voices and personality across the ocean with me. This gave me a unique opportunity to become personal and to raise sensitive issues in our family. The tape recorder was a big hit in both countries.

Purpose of First Trip to Italy

My goal was to gather information about my extended family in Italy, especially about my father's side of the family. I was prepared to raise issues I thought would produce confirming information about family emotional patterns. An inner motivation was the desire to reestablish the tie between my mother and her two living sisters. My efforts to work with my siblings were having the effect of improved relations between my mother and her children, and that pleased me; so the role of bridgebuilder was one I was more consciously and willingly taking on. I was hopeful that more would come from the trip, but was unclear what that might be.

FIRST TRIP TO ITALY

I had tried to convince my mother to go with my family and me to Italy, but after agreeing and purchasing a ticket, she backed out. The physical cut-off of forty-five years and the many years of emotional cut-off were not easily overcome.

I had read books about Italy and I had spoken to people who had visited there and they all told of its glories; yet I did not believe them because of my childhood attitude about Italians and Italy. But I began to undergo a change as soon as we left New York. The plane was full of Italians and American-Italians, and it burst into spirited conversation and groupings of people as soon as it was aloft. I was immediately impressed with the friendliness and personal interaction. Similar experiences occurred everywhere on Italian streets during our trip. I was so impressed with everything Italian that I saw, that the embarrassment I had felt as a child was totally replaced by pride. I had done so much of an about-face that by the end of our trip my wife was downplaying Italy and Italians, to keep things in balance for me.

Confirming Emotional Patterns

The generally positive feelings I had in Italy were intensified in the town of my parents' birth, Campolieto. I was so stirred emotionally that I found myself babbling much of the time, and was unable to keep the clear head needed to accomplish the work I had come to do.

My initial meeting with my mother's sisters and my father's relatives was, understandably, restrained. Emotion built during the stay, and it was particularly evident in their eyes, even though other manifestations were reserved by both sides of the family. My family in America was mirrored in the family I was discovering in Italy.

My role as ambassador was quickly confirmed. I knew instinctively how to present my mother and her life in America to her sisters. To my father's family, I was a resurrection of my father as well as ambassador of my mother. It seemed to them as though my father's 1950 trip to Italy had occurred just a week before and my father's and mother's labor on their house was just completed a year before.

My mother has difficulty accepting a gift she is not pleased with. I have the same problem. An identical reaction occurred, when I presented my maternal aunts with gifts from the United States.

Family generosity from both sides was abundant. My family and I were treated to great banquets, which reminded me of the Sunday feasts over which my father had presided. Now I understand better my social habit of seeking entertainment in which food is focal.

Everyone remembered my father as a hard worker. It was a label he wore in Italy, as he did in the United States. In fact, it was the whole family's label in Italy. His characteristics of honesty and simplicity were strikingly evident and attractive in his relatives. I was surprised by the spirit of religion on his side of the family: I found two nuns and a priest. Feelings I had experienced in religion were evident in these persons too, as well as in other family members: dogmatism and emotional distancing, modified by integrity and simplicity. I remember, too, from my teenage years, when my father was having physical problems because of his falls and emotional difficulties with my mother and me, how he suddenly began going to church by himself on Sunday mornings after years of not going to church at all. I concluded that religion had provided my father's side of the family with a convenient avenue for the expression of these family emotional characteristics.

The main question I asked relatives on my father's side of family concerned the conflict he had with his family when he returned to Italy in 1919, and why his parents did not approve of his marriage to my mother. The response was always the same, traditional one: Children were supposed to do what their parents wanted; my father had obviously done wrong; no explanation was needed from parents and no criticism was permitted, even if secretly felt to be justified. Although many people I met were very young when my father returned in 1950, it was evident that his return had been a festive event for the family, and in the village. In light of the family characteristic always to see wrong as such, but to forgive, the 1950 reunion must have been like the return of the Prodigal Son. I suspect that my father had accomplished some reunion with his family then, but it was not felt by his family in the United States.

When I presented myself to his family, I also felt their judgment. It was clear that my leaving the priesthood and the behavior of my siblings against my father (which he had talked about when he was in Italy) were considered wrong, but these acts could be forgiven. What I felt even more was that I was a link to the living family in America; and having taken the initiative to present myself to them, as if to confess, I was being forgiven and reunion was accomplished.

The one major family pattern of withdrawal into emotional distance in the face of conflict was evident everywhere in both families. Brothers and sisters who literally lived on top of one another were not on speaking terms, and the bitterness toward one another could not be held back in conversation with me, even though great efforts were made to be reserved. A 17-year-old cousin on my father's side of the family used the noneuphemistic English word "hate" to describe the tone of feeling between family members. Open hostility was absent, but their emotional distance was easily sensed. I felt right at home!

Likewise, the subject of death was treated as much a matter of fact as it is by my family in the United States. I couldn't help wondering how much this fact is a reflection of the feeling of emotional distance that family members live with daily.

It was not clear why some members of my father's and mother's family had left home to go to other places to live, but it was very clear why those who remained did so: They stayed at home to look after and be close to their parents. This second major family pattern of staying close to mother was particularly evident in *my* mother's family.

I found myself caught up in this pattern through the competition that developed between my two maternal aunts over me. I found myself trying to keep even the amount of time spent with each and the number of meals I ate at each one's house. One of the aunts had an advantage, because she had a bathtub, which I was glad to use! The emotional pull to keep closer to one than the other was so strong that after the two days we had allotted as our stay in Campolieto were practically over, I realized that I had not been able to break out of my mother's family's emotional pattern to go visit the many relatives on my father's side of the family who lived in the village. I managed to get myself unstuck enough to send my wife and children on to Naples and Capri without me, and I moved out of the hotel and into my paternal aunt's home, where I spent the next three days visiting my father's family.

I had realized how the two family patterns of emotional distancing in the face of conflict and getting close to mother had merged in my family from the two families in Italy. When my oldest brother was born, he was given a first name after his mother's deceased brother and a second name after his paternal grandfather. Every first-born son among my father's relatives carries the first name of my parental grandfather. Members of my father's family referred to my brother according to his grandfather's name, whereas my mother's family refers to him by my mother's brother's name. I appreciate better the struggle he has had since his marriage in distancing himself from the parental family and associating more with his spouse's family. His children bear entirely neutral (nonfamily) names.

My past anger at the guilt induced by my mother's self pity also exemplifies these merged patterns. In my family of origin, when one cannot freely be close, it becomes necessary to introduce emotional distance even though physical proximity remains possible.

As the sixth day ended and we prepared to depart for other parts of Italy, I was equipped with many photographs, an amplified family tree, tape recorded messages to my mother—and overflowing emotions. The isolation I had experienced for forty years had suddenly been dispelled, replaced by the presence of many new people bearing the same name. My family had grown so fast that it was joyfully overwhelming.

Between the First and Second Trips

Once back in the United States, I was in a state of euphoria that lasted for about a month. I made the rounds of my extended family, sharing all with them. At Christmas, I wrote a letter to all the people I had met in Italy. Correspondence between my mother and her sisters began once again. As time went on, depression and anger set in at certain places of my life. I experienced increased difficulty in my marriage, with my in-laws, and on the job. I discovered that it is very difficult to focus on one's family without some let-up in other systems. However, with my extended family I was flying high.

There appeared a bright spot on my mother's seventy-fifth birthday party, which made clear to me the role I had been destined to play in my family. I am a middle child, first-born of this country. Photographs were taken at this party. One was of my mother and her children. My mother was in the center of the front row of the picture. I was in the center second row, behind my mother, the middle child among the siblings. Another photograph of the in-laws and my mother was taken, and almost the same configuration occurred. The position of each sibling and in-law was also very clear from the photographs and the random seating arrangement at the tables. As in the picture, I was central in the arranging of the party and had to deal carefully with each family member and in-law to achieve a family first: all siblings agreed to—and in fact did—contribute equally to a birthday party for my mother in a fine restaurant to which all family members and my mother's friends were invited. My attempts to pass this arranging responsibility on to my oldest brother were vigorously resisted. I also acted as master of ceremonies at the party, and was able to poke fun at my mother, siblings, and in-laws while raising all the sensitive family issues here and in Italy, as well as that of the inevitable death of my mother. The emotional reaction was heartwarming, and I found my siblings much freer about sensitive family issues. I had come to accept my position of middle child in person-to-person relationships with my mother, siblings, in-laws, and family members of both parental families. In Italy, emotional ties were beginning to emerge and the distance and isolation was beginning to lessen. I was willingly functioning as a bridge and my mother was the main beneficiary in her old age.

I knew that when I told my mother about the response my family and I received from relatives in Italy she would want to return to Italy to visit her family. Therefore, I took every opportunity to persuade her and enlisted the aid of my siblings to do likewise. During the year following my first trip to Italy, my mother was together with her children and the siblings with each other on a number of extremely satisfying occasions. On July 4, my mother surprised me by announcing that if I wanted her to go to Italy that year, she would, provided her doctor gave her the clearance. She then announced at a family gathering later in the day that she would go to Italy with me because her children were so insistent about it.

Second Trip to Italy

Resistance to my mother's going first emerged from my youngest sister, with whom she has always lived. However, this did not prevent our departure; but I was surprised by my mother's attitude once we arrived in Italy. She had taken my sister's resistance, as well as her own, and expressed it as displeasure with everything Italian; America was better in every conceivable way. I understood my mother's resistance as a statement of loyalty to her daughter with whom she lives. As the time approached to go to Campolieto, my mother's attitude began to change. She was eager to get there, even a day early to surprise her sisters. The initial reunion after forty-six years was, unexpectedly, tame and reserved, but after a short while it was as if my mother had never left Italy.

What I consider the major family fusion characteristic of my mother's family emerged immediately. Contrary to my expectations, my aunt, with whom we were not staying, and who lives down the road from the house of the aunt who housed us during our stay in the village, was not immediately summoned to see her sister so long absent. Throughout the stay, the conflict between the two sisters over my mother grew until I found myself trying to influence my mother to spend more time with her other, older sister, who in my mind was my mother's favorite sister. My mother was so drawn into the pattern of "who is closer to whom" that she left Campolieto with cooler feeling toward her favorite sister. My mother expressed hostile feelings toward that sister's daughter, who failed to show up for a dinner party for my mother and never offered an explanation. The fact that we stayed at the home of my mother's younger sister set up the possibility of conflict between sisters, but the way my aunt and her children spoke about my mother's favorite sister and her daughter convinced me that the conflict has deep roots. There was continual comparison of which sister was doing more for my mother—especially which one was feeding her better. This so affected my mother that she couldn't judge an excellent meal when she saw and ate one. My mother continues to hear about the conflict in letters from her younger sister.

Another striking example of this pattern manifested itself in the conflict between my mother's younger sister and her brother-in-law (her deceased sister's husband), with whom she was not on speaking terms. I had experienced this problem the previous year when my aunt tried to persuade me not to attempt to contact my uncle because of the conflict that he and my aunt had had. My mother had positive feelings toward this man, who was her brother-in-law. The previous year he had avoided me—I am sure, because of my association with my aunt. On this second trip, he also avoided my mother, who, from the day of her arrival, was told how cruel he had been to my aunt. When their paths did cross in the presence of my aunt and her family and me, my mother found an excuse to go into the house and change in her bedroom into a housedress. She claimed she was too tired to go outside any more. I had to become physically involved in order to have these two people—my mother and her brother-in-law—meet after forty-six years of absolutely no negative communication between them. I could feel the tension in his arm as I walked him across the street to meet my mother. I had to push my female cousin out of the way, and I'm sure I must have been speaking very angrily to her and my aunt as I practically dragged my mother down the steps to meet her brother-in-law. The meeting was very strained, and they could not move beyond the present family tension to the uncluttered, positive emotion I could sense they both had known at one time.

This dominant pattern in my mother's family spilled over into the relationship with my father's family also. My mother was reluctant to visit her husband's relatives, and then showed surprise when she was so warmly accepted. I felt that the pressure from her sister and her sister's children to stay close to them, and away from my father's family, created much of this hesitancy. I managed to free myself to revisit these relatives and to discover a new part of the family, my paternal grandfather's sister's family. But I had become so angry and depressed that I did not investigate church and civil records in the town and delayed too long in seeking leads to other relatives, and thus did not investigate another part of my father's family, my grandfather's brother's family. With all these conflicting feelings, I felt trapped and wanted to run, a feeling I know well and have given in to many times.

During these emotional upheavals my mother and I experienced some painful moments with each other. However, we both were able to think while in these situations, and for the first time I can recall I was able to be apologetic to her without guilt and she was gentle and forgiving to me. The month with my mother alone proved very rewarding, since we shared a lot. I could see where and when she was giving in to my needs. I grew in understanding and acceptance of hers. We spoke much about the experiences of our stay in Campolieto. She came away with a richer appreciation of her family and her husband's family. Issues were no longer black-and-white, and people were not divided into the categories of good and bad that forty-six years of absence and one-sided and second-handed reports had helped to form in her mind.

When we left Campolieto, it was a warm departure, with the issues sufficiently uncovered, understood, and probably laid enough to rest to make the reunion a happy memory if she and her relatives never see each other again. My mother was exhilarated by the visit. Her health was very good while there. At home, she constantly complains of arthritis. Thus, she ate well, rested well, walked a lot, and appeared younger. Her Italian improved 100 percent. She even regained her ability to haggle with merchants. A salesman in Venice in a famous glass shop where bargaining is out of place ended up giving her a $2 discount and a very fine compliment when he told her that even after forty-six years in America she had not lost her native ability to haggle.

My mother had reopened a book about her family, her husband's family, her friends, and the place of her birth that had slowly been closing for years, and was pretty well closed for the last twenty-five years. For me it was a unique experience to observe her reopen this book, which my siblings do not share, and an experience common only to my mother and me.

I had been advised by the extended family study group not to raise issues deliberately. And it was not necessary, since the issues emerged easily. My mother has felt that she was effectively excluded from her father's will by being given only a small tract of wooded land. This seems to have been the result of selling my father's house, on which her father had labored so hard. My maternal grandfather's resentment seems to have been so strong and his displeasure so great, that this was shown in a lesser gift—a way of acting familiar and usual with my mother, who rewards when pleased and withholds when displeased.

I felt sure (even though my mother denies this) that my mother had considerable guilt about leaving her family forty-six years ago to come to the United States, especially when her aging father required the care of his children. That chore was left almost entirely to the youngest sister, but she never did it well enough and probably gained a profit in the process, according to my mother. My mother and her sister were able to talk about the care their father needed, and it was clear to my mother that her sister performed her duty faithfully. She was also able to say to her sister that she would have wanted to bring her father to America to care for him had it been possible. Her sister responded that he would not have wanted to leave Italy—as if to say: "The duty to care for him fell to those in Italy, not the U.S.A., so no need to feel guilty."

The misunderstanding over my father's lost wallet in 1950 was also cleared up with the nephew who had been accused of taking it by my father. If my father had left Italy unconvinced, my mother was convinced. Hard feelings over land sold by my father in 1950 were sufficiently talked over with my paternal aunt that my mother left with good feeling toward her as well.

CONCLUSION

In drawing conclusions from the foregoing material, I wonder whether what will be said is as clear as it appears to *me*. Certainly I understood less of what was happening at the time than I did after giving it considerable thought. Further reflection may make them clearer, but my guess is that the process of isolating and focusing on certain patterns tends to give the appearance of clarity, whereas the integrated, overlapping, complicated emotional patterns leave me wondering.

My father distanced himself emotionally from his family (especially his parents) when he came to the United States to stay, and did not maintain contact with his family. In the face of parental displeasure about how he was living his life, he could not fight, because parental authority could not be challenged; and so he withdrew. In 1950, he reopened the cut-off relationships by returning to Italy in what was, at least in part, an emotionally explosive situation. Although I do not have sufficient information to document this, my guess is that the deaths of six family members within four years of his visit (from both his and my mother's families, including my father's own death) are part of the shock wave of his visit. Further patterns of emotional distancing occurred between my father and his children for exactly the same reason, and it appears to continue into the next generation with some of my nephews. The realization that this was happening with my own children has helped me to retard the transmission process in my nuclear family.

My mother denies guilt about leaving her family in Italy, but she has been quite capable of projecting feelings of guilt onto her children, who are willing receptacles. My older siblings claim that they feel no guilt about my father's death, but their actions express guilt in their relationships with our mother. Mother's expectation of how she should be treated by her children keeps her and her children dissatisfied about their relationships. For my younger sister and me, guilt was present over my father's death and in the relationship with our mother.

It is my contention that the role of bridgebuilder, which I have come to play in my family, has its roots in these two patterns: emotional distancing and guilt resulting from not meeting mother's expectations.

In the projection process in the family, I seem to be the most willing receptacle of these two patterns, and it is acted out as bridgebuilder.

When I began working on my extended family, I started by resurrecting the primary triangle of father, mother, and children, with special emphasis on myself. With information about their relationship, I was able to travel the distance to my father and remove the negative feeling I had toward him. There was an accompanying sense of diminished anger and guilt toward my mother. Exchanges with my mother regarding my father released a positive side of him in my mind. Changes in his behavior and my parents' relationship owing to physical and emotional problems he was having had precluded this experience while I was a teenager. As my mother's and father's relationship was becoming more balanced with the positive elements, I was able to detriangle myself considerably.

As this primary triangle became less fused, I was able to turn my attention to the interlocking triangles of father, older siblings, and me. Here too I have discovered positive aspects of my father and his relationships with my siblings. The distancing from my father, which I always knew was present in their relationship, was tempered by the relative absence of anger. Personal visits with my siblings resulted in improved relationships with each of them. I had experienced distance from them most of my life, as a child because of the great age differences and as an adult because of a judgmental position I had taken toward them. I recall that as a teenager I found myself taking what I considered my father's judgmental position about each of them. My timidity in approaching my older siblings seems to have been related to the expectation of hostility from them. I was surprised by its absence just as I was when I learned about their relationship(s) with my father. The resurrection of those triangles resulted in my seeing myself in a different way with my siblings, which allowed me to experience their personal concern. In my actions toward them, I now presented myself to them as a younger brother, very different from my previous position.

When I focused on the triangle mother–sibling–me, the situation was different. There is a history of guilt that we share. This has a joining influence among us. However, my own efforts to become somewhat free of that guilt and to replace it with a personal relationship served as an example to them, devoid of comment or recommendation. I think this has contributed to alterations in their own relationships with mother.

My focus continued to broaden as I looked toward Italy and the families of my parents. On the basis of my experience of the interlocking triangle of my father's family, my father, and me, I concluded that emotional distancing seemed to exist with a minimum of guilt, and all that was needed to bridge the cut-off was to present oneself to those from whom one was cut off. I found myself standing in the place of my father and of the family my father brought to the United States. It was as if I were a symbol of my father and my presence in Italy were a representation of his and his family's return to surmount the cut-off relationship with the family of origin. I felt the judgment of having done wrong, as had my father; yet the fact that I neither fought the judgment nor ran from it, but remained to receive the warmth and generosity of his family, was enough to reestablish the relationship. My father had done most of this on his own when he returned in 1950, but it was now being done for his wife and children. My mother's return to Italy and to my father's family modified the cut-off even more profoundly. For me, the isolation disappeared and was replaced with belonging. I think it would be beneficial for each of my siblings to reestablish ties with my father's family.

My presence among my maternal family helped me to overcome a long-standing cut-off. My mother indicated to me recently that she was astonished at the positive reception I received from her sisters and how her fear of not being well received had made her own return so difficult. My own wrongdoing in my mother's eyes had widened the cut-off. I think that the fact that I presented myself and my life history to her sisters was sufficient to break the ice. Her sisters, especially the youngest, who had cared for her father and who now lives in her father's house, immediately brought up family problems (as I taped our conversations) to be taken back to the United States for their sister to hear. Thus when my mother visited, each sister gave her side of the story over which feelings had been hurt. My mother's opinions of her sisters changed a little, but more important, relationships that had been cut off were reopened and emotions began to flow again.

What I draw from the study of the interlocking triangles in Italy is that the one major pattern of distancing comes predominantly from my father's side of the family, whereas the feelings of guilt that result from trying to get close to those who have high expectations of one come from my mother's side of the family. These two patterns have merged in the family that emigrated, of which I am a member. Both patterns have been projected onto me, the first to be born in the United States, a middle child like my father. I took on the role of bridgebuilder and acted it out for years in an emotionally fused state. Within recent years, I have been able to separate myself somewhat from the fusion and have taken on the role of bridgebuilder with a minimum of guilt and with initiative in personal (one-to-one) relationships with family members. The results have been increased freedom from guilt, anger, and depression, increased feelings of belonging, and more satisfying relationships among family members, nuclear as well as extended.

The experience of the triangle of mother, me, and mother's family confirmed the pattern of guilt resulting from the struggle to see how close one can get to another—especially mother. I have indicated that I perceived the competition over me by my two maternal aunts on my first trip to Italy, and felt the need to keep things balanced between them. During the visit the following year with my mother, her youngest sister told her that her return was as if her mother had arisen from the dead. Furthermore, the competition over my mother by her two sisters exemplified the family expectation that it was important to struggle to get close, this time not to their mother, but to the oldest sister. I do not know if my mother felt guilty, but the behavior of her sisters fairly *exuded* guilt.

Chapter 13

AT LEAST THREE GENERATIONS OF MALE DISTANCING

James C. Maloni, Ph.D.

In this chapter I shall explore and describe patterns that I have observed in myself and family of origin as a result of seven years of utilizing the Bowen approach to family work. At the outset I began this work in order to understand better my own behaviors in relation to my nuclear family and to change some of these behaviors. After finding this approach quite useful in improving myself as husband and father, I began applying it more and more in my work as a clinical and community psychologist. This in turn gave me an added incentive to continue studying my family of origin. We shall focus herein only on the study of my father's family, and for the most part, on behaviors of my paternal grandfather, my father, and myself; these will be related to closeness–distance, responsibility, and reentry work issues. My father and grandfather were first-born children, and although a fraternal twin myself (older by an hour or so), I have also demonstrated certain first-born behaviors. A fammily diagram is presented in Figure 13–1.

The most dramatic phase of this family work was a trip to Italy in October of 1976 with my parents. It was the first time my father had visited his birthplace since he emigrated almost sixty years ago. Two subsequent trips on his part have helped him to gain interest in learning about his father's family, about which he knew only from information (mostly negative) received from his maternal family of origin. Although at the present time there are still more questions than answers in relation to my paternal grandfather's family of origin, the effort has had dramatic effects on my relationship with my father, as well as helping him to reconnect with his ancestry. It is perhaps more than co-

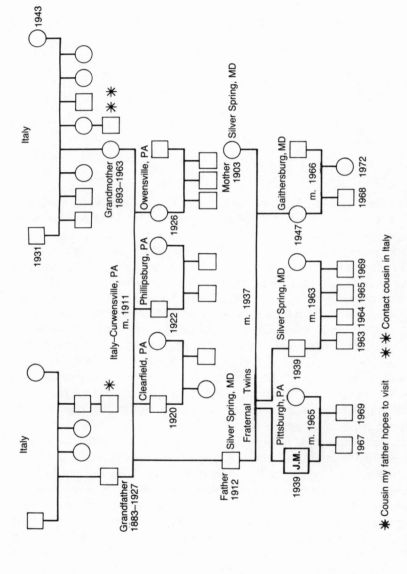

Figure 13–1. Paternal family system.

✳ Cousin my father hopes to visit   ✳ Contact cousin in Italy

250

incidental that I am writing this a few weeks before my fortieth birthday. My paternal great-grandfather died in his early forties and my grandfather died at age forty-three. My father moved his nuclear family 200 miles away from his mother's place of residence, where both he and my mother had lived throughout most of their married life and for sixteen years of their parenting life, a few months before his forty-third birthday.

CLOSENESS-DISTANCE

My paternal grandfather, my father, and I have all exhibited a pattern of behaviors reflecting considerable difficulty in establishing a comfortable closeness–distance position in relation to our families of origin. This has resulted in one or more forms of physical and emotional distancing. In all three cases, the manifest content involved bettering ourselves in the area of work or potential work. With my grandfather and father, the pattern was delayed emotional distancing, whereas the pattern in my life was instant emotional distancing, which eventually was reversed through systematic reentry work.

Another manifestation has been a general pattern of difficulty in separating from family of origin to become involved with the nuclear family. This is most dramatically portrayed in the case of my grandfather, who was disowned by his family of origin at the time of his marriage. My father's full-time commitment to his nuclear family occurred only after *his* geographical move away from his mother. This same pattern was initially disguised in my life. It manifested itself more directly only as I allowed myself to reconnect with the issues involved between me and my family of origin.

My grandfather was between ten and twelve years of age when his father died. Sometime before age twenty my grandfather emigrated from Italy to this country, ostensibly to provide better financial support for his mother and younger siblings. Approximately five years later he went back to Italy and married my grandmother. Although there is much missing information concerning the details and the timing, shortly thereafter he was disowned by his mother, ostensibly because he would no longer financially support her and his siblings as he assumed marriage responsibilities. Apparently there was no contact between him and his family of origin for the remaining sixteen years of his life. He did not speak much of his family, except to cry out for his mother on his deathbed.

The severe and permanent nature of this emotional cut-off reflects and reinforces a highly intense relationship system which is still reverberating in the extended family today. When my father attempted to speak by telephone to a female cousin on his father's side two years ago, he was virtually cut off in his attempts to initiate a reconnection. The only message communicated to him in the abortive conversation was that there was no reason to reestablish contact now, since his mother had failed during those years to carry out her responsibility of maintaining contact with her husband's family. Thus, sixty-five years later the heavy underpinning of this emotional cut-off is still active in the extended family system. Through the aid of a cousin on his mother's side, my father is hoping to make contact with newly discovered relatives on his father's side when he makes his fourth trip back to Italy, planned for May of this year (1979). Reentry on the part of a distancer in this type of system is not an easy task, particularly if the distancer is still highly sensitive to rejection themes.

The fact that there is still much missing information concerning the specific circumstances surrounding the disowning of my grandfather makes it difficult to analyze this event. There is no information available yet concerning similar cut-offs in previous generations of Malonis (spelled Milonni in Italy). It can be stated on the basis of family systems theory that my grandfather was not merely a passive recipient of this disowning event. Rather, there was probably an inherently reciprocal relationship between his distancing and becoming disowned, particularly since he apparently made no effort to reestablish contact during the remaining sixteen years of his life. (The issue of responsibility is discussed and related to this disowning event beginning on page 256.)

The available information indicates considerable tension between my grandfather's and grandmother's families, who had lived near each other. My grandmother's family owned considerable land and had had more formal education than my grandfather's family. They clearly viewed their daughter to be marrying below their level. This tension between her and her parents served to delay her coming to this country to join her husband until my father, their first-born, was five years old. To what extent and in what ways the relations between the two families both before and after the marriage contributed to the disowning of my grandfather is not known. Apparently neither family approved of the marriage, for different reasons. My grandfather's mother evidently expected her first son to continue being the breadwinner for her and her other children. My grandmother's family was expecting their daughter to marry another young man, whose family was more similar to theirs. (There is information concerning my grandmother's relationship with her parents that helps to explain how she came to choose a marriage partner whom they considered unsuitable. However, further discussion of her family system is outside the scope of this chapter.)

My father was fourteen years old when his father died. My grandmother changed her plan of returning to live with her parents in Italy, it was said, because my father refused to go. Even though he had only nine years' personal exposure to his father, he nevertheless carried out in an equally determined way the Maloni male pattern of distancing from and at least partial disowning of the homeland. This pattern was probably reinforced in my father's life by overt acts of anti-Italian bigotry directed toward him by people of English descent. Although he describes numerous occasions of physically defending his ethnic ancestry against those who challenged the quality of this nationality, my father's more consistent behaviors tended toward proving that he was a total American. It is significant that this pattern was not altered until shortly before his retirement, in 1975. Several months after this event, he suggested that we make a trip to Italy, an idea that I had attempted to plant a few years earlier but was no longer expecting to bear fruit.

During most of the twenty-eight years between the time of his father's death and his moving his nuclear family from a small town in rural Pennsylvania to the Washington, D.C. area, my father lived close to his mother and helped her much of the time in parenting his younger siblings. There were a few years of being away to pursue a college education (which was sanctioned by his mother), obtaining a job after college, where he met and married his German wife (temporarily cutting-off by being married at a neutral site), and two years of serving in the armed forces during World War II. Whereas my grandfather made a definite split with his family of origin in order to begin a nuclear family, my father attempted to blend his two families. This not only pleased my grandmother but also may have helped my father at least temporarily to mask the closeness–distance issues that he had "inherited" as a first-born Maloni male. During most of the eighteen years that his families were blended, his work kept him away from home a few days each week. This provided him with a physical way to live out the closeness–distance theme with respect to both his family of origin and nuclear family. (My twin brother and I have recently discussed how being away has helped each of us to relate better with our nuclear families. From what I have learned from informal discussions and from my clinical practice, this may be a common experience for a large number of men.)

The tendency in this family to think about major decisions in terms of financial needs or concerns for the children contributed to the timing of my father's move away from the small town in Pennsylvania. This town, which my grandfather had emigrated to, had by now developed a family significance similar to that of the hometown in Italy. My grandfather's choice of a particular town in America was due to the presence there of other families from the same hometown in Italy as previous immigrants. Moving to a suburban area of the national capital not only provided more gainful employment for my father and better post–high school educational opportunities for the children, but probably also signified for my father that he and his family had finally become totally American. The more ambivalent aspect of this move involved leaving my grandmother. Although my father earnestly attempted to persuade his mother to come with us, she was determined to live the remainder of her life in the place that had become the next best thing to being at home in Italy—she was not going to allow her first-born son to decide once again for her where her home would be. A few years later an advanced case of breast cancer was discovered and she gradually gave up living. She died seven and one-half years after her son had left home.

Being sixteen years old when this move occurred, I have first-hand information about the emotional reactions that occurred in many parts of the family system, including myself. Emotional cutting-off had become at least the first-born Maloni male way of dealing with feelings inherently associated with the physical distancing. While my father was vigorously carrying this out before and during the move, I was flooded with emotions. Whether my family system only requires one first-born male at a time to distance, or I had not learned my role yet, is uncertain. My twin brother and I teamed up with my grandmother to keep my father constantly reminded of the "inhuman and destructive nature" of his decision. (It was only a few years ago that I could admit to him that he had made a wise and courageous decision, and that I was exceedingly grateful.) The interesting point about this process was how the emotional distancing component, carried out primarily by my father, and the emotional reactivity component, carried out by his mother and two sons, seemed to reinforce each other. I can remember how I would react more intensely when my father attempted to negate the loss experience associated with the move. Conversely, he probably adjusted the "distancing switch" from low to high, which activated the "cut-off valve" according to the "degree of heat" being transmitted through the family system at any given time. Most likely my grandmother had a primary role in "setting the thermostat."

Shortly after our move, I began living out the Maloni style of cutting off from closeness feelings. My grieving for the lost homeland in Pennsylvania was soon interrupted by a process composed of such ingredients as stoicism, overresponsibility, and "burning my bridges." Four years after the move, I developed a dramatic urge to move away from home as soon as possible. This had been preceded by a couple of years of conflict between my father and myself concerning my wanting to go away to college. In his thinking, our move to the nation's capital had replaced the need for his children to leave home when attending college. I suddenly announced to my parents one day that I would be going away in a few weeks to a seminary in Canada, 600 miles from home. Going away to a seminary was a way to neutralize my father's objections to my leaving home because of a long-time religious emphasis in the family. My grandmother had often expressed concern that the family had not yet generated a priest. The other common family theme of money was also instrumental, since this form of education would involve minimal family financing. During the two years spent in the seminary, I lived out the emotional distancing role with as much vigor as my two first-born male predecessors. During that period, I expended considerable energy in providing that I no longer needed my family or, for that matter, anyone else on earth. My goal was the letter of the law as it served my distancing and disowning. Fortunately, I was not successful in this two-year demonstration project and, after terminating my seminary studies, gradually made my way back to the world and family. My father and I engaged in several low-key discussions that aided me in choosing to pursue my studies in the field of clinical psychology. (Incidentally, my grandmother died one-and-a-half years after I left the seminary.)

My susceptibility to the established pattern of the first-born Maloni males—i.e., being unable to achieve sufficient psychological distance when living geographically close to the family of origin—helps to account for my being the only one of my parents' three children who married and established his home away from the Washington, D. C. area. In marrying a strong female, I was reconnecting with the matriarchal structure of the family system prior to our move away from Pennsylvania. My choice of site may also have been the beginning of a circuitous route back toward the past homeland, a retreat from reaping the harvest that comes from living and working in the hub of America. Deciding on a graduate school that was espousing a heavily European view of thinking and living was an intellectualized (and thus distancing) way of going back. It is perhaps significant that I learned about the orientation of this graduate school from my cousin, who is the first-born and distancing daughter of my father's next youngest brother. This turning back may have been serving a need of the Maloni family to begin reversing the distancing/disowning patterns of my grandfather and father. Their courageously pragmatic behaviors and decisions were important for a family system that was, perhaps, seeking to make adaptive changes in order to continue living. It is as if the family needed to turn outside of itself, and moving to the New World was a way of doing so. It adopted the theme of "not looking back in order to keep going." My turning backward and inward may have served as a temporary balancing act or rest stop in the family journey. Fortunately, the reentry work (discussed below) provided a more systematic way for me, and to some extent my father, to make necessary reconnections. I hope that my two sons and possibly other extended family members will be helped thereby to participate fully in the mainstream of American life without having to pay the price of "melting into the pot."

RESPONSIBILITY

The inability to find a comfortable degree of closeness in relation to the family of origin on the part of us first-born Maloni males may be related, at least in part, to my father's and grandfather's assuming of heavy family responsibilty at an early age. Both of their fathers had died relatively young, leaving the first-born to help take responsibility for three younger siblings. This was strongly reinforced by Italian custom, in which the first-born male was clearly expected to replace the dead father. Both my grandfather and my father assumed responsibility for part of two generations of the Maloni family. My father's parenting responsibilities encompassed forty years from the time his father died to when my sister was married. My grandfather's coming to America may have been undertaken not only to gain better job opportunities but also to remove himself from an environment that reminded him of his being responsible for others. The emotional intensity associated with closeness may have included for my grandfather the "having to take care of the others" imposed by family, culture, and self. The *self* component of this expectation was perhaps dependent upon the norms of the immediate surroundings. The notion current in America of "freedom of the individual" could thus have provided a way for my grandfather to gain sufficient physical and emotional distance from the burden of his responsibilities. Sending money to his mother, which he did for several years before marrying, was a way to meet his obligations without having to experience on an every day basis the others who needed him to "carry" them.

By the time he was ready to marry, my grandfather had apparently distanced himself sufficiently from his family of origin to redirect his energies toward taking care of a wife and, perhaps, being taken care of by her. Conflict with his mother over this event probably made it easier for him to cut himself off totally and permanently from any remnant of feeling responsible for his family of origin. Emotional intensity creates extreme positions. Emotionally intense closeness begets sameness and possession of others, as well as the burden of overresponsibility (responsible for others), but in turn breeds intense anger, which justifies distancing, disowning, and underresponsibility (absence of responding to others). Owning her first-born son gave my grandfather's mother the option of dis-owning him, which in turn afforded my grandfather the right to disown his responsibility for her and family. From the limited information available, it appears that my grandfather's severe emotional cut-off from family of origin deprived him of ever being able to resolve his responsibility issues. Underresponsibility appears to have been his general pattern of behavior with his nuclear family. In fact, my father recalls that when he was twelve years old, he had to drive the family relatively long distances home because his father had consumed excessive amounts of alcohol and was well beyond the point of being able to drive responsibly. My grandmother obviously contributed much to such underresponsibility patterns in her husband (but again, this issue lies outside the scope of this chapter).

The overresponsible behavior of my father in relation to his family of origin is related to numerous factors. These include living with his mother and her family of origin in Italy for his first five years before he and his mother joined his father in this country, and the unresolved triangular relationship among his father, mother, and himself, as well as the obvious factor of his father's early death. Being conditioned at an early age toward emotional responsibility for others, as well as hardly ever relating to his father on a constructive, nonreactive, one-to-one basis, my father apparently welcomed the opportunity to assume the first-born male's responsibilities after his father died. He readily shares information concerning his mother's several opportunities to remarry. She would seemingly base such a decision on a majority vote of her children. My father humorously recalls how he always succeeded in persuading his younger siblings to vote against their mother's remarriage. When asked why this was important to him, my father's immediate answer was that he wanted "to be the big man."

Although the above response points to the novelty and privileged aspects of overresponsibility, my father has described numerous examples that illustrate his experience with the burdensome part of such a position in the family. A mild heart attack in 1975, eight years after my sister was married, allowed him to retire from teaching prior to age sixty-five. Thus, forty years after his father's death, my father's body decided for him that being responsible for others was no longer possible if he ever wanted to live for himself. Whether or not a more thorough resolution of his responsibility issues would have lessened the need to emotionally distance when moving away from his mother is now an academic question. However, it does appear that the heart attack and his subsequent retirement allowed him to begin reversing the long-term patterns of distancing from and disowning of his homeland. The disowning of his birthplace in order to become a total American and thus be given the opportunity to discharge his responsibilities for other family members was no longer necessary after retirement.

Fortunately, I was spared the circumstances that required my grandfather and my father to assume responsibility for their families of origin. It is nevertheless interesting that I absorbed some of the emotional components of the overresponsibility pattern. An earlier triangular relationship between my father, mother, and myself included my overconcern about and responsibility for my mother's feelings. As I was highly sensitive to her continual grieving for her homeland, I promised my grandmother that I would one day take her back to Italy for a visit. After she died, my concern was redirected to my father's return to his birthplace. During our trip to Italy of 1976, it was sometimes difficult for me to separate tasks I had set myself from my concern that the trip be beneficial for my father. My need for physical distance in order to attain necessary emotional distance in relation to my family of origin was definitely related to these overresponsibility tendencies. The reentry work has been helpful in diminishing not only my need for distancing but also my ability to assign priorities to various areas of responsibility in my life.

REENTRY WORK

My reentry work began seven years ago. For the first three years, I was coached in the work. This involved systematic planning and implementing of family systems methods with my extended family. For the past four years, my work has become considerably less formal as the results of the earlier work have allowed for more straightforward and spontaneous interactions. My tempo or style of working has been generally erratic and inconsistent. I started very slowly for the first several months, picked up considerable momentum, and eased up again towards the end of the third year. During the past four years I have enjoyed some dramatic experiences involved with the applied genealogy aspects of the work, including the trip to Italy in 1976.

That trip evoked much excitement and fulfilled many earlier wishes, particularly in regard to meeting people and seeing places about which my grandmother had often spoken. Probably the most fulfilling aspect of the trip was the opportunity to observe my father's vitality and relatedness as he reconnected with his homeland. The exciting and wish-fulfilling nature of this trip also made it difficult, however, to remain focused on reality tasks. The more mystical aspects of past stories of my grandmother, as they came alive in the present, led to some temporary confusion on my part in delineating past from present realities. On the basis of my experiences, it appears that reentry into a family system full of long-term emotional cut-offs may lead to temporary disorientation and resurfacing of earlier feelings and fantasies. Although the latter involves a state of fusion, it does provide ample material for continuing one's work.

In addition to the above, I became highly reactive to my feelings of disappointment when I discovered during the trip that little additional information concerning my paternal grandfather's family would be forthcoming. My excitement before the trip prevented me from carefully planning realistic information-gathering procedures. Instead, I allowed my level of expectation to stay far too high in relation to my ability to connect spontaneously with my grandfather's family system through a visit to the hometown. It is, then, not surprising that I am writing this two and one-half years after the trip. That is probably the time I have needed to work out a comfortable closeness–distance position in relation to the material.

During the seven years of work, I have reaped considerable rewards in regard to my relationship with my father. This includes more direct one-to-one communication, which in turn has helped me to detriangle my relationship with my parents. In the past two years, my father has seemingly enlarged his perception of his father. Seven years ago, he eagerly shared with me negative feelings he had toward his father. Resentment still lingered regarding his father's obvious preference for the second son, who was openly referred to as "papa's boy." My father generally remembers his father as never "being there for him." Regarding this, my father cited his vivid recollection of the time he and his mother first came to this country and his father did not come to greet them. In addition to these first-hand experiences, my father created an image of his father based primarily upon negative information communicated by his mother regarding her husband and his crude and uneducated family heritage.

In the course of the 1976 Italy trip, my father began to ask his own questions regarding his paternal family. It was apparent that he was becoming more interested in viewing his father through his own eyes rather than those of his mother and her family. The early summer of 1978 was the first time I ever heard my father speak spontaneously about positive attributes of his father. Specifically, he was discussing his father's musical interests and his playing musical instruments in the evening with the family. My mother said that it was the first time she had heard this information.

It is difficult to assess what part of my father's new attitude toward his father was a direct or indirect result, or even by-product, of my extended family work. It is my distinct impression, however, that the timing of my work was related not only to the specific context of my nuclear family, but also somehow connected with my father's issues concerning retirement from work. It appears that these issues helped to motivate him to reconnect with his own background. The paradoxical nature of the seeming interrelationship between my issues and those of my father is that although each has been useful for the other, it is difficult (but necessary) for me to treat them as connected but clearly separate tasks that require separate doers. New levels of closeness sometimes involve a seductiveness that leads to the erroneous expectation of permanent togetherness. This expectation was probably a primary independent variable in the three generations or more of male distancing and emotional cutting-off in my extended family. Needless to say, it is no easy matter to change this expectation in my generation. The aftermath of the trip to Italy includes the painful task of facing and dealing with the loss of this "togetherness fantasy island."

Part IV

Illness and Death

Chapter 14

NO SYMPATHY: A RESPONSE TO A PHYSICAL DISABILITY

Susan W. Graefe, A.C.S.W.

Thirty years after polio's crippling assault on my 7-year-old body, I began to experience an intense need to cut through years of denial and overfunctioning, to look squarely at the facts, and to allow my feelings about that most painful part of my life take their rightful place.

I needed to make peace with the years of silence, denial, intellectual and emotional overfunctioning, and compensations for physical incapacities. I needed to explore what that illness meant for my family and friends, and then for colleagues and clients as I moved from the dependency of a child on crutches to marriage, motherhood, and a successful career as a clinical social worker. I needed to start to listen more carefully to my inner thoughts and to observe my life patterns in broad and open ways. The key to the process has been, and is, the sorting of facts from emotions in this highly charged area.

As I near the thirty-third anniversary of polio's intrusion into my world, the pieces of the puzzle are coming together. I am freer of the need to overfunction as a way of proving to myself and the rest of the world that I am a capable human being. I am aware of my nuclear and extended families in new ways, and of their patterns of functioning in response to crises and to family illnesses. In addition, I can recognize a connection between my choice of a career as a clinical social worker specializing in the treatment of elderly people and their families and my responses to illness and family systems, both conscious and subconscious.

At the time of my graduation from high school, twenty-two years ago, a local newspaper interviewed my mother and me about the impact of polio on the family. My mother said that "no one can estimate the endless effort parents put forth during a child's long illness, as well as the worry, constant care, and draining financial expense." She credited the success of my struggle to the fact that my family gave me "lots and lots of love and no sympathy." That clearly stated philosophy became a permanent part of the basic fabric of my being.

FAMILY SYSTEMS UNDER STRESS

As one begins to look at the effects of a major illness, several major areas emerge immediately: (1) the patient's and the family's emotional system at the time of illness begins; (2) subsequent development of both as the illness continues; (3) response of the patient to the physical limitations imposed by a crippling illness, and (4) response of both the nuclear and extended families to the needs imposed by these limitations.

With respect to both my needs and my limitations, denial was the cornerstone of my nuclear family's behavior. My extended family, however, provided some sympathy and indulgence as a balance to this. My maternal grandmother and maternal aunt relieved me of general housekeeping tasks when I was in their presence, and they chided my mother for involving me in too many activities, as well as housekeeping chores. However, I was continually reminded by my mother that if I allowed myself to be "pampered," I might never regain my strength or walk again. My mother's prescription was powerful, and she enforced it vigorously. I believed her fearsome assessment, but it was difficult to concentrate only on the sheer drive she demanded when within me I often wanted to be pampered and taken care of. This anguish always intruded.

Cheered on by my parents, I pursued life with a vengeance. I did not allow my two Canadian crutches to get in the way of being an avid softball player. Although I could not run, I could hit a line drive, and one of my friends ran bases for me. Football and basketball were a little more difficult, but no matter what the sport or activity, I found a way to adapt. In high school I was known as the "nonjumping" cheerleader, and never missed a game in three years.

In all, these achievements contributed to the illusion that I had few, if any, limitations. My family and I defined, by our own attitudes and actions, the view we wished others to accept.

Achieving this projection of competency despite adversity was a triumph over the initial facts of my case. At the onset of my illness I lived for two weeks in the terrible loneliness of an isolation hospital. I was completely paralyzed from the waist down and also in my left arm. It was a crucially traumatic experience for a seven-year-old.

The next three months were spent in a chronic care hospital. I remember my mother's words as I was being put in the ambulance for the trip to that hospital: "You have been very ill, but now you are going to be fine." At the time, I thought being "fine" meant running and jumping with the rest of the children. These hopes were dashed by three months in a ward with forty other polio victims in various stages of affliction, living out their lives in iron lungs, rocking beds, wheel chairs, walkers, and crutches.

I remember feeling very frightened, as well as experiencing indescribable physical pain. My limbs were immobilized for a time by sandbags weighted to keep the muscles stretched. Many times a day my body was covered with wet wool hot packs; I never was told the purpose of this treatment (Even now, the odor of wet wool stimulates body aches and nausea.) I was among the youngest patients on that polio ward. Many of the patients were adults, and several of them died while I was there. There were a number of high school and college students, and also some very young children who were unable to express their feelings in words. I was shy and timid, fearful of asking for help, and frightened by the atrophying bodies surrounding me. How could I ever be "just fine"?

I discovered the radio. Its soap operas and adventure stories were my beside companions. Every day there were visitors, usually one or both of my parents, a family friend, or a neighbor. I have little or no memory of the presence of extended family—my parents were the key figures.

MOTHER'S DETERMINATION

My mother pushed constantly for the best possible treatment for me. She worked hard to convince me that I would walk again if I would do even more than what I was told to do. If I was told to exercise for ten minutes, she encouraged fifteen or twenty. If I was supposed to walk one length of the hall in my walker, then she pushed me to do two lengths.

In a recent conversation, I asked my mother what this period was like for her. She focused on two words: fear and determination. Her fear was of "the dreaded disease" and her sense of lack of control over its crippling effects on my body. My mother, an overly responsible eldest child, was always in control of everything, or so she and we believed. Her determination was the cornerstone for overcoming my illness, and she went to great lengths to help me recover. I was awed by her persistence in knocking down barriers to good treatment. She confronted complacent doctors with demands for answers to her many questions. She worked on my body for hours, following carefully the instructions of the physical therapist she had searched out; I became my mother's project.

During the first year of my illness she quite neglected herself. That self-deprivation created a kind of backlash in me, keenly felt over the years. I always assumed that her pent-up anger was caused by my failure to live up to her expectations for coping with adversity.

While my mother and I were on a trip alone four years ago, she asked what it was like for me during that first year and the subsequent dealing with the effects of polio. I had waited for her to ask that question for almost thirty years.

It was a year before I could respond effectively. I was then able to share my feelings of physical and emotional pain that I had always believed she did not want to hear. I also shared my perception that she felt that my illness had nearly ruined her life. This open and direct conversation was a turning point in my relationship with my mother. We were able to share long overdue tears.

During my childhood she had finally accepted the fact that my recovery would be long and slow, but she did not share that fact with me until these conversations several years ago. As we finally discussed our perceptions of my childhood years, she related having experienced an immense sense of loneliness in not having any help, either physically or emotionally, from her family or from my father's family. They were present for visits and for giving gifts to me, but not for pitching in and helping with respite care and relieve her and my father. My grandparents, aunts, and uncles tended, instead, to be quite critical of the extent to which my parents "pushed" me into the normal activities of daily living. The determination of my parents to see me succeed in overcoming my illness and their sense of denial kept them nonreactive to criticism and to the anxiety of others. This, in turn, enabled me to engage in many activities, which were both healing to my body and effective in helping me develop a sense of self in which I viewed myself as more normal, than disabled.

Recently my mother acknowledged that although she allowed me a great deal of freedom and independence, internally she had experienced tremendous anxiety over my safety, and my vulnerability. I had been totally unaware of her anxiety, as well as of the physical risks involved in many of my activities and adventures. I am thankful that she kept her anxieties hidden, for this allowed me to take risks. And while I admire her ability to conceal her fears, I know the costliness of such a gift.

I am now aware of the extent of the trusting bond that actually existed between my parents and me, an extremely crucial trust for someone as physically dependent as I was. Learning about my mother's anger and disappointment in her family's response to my illness was helpful. I had always believed that all of her anger stemmed from me and my illness, that through my illness I had been responsible for "messing up" her life. Now I know that at least some of her anger belonged elsewhere—with her family. With these new realizations, I feel a lessened need to maintain the superhuman stance I always felt necessary to make her happy with me.

FATHER—STEADY AND DEPENDABLE

My father's steady presence, as the nonaggressive parent, brought a balance of quiet and levity to my mother's intense, action-oriented reactivity. He provided much actual physical care in the early stages of my illness. My need to be carried in his arms, I now realize, was emotionally—and physically—difficult for him. He never complained and never shared his emotional pain. Looking back, I recall feeling that he always appeared unhappy, as if he were carrying heavy burdens. He had to work hard for the financial support of the family.

His time with me was often spent in just talking about things unrelated to my illness. He introduced me to sports, and I became a New York Yankees fan, endlessly reciting statistics on American League players and important games. He pitched balls for me to hit and shot baskets with me in front of the garage.

His quiet, unwavering support was always there. If he saw me struggling with a physical task, he intervened with possible adaptations, but not with discouragement. He encouraged new interests: cheerleading; rifle matches, in which I proudly won target shooting prizes; swimming; fishing; sailing—he taught me to fish, I taught him to sail. His interests extended to my academic pursuits, particularly mathematics, which was his strength and my downfall.

The message from my father, though not verbalized, was clear: I was capable of doing anything. Even though this was my mother's message also, my father conveyed it in more expansive terms.

Over the past nine years, in a reversal of roles, I have spent considerable time visiting my father during his several hospitalizations. Typically, he protested the necessity of my travelling a considerable distance to visit him. Once, in 1977, when he was close to death following the removal of a kidney, we had a very quietly significant visit together. I was able to reminisce about the importance and meaningfulness of his hospital visits to me as I went through polio and a series of rehabilitative surgeries. I was able to share my sadness over his illness, and we both struggled to hold back our tears. Gently I suggested that it was important for us to be able to shed our tears together. In those few moments of blended tears, we felt permission to thank each other for our mutual presence and support over the years. We were able, in the usual quiet and understanding ways in which we lived our lives together, to grieve over his illness and to speak of the possible loss of his life.

My father recovered from his kidney surgery, but is currently in declining health. I have yet to ask him exactly how my illness affected him. I think, however, that we can now share—verbally—this particular bond.

SIBLINGS AND PEERS

My brother, who is three years younger than I, was too young to understand events during the early years of my illness. Very caring neighbors and friends took care of him when my parents visited me in the hospital. He became my primary friend and companion during those early years when I could not keep pace physically with peers who were running around and riding bicycles. We shared an emotional closeness even though his interests developed in very different directions from mine. Neither academically nor athletically oriented, he was encouraged to pursue his artistic, and later his entrepreneurial, talents. Despite our closeness, he and I have yet to be able to talk about what it was like for him to grow up with a handicapped sister, or about its effect on our continuing relationship. Breaching that particular silence is part of my continuing work of healing.

Peer relationships became difficult for me, beginning with the loneliness and isolation of the months of hospitalization. There, the gnawing fact that our bodies were different from those of other people was something none of the polio victims on my ward could talk about; it was easier to stay in touch with the inner persons who had existed before the illness and to ignore or deny the existence of the distorted and atrophied bodies we inhabited. For all of us, there was one vital deprivation: the permission to grieve the loss of physical functioning that each of us had experienced.

I made a promise at that time that someday I would help people who were sick to talk about what they were going through. For me, however, there was no one to acknowledge and listen to my physical and emotional pain. When I cried, I was told I should not, because other people were worse off than I, even dying. In my own quiet way, I began observing and listening to the pain of others at that early age. Listening to them speaking about their feelings was a comfortable way of relating to people and, of course, a way to circumvent acknowledging my own. In the hospital I was always the friendly visitor for other patients. I know now that I was defining a sense of purpose for myself that was beyond my own physical rehabilitation.

Relating to my peers was a different matter. They were not sick, and my crippled body was outside their experience and comprehension. How could they relate to a peer who could not run and jump and ride bicycles? Occasionally they came to visit, and played games or watched television with me, but I could sense that they did not really want my slow, awkward, ugly body in their active 7-year-old lives. Later, at school and in the community, efforts were made to integrate me into normal activities, but my embarrassment about the way I looked and walked made these efforts difficult for me to accept.

Returning to school was not easy after being away for a full year and being taught by a teacher for the home-bound. I had missed socialization, and third grade went badly. I felt very conspicuous dragging my weakened body with two Canadian crutches.

However, in the fourth grade I had the first of a series of teachers who took a special interest in me. My fourth grade teacher took me aside one day after I had sat for an hour wistfully watching my classmates learn to square dance. "It must be hard for you to watch the other kids do things that you cannot do," she said. I cried. She was the first person to acknowledge and address my feelings. I thought no one would ever recognize the depth of my anguish, the deep hurt I could not allow myself to voice. Then she expressed her admiration for my courage and the strength of my family. She was very specific in identifying the number of intellectual and creative talents she observed in me. Unfortunately, she was only one person. No one else gave me permission to feel sad and grieve, and I could not allow myself these essential feelings.

FAMILY PATTERNS

Looking back into those years is still painful. Today, as a therapist based firmly in a family systems orientation, I must consider the compelling issues involved. Of particular interest to me is the history of illness and loss in my extended family system and the way in which illnesses and deaths have been dealt with over time. The maternal side of my family furnishes many examples. Figure 14–1 presents a maternal family diagram.

My maternal great-grandmother died at age forty, leaving four children, aged sixteen, thirteen, eleven, and six. She is described as a model mother, attractive, hard-working, and mild-mannered. The story goes that several days before her death she was struck by lightning, which left her feeling ill. Several years ago I learned from her death certificate that she died having a miscarriage. As far as I know, her own children either did not know this or simply never talked about it.

After her death, my maternal great-grandfather provided well for his family, even hiring a live-in housekeeper to help with child care. He became the patriarch; everyone turned to him for answers to life's problems and for financial and emotional security. He built a summer home for his adult children to "keep the family together" — a successful effort.

Despite my great-grandfather's efforts to normalize family life after the death of his wife, all of his children had serious, continuing problems with coping with the stresses of their lives. The oldest child, my great-uncle, went to work to augment the family income and later went into the U.S. Army, with which he served in France during World War I. He married, had one daughter, and held a responsible job. However, he drank heavily throughout his life as a method of coping with his demanding father, difficult wife, and arduous job.

The oldest of the daughters, who was described as the "most fun-loving" of the four siblings, died at age twenty-one in childbirth. Her death was seldom talked about; apparently she had become pregnant out of wedlock. This was not acknowledged until recent years, when my great-uncle's granddaughter became pregnant before marriage.

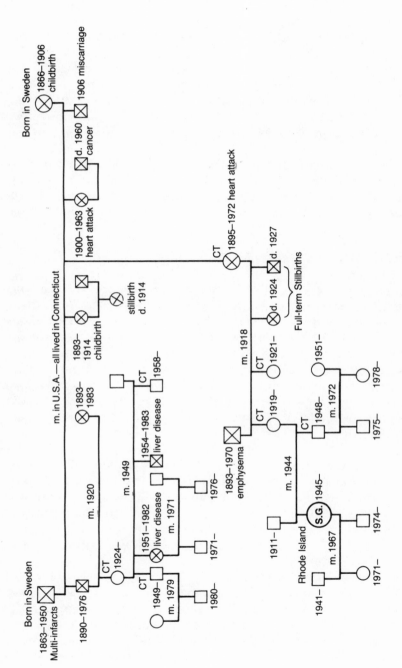

Figure 14-1. Maternal family diagram.

271

My great-aunt married several months before she and her child died in childbirth. Her husband disappeared from the family shortly after her death.

My grandmother was the third child and second daughter in this family. She developed St. Vitus's dance (chorea—a "nervous disorder") at age eleven after a serious fall at a house construction site. Although she married and had two daughters, she had numerous physical problems and two miscarriages, and was known for her nervousness.

The youngest daughter developed diabetes mellitus at age twenty-three, not long after her marriage. She never had children. She was one of the early users of insulin, but also dealt with her illness through denial, frequently neglecting her diet and suffering diabetic comas.

EMOTIONAL SHOCK WAVES

My maternal great-grandmother's death in 1906 and my maternal great-grandfather's death in 1950 both produced what Murray Bowen calls the "emotional shock wave" phenomenon. The emotional shock wave is a complex network of "after shocks" following serious life events occurring anywhere in the extended family system in the months or years following serious emotional events in a family system. The phenomenon operates on an underground network of emotional dependence of family members on each other (Bowen 1976a). The emotional dependence is denied and the serious life events thus appear unrelated.

Although the shock wave phenomenon occurs most often in families with a significant degree of denied emotional fusion, it also may occur in families that are closed to discussing sensitive issues, such as death and illness. The closed communication system is an automatic emotional reflex to protect self from anxiety, although most people will say they "avoid taboo subjects to keep from upsetting the other person" (Bowen 1976a, p. 336). It is as if the shock wave triggers the physical process into activity.

Following the deaths of key family members, a pattern of physical and/or emotional dysfunction often emerges. In my own family I have explored this as far back as the deaths of my maternal great-grandparents. As noted earlier, there was a high degree of dependence on my maternal great-grandfather. His adult children and their families cared for his physical needs in later years, but all were emotionally dependent on his presence. As long as he was alive no one else had to take much responsibility for family life.

Following my great-grandfather's death, there were many instances of physical and emotional dysfunction within the family. Both my mother and my maternal grandfather developed serious asthma, which was the beginning of life-long chronic bronchial disorders. My great-uncle and his wife began a pattern of heavy drinking, which has continued into the next two generations: their daughter is an alcohol abuser, and two adult grandchildren have died from alcohol abuse. My great-aunt's diabetes worsened and she suffered several diabetic comas. Although my grandmother became the clan leader, she developed myriad chronic physical problems, including leg ulcers, stomach ulcers, breast cancer, and heart disease. She also became somewhat reclusive and was, perhaps, phobic. She died in my presence on December 23, 1972 of a sudden, massive heart attack while entertaining the family for dinner. I contracted polio just two years after the death of my maternal great-grandfather.

My illness was contained in a matrix of anxiety about polio from a national perspective. People actually bought polio insurance out of fear of the summer epidemics of the disease.

Throughout the continuing shock waves of illness, denial was the prevalent pattern. It is important to understand that the loss of significant family members did not cause the subsequent illnesses; rather, the illnesses were part of the response to anxiety as the family tried to realign itself.

REPLICATIONS

In Bowen theory, the nuclear family emotional system is described as having patterns that replicate past generations as they repeat in future generations (Bowen 1976a, p. 78). Bowen also says that in every family system there is emotional fusion, and the greater the fusion, the more likely the family is to become symptomatic in periods of high anxiety. He notes that there are several important ways in which a family handles such anxiety: emotional distance between spouses, marital conflicts, dysfunction in one spouse, and impairment of one or more children. I was a likely candidate for absorbing a large dose of family anxiety. I had been seriously ill with measles several months before contracting polio and had had a tonsilectomy the previous spring. I believe that as the oldest and highly valued grandchild in a very enmeshed family, which also worked hard to deny grief and crisis, I lived out the role my parents covertly assigned me—that of an extremely competent child without limitations.

This family environment of illness was perfect for compounding the emotional effects of polio, whose victims were often so glad to have survived, or to be able to walk, that they felt guilty about complaining or being concerned about symptoms or residual effects. Polio victims often denied their disabilities and were encouraged to "count their blessings."

In reexamining my own history, I have observed two models of reaction to illness and disability in my family: (1) denial and (2) the use of illness or disability as an excuse for not functioning. I learned denial from my parents, who persisted in all efforts, no matter how they felt or how many obstacles were inherent in the illness and in its rehabilitative aftermath. From my maternal grandmother and my mother's sister, who both suffered from multiple physical maladies, I learned the "convenience" of illness. That is, if no one was available, my grandmother got around well, took care of herself, and even met the needs of others. However, if someone was there to wait on her, she took advantage of the fact. It was, therefore, hard to assess how functional she actually was.

I notice a similar pattern in my own behavior. I can usually find a way to do anything I really want to do; however, at times I *like* to be dependent, although I still have difficulty communicating my desire for help. How much of "functioning" is actually function, and how much is really dysfunction? What are my physical capabilities, and what are my actual limitations? Never having been allowed to recognize limitations, it is difficult to concede that there are barriers of any kind. My mother's "no sympathy" was a challenge, indeed a command, to do my best. However, since my mother never allowed any limits, how could I learn them?

THE CONTINUING EFFECTS OF POLIO

The spectre of polio is again in the news in 1985 as the *postpolio syndrome* (or *postpolio sequelae*) begins an insidious debilitation of an estimated one-fourth of polio survivors and strikes dread in all who have a history of polio. Symptoms of the postpolio syndrome include fatigue, muscle weakness and pain, debilitating joint pain, breathing difficulties, and intolerance of cold. I now have an additional reason to examine, using all my resources, both the facts and the feelings inherent in the painful legacies of this illness.

In a *New York Times Magazine* article (July 7, 1985) regarding polio's legacy, Dr. Jaquelin Perry notes: "These people push themselves more than most of us. They've put up with signs of strain to live a normal life. I always say that people who have had polio are over-achievers, because so many of them are out to prove they can do as well as those who didn't have it." In the same article, Susan S. Turner, a social worker, confirms that many postpolio patients "view themselves as super-achievers or workaholics." Turner states that "part of the panic people are feeling is the nightmare of not feeling self-sufficient" (Horowitz 1985).

Whether I become a postpolio syndrome victim or not, the manner in which I deal with function and dysfunction is important: By adopting my family's denial, I was enabled to lead an essentially active life; and it was not until my junior year in college, while seeing a therapist, that I finally acknowledged and began to mourn the fact that I could not run or jump or walk long distances. Even more telling, it was only three years ago that I showed a long-hidden photograph to a group of social work colleagues as we worked on family systems issues in our own families. I am shown seated in a wheelchair, accepting a plant from my Brownie Scout troop. Sharing this photograph was a major breakthrough in facing the many years of denial and embarrassment about that part of my life. I had never wanted people to feel sorry for me any more than I would have wished them to make fun of me—I wanted to be treated as a normal human being. While symbolic of many things, the photograph primarily serves to dramatize my differences from others rather than my similarities to them.

The central issue in recounting my experience with polio concerns limits and the awareness that physical limits and emotional limits are not always effective partners. Indeed, they are often at odds with each other. My inability to allow myself to recognize physical limitations is frequently counterproductive, resulting in serious fatigue and pain in my limbs. As a result, I do not always perform well in my roles as wife, mother, daughter, community organization volunteer, or clinical social worker. My superfunctioning sometimes makes the other people in my family and work systems less functional, which is not helpful for them or me.

I do not want to help replicate the pattern of past generations, in which one or two superfunctioners in each generation carried along the family members who functioned minimally, or underfunctioned. I try to achieve a delicate balance which allows me to be less functional at times, knowing that I am a solid enough self to return to normal functioning again, and further allows other family members and my clients to develop as normal functioners.

PROFESSIONAL DETERMINATIONS

In the process of training to become a clinical social worker, I realized that there were many areas in my own life where I was stuck. This realization in turn revealed impasses in similar areas of my clinical work with individuals and families. In view of this difficulty, I began additional training in family systems thinking. In 1974, I participated for a full year in a group with other therapists, facilitated by Paulina McCullough at the Family Institute at Western Psychiatric Institute and Clinic in Pittsburgh. We studied our own extended families as a way of learning more about family systems. As I worked on the process of differentiation in my own family, I realized that I was already manifesting the behavioral characteristics of an overfunctioning oldest daughter, just as my mother had done before me. I also saw the extent to which I was overfunctioning in both my nuclear family and work systems. In addition, I experienced severe panic attacks for six months, beginning within a month of my grandmother's death (at which I was present). I gasped for breath, just as she had done. I did not realize fully the impact of her loss on the unresolved anger that I had directed toward her passive domination of the family system. My mother now moved to the position of being the clan leader, and the message became clear that as the oldest daughter I would be the next in line.

The differentiation process has continued over the past eleven years with ongoing efforts to remain detriangled. Though difficult, this work has been invaluable in my personal life and professional growth and development, and in my clinical work with families. Work on one's family issues is clearly a birth-to-death process, with new developments at each stage of the life cycle. Every year I uncover new information, which, although helpful in understanding patterns, rarely brings immediate gratification or a sense of useful direction. Instead, it usually surfaces in unexpected ways and at unexpected times.

During this past year I took a risk in my relationship with my parents and several of my friends and colleagues by showing them a video tape of a consultation done by Murray Bowen with me at a conference for professionals in March 1984 in Northampton, Massachusetts, sponsored by the Family Living Consultants of the Pioneer Valley. Doctor Bowen interviewed me about the work I had been doing on my extended family during the preceding ten years. In addition, I decided to show my initial drafts of this chapter to the same individuals.

Taking such risks is dangerous, in that family members, friends, and colleagues are often negatively reactive to spoken and written perceptions of family events and interactions. They may become defensive, may attack, or even withdraw from contact. There is also the risk of having the viewer or reader become fused with any emotions expressed and thus be unable to view the material objectively. This can lead to overidentification with the writer and lack of separateness.

My experience with both the tape and the writing has been very positive. I believe that it has provided a new level of understanding with my parents and has opened conversation about topics we had been unable to address. They have both expressed appreciation for my sharing, and have said that it added something to their lives. The effect on my friends and colleagues has been much more varied. Their questions and comments have been helpful in enabling me to think more clearly and in broader terms about my family and the experience of illness. Through sharing, I have also learned a great deal about their families, which speaks for the universality of coping with human suffering and trauma.

In view of my family history and life experiences, it is no accident that I chose to become a family therapist. The awareness of my capacity for observation and listening to people's pain began when I was a seven-year-old patient in the polio ward trying to make sense of what had happened to my body and those of my fellow patients. I was puzzled and frustrated at the time by the fact that there was no one who would acknowledge my physical and emotional pain, extreme fear, and loss of function. Such an experience of illness often results in a particular sensitiveness, which may become evident in a number of ways. I developed "antennae" that are particularly sensitive to people experiencing physical and emotional trauma from external circumstances beyond their control. I experienced the effects of living in a closed family system that perpetuated the myth that I had no physical limitations from the polio. It was not until psychotherapy during my college years that I realized the fact, and the extent, of my unresolved grieving. With the nurturance and acceptance of a listening therapist who herself had experienced an incapacitating physical trauma as a young person, I became aware of my own capacity for listening and reflecting, as well as the value of my experience as a strength in helping others.

Any vocation coming out of a strong life experience should be followed with caution, lest personal factors override professional performance. As a family therapist, my personal inclination to overfunction must not be allowed to deter my clients from reaching their maximum levels of functioning. On the other hand, personal awareness of the potential for emotional shock wave patterns can, indeed, be helpful in encouraging clients to be more open and communicative at the time of loss or serious stress and to avoid harmful denial. When shock waves are evident, my experience allows me to be less reactive to them and to understand the natural cause of their existence.

A "given" in my life is that my extended family remains locked into shock wave patterns. I continue to try to facilitate communication with and among extended family members by stressing the facts of any given situation and seeking to allow the release of feelings, both of which bring healing. I realize that my own differentiation is not easy for my extended family to accept and will not necessarily change their life patterns.

My professional orientation and experience influence and inform my personal family systems, promoting the continuing growth and challenge that lead to more personal integration. I can see also that my personal experience with family systems under continuing stress is an enabling force in my work with clients.

The interplay between the professional and the personal aspects of my life brings a particular kind of balance and perspective. My hope is that it serves to free my nuclear family and provide increasing liberation from replicating harmful patterns of the past.

The *value* of the past is the perspective it brings to the work of the present and to the hope for the future.

REFERENCES

Bowen, M. (1976a). Family reaction to death. In *Family Therapy: Theory and Practice*, ed. P. Guerin, pp. 42–90. New York: Gardner Press.

Bowen, M. (1976b). Theory in the practice of psychotherapy. In *Family Therapy: Theory and Practice*, ed. P. Guerin, pp. 335–348. New York: Gardner Press.

Horowitz, J. (July 7, 1985). Polio's painful legacy. *The New York Times Magazine*.

Chapter 15

THE USE OF TERMINAL CANDOR

Lorraine David, M.S.W.

I am a forty-eight-year-old mother–wife–social work educator– family therapist who became ill with acute myelomonocytic leukemia over four years ago, in April 1973. I explore here the impact on several systems of which I am a part, of my insistence, from the beginning, of handling the issues of my terminal illness and impending death in a publicly open and candid manner. Especially I examine the changes that have resulted from my sharing of thoughts and feelings about facing death in my own family, feelings that are intensified every four weeks when I must return to the hospital for bone marrow aspiration and five days of harsh chemotherapy.

As a result of totally open communication between the medical team and myself, I was enabled to be completely open with my husband, children, extended family, and friends. Needless energies have not been dissipated in "keeping secrets" or playing the draining charade of "protecting each other." In their candid communication with my husband and me from the very beginning, the medical team has modeled all the positives that can accrue from openness, mainly a sense of trust in one's environment.

This openness has enabled me to accept my physical reality while at the same time instilling hope that I might live a full and rich life for however long that may last. Although originally given a statistical av-

---

This is a fictitious name to provide confidentiality for the deceased author's family.

erage of a year to a year and a half to live, I have never been treated as a "dying patient" but rather as one of the living—with respect, compassion, and good care. The medical team has treated me as a partner, not as an impersonal object who might be too fragile or dumb to understand. Yet they have not mystified me or my husband with language or terminology for which we have no background. Consequently, we have been able to explain to our children, family and friends what has been happening and why, and thus to take away the mystification and share our mutual feeling and concerns.

During the first seven and a half weeks I was hospitalized, I became painfully aware of the sense of isolation and abandonment that dying patients feel as they approach death. I am not talking simply about the sense of aloneness that comes from having no people about one, but from being unable to communicate the things that are important to oneself, or from having certain feelings that others find inadmissible. This stems from the fear that if one communicates one's deep and often painful feelings, this will stir up so much anxiety in the other that he or she will distance all the more—which is the last thing the patient wants.

When I went back to my own hometown community, I became aware of how people I had known well and intimately seemed to avoid me, by walking across the street, by avoiding eye contact, or shying away from the fact that they had been unable to visit or contact me when they heard I was on the brink of death. When I confronted them with "Hey, you're avoiding me; let's talk about it," they would become teary-eyed and confess that they did not know what to say or how to say it.

It began to dawn on me that the "avoidance syndrome" was not merely due to the fact that my terminal illness stirred up their own unresolved death anxieties. It became clear that people were often totally unrehearsed in interactional styles of communication with the dying. I began to read up on the subject and found that eighty percent of people today die in institutions, not at home. I began to understand the impact of the "invisibility" of personal dying in our society on our family, educational, and caregiving systems.

My confronting death head-on—talking about it, reading about it, teaching about it, writing about it—is undoubtedly a counterphobic way of dealing with my fears and anxieties. However, it has also been a desensitizing process, for the more I read and talk about and encounter death, the less I have come to fear it.

MY PAST EXPERIENCES WITH DEATH

My own close brushes with death throughout my life had conditioned me to expect salutary outcomes. Although I was born prematurely at seven months, I weighed five and a half pounds and was fully developed. Fortunately, I did not require an incubator. Instead, for nine months I shared a room with my mother, who constantly attended me and surrounded me with warm water bags for sleeping. So while I had a precarious introduction to life, my mother's constant care and frequent breast feedings, and the warmth and comfort of sharing a room at home with her—not in the hospital—undoubtedly gave me the message at a very early age that a human being who really cares can make a difference between prolonging life and death.

My next near-encounter with death was at age 6, when I suffered a ruptured sinus and needed an operation in order to save my life. I was hospitalized across the hall from my brother, who was ill at the same time with a double mastoid infection. While we both experienced gradual and successful recoveries, I was not permitted contact with other playmates for a year in order to avoid infection. Again, my mother's constant and attentive ministrations of care and concern conveyed the message, "I will not abandon you and my care will bring you back to health." This experience undoubtedly predisposed me toward a kind of social hunger that urged me toward gregariousness, and implanted a permanent determination not to be isolated from my peers ever again.

My only other contact with near-death in regard to someone highly significant to me occurred when our youngest daughter was seven months old and was almost fatally scalded by an overturned vaporizer. Although it was "touch and go" with her for a year and a half, she emerged from this experience physically and emotionally "whole," with an uncanny sensitivity and profound ability to endure.

The one direct experience with death I had previous to my illness occurred about fifteen years ago, when an elderly Orthodox Jewish woman in our small community died. She had requested the traditional washing of the body for burial preparation by a female ritual committee, called the *Chevra Kadisha*, or Holy Society. While assisting in the preparation and burial of the dead is one of the greatest *mitzvot* (*good deeds*/"God's Commandments") in Judaism, members must be Sabbath observers, of high moral character, and conversant with the laws and customs of this undertaking. Only the elderly were generally accorded this privilege, but one by one, our most "holy" congregants died and only one lone person remained on the committee. Our congregation, the only one in our community, had by then moved from being Orthodox to Conservative to near-Reform, and so potential candidates and/or volunteers for the Cherva Kadisha had dwindled considerably. Knowing my love and admiration for this beautiful lady, who had given so much of herself to others during her full life, the committee head asked if I would assist her in the ritual. This turned out to be one of the most moving and meaningful experiences of my adult life, since this ritual is done with great respect and care for the deceased and for his or her integrity.

After the body is lovingly and carefully washed, it is dressed in a traditional white cotton shroud, so that everyone is buried simply and equally. This moving ceremony put me in touch anew with the vitality of my faith that treats death as a part of life, that even in death insists "one not be separated from one's community." According to Jewish tradition, what one does here on earth is far more vital than what one believes, and while the body may die, the spirit lives on in the minds and hearts of those the deceased has touched. Undoubtedly, the fact that this woman died from old age and not from a ravaging disease, so that her body and face reflected a complete sense of peace, helped predispose me toward thinking of death as a peaceful rather than traumatic experience. Raymond Carey's (1975) research at Lutheran General Hospital in Park Ridge, Illinois has demonstrated that one of the main predictive factors of emotional adjustment to a limited life expectancy is having been close to a person who accepted death with inner peace.

All the foregoing experiences have given me a rather optimistic and salutary attitude about life-threatening situations and death. Besides, I had felt very good about my life as having been full and rewarding, and fortunately I had been able to live it much the way I had desired. Perhaps this is why death held no particular terror for me; only the process of dying frightened me, in particular, the threat of being isolated and abandoned.

FAMILY: CHANGING MY POSITION IN THE SYSTEM

In recounting my odyssey with terminal candor, I must begin with the impact of my life-threatening situation on my own immediate family. The threat of isolation and abandonment that I encountered during my first hospitalization made me all the more determined that this was not going to happen to me. While my husband and I had no difficulty sharing fears and angers and sadness with each other and with our four children, who then ranged from ages fifteen to twenty-three, my main problem was with my own family of origin. My mother and father, seventy-five and in good health, and my brother, fifty-two, a radiologist, were all living a thousand miles away in Georgia. Figure 15–1 presents a family diagram.

My concern was that I came from a family in which, as far as I know, death or anything unpleasant had never been discussed for at least three generations on both my mother's and father's side. Although my mother had come to America as a small child from Russia and my father was born in New York City, they grew up in a Southern ambience of magnolias dripping with honey, where even the Civil War was referred to as the recent "unpleasantness." Both my mother, the oldest of five still living sibs, and my father, the youngest of four sibs (all dead but himself), grew up in Georgia. The one abiding family theme was that everything and everyone should look good on the outside; one should keep deep feelings inside and never make trouble for anyone. Family values and goals focused on "living a good life" materially and being convivial with one's family and friends.

Although my parents are extremely loving and caring, and called the hospital almost daily those seven and a half weeks of my first hospitalization, they never insisted on flying to Pittsburgh, as close as I was to death. When I returned home, minus thirty pounds and all my hair, they finally flew up to Pennsylvania to visit. My father's first remark when he saw me was, "Don't ever let me see you without a wig," so unhinged was he by my appearance.

Before my illness, I always had had great difficulty expressing anger generally, and particularly towards my parents. Now that I had become terminally ill, I was afraid that in my desire not to alienate people and to keep them close and loving and supportive, I would tend to suppress negative feelings even more. I knew I wanted to get out of that trap. In addition, I was concerned about the effect of my illness and impending death on my parents' emotional health. Not only was my father the only remaining member of his nuclear family, but there had been a siege of clinical depression in my mother's family that manifested itself between sixty and seventy years of age when social roles changed. For instance, my mother's oldest brother, who headed a lucrative manufacturing company with his two brothers in Maryland, was hospitalized for manic depression when he reached retirement

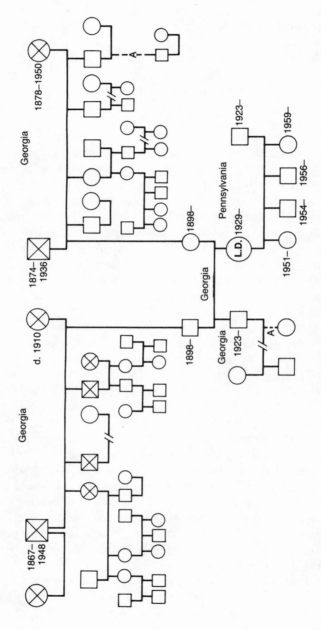

Figure 15-1. Family diagram.

age. This was followed by the depressive reaction requiring hospitalization of his youngest brother, who fell apart when he could no longer lean on my oldest uncle. The middle brother began to drink excessively, and shortly thereafter my mother went through a period of psychomotor retardation from a depressive reaction that required short-term psychiatric help. Around the same time, her sister's husband was hospitalized for a psychotic depression shortly after their youngest son married and left home.

In spite of my mother's family history of depression, I felt sufficiently stable emotionally to handle my own impending death. For one thing, I have a very strong, stable, loving, and caring husband, whose own mother had died when he was twelve from a long, debilitating illness. Although he was the middle of six sibs, he was left with the responsibility of "looking after" his three younger brothers, since his older sister and brother were soon out of the home and away at college. Thus, he had had a great deal of experience in having to support family members as well as obtaining the support of his entire family, all of whom still live in the same vicinity and remain emotionally close.

Having learned of Murray Bowen's (1972) research on the *emotional shock wave phenomenon* that often occurs after a death in the family, especially where communication about death has been closed, I became determined to change my own position in the family. For one thing, I had become the main emotional domino on whom everyone in the family leaned for solace, support, and conflict resolution. My parents, aunts, uncles, and brother tended to go through me to avoid direct conflict with someone else in the family, thereby triangulating me to dilute their interpersonal tensions. I suddenly realized how much I had previously enjoyed this pivotal role. The problem was that now I needed to conserve my energies for myself and my immediate family. Secondly, I was determined to change our family's pattern of avoiding unpleasant topics, such as death, or expression of strong feelings of anger and sadness, so that we could all be more comfortable and less vulnerable during this period of stress.

While I felt no need for traditional psychiatric intervention during this two-year period, I did determine to get outside help for dealing with my own behavior in my family system. About a year after my illness, I joined Paulina McCullough's family therapy seminar at Western Psychiatric Institute in Pittsburgh, where nine family therapists met weekly to work on changing their own positions in their various family systems, based on Murray Bowen's (1974) approach on "differentiation of self in one's family system." Helping myself with the support of consultation from peers has taught me the value of self-help groups generally, as well as enabling me to maintain my own autonomy and sense of control, a condition so vital when one is confronted with a terminal illness.

My first thrust toward changing my position was to reverse the usual procedure of my brother calling for information about me from my husband and then filtering it through his medical sieve and relaying it to my parents. The other pattern was for my mother to call me with my father on the extension, and then to relay information to the rest of the family. I began rotating calls directly to my father, and mother, or my brother, so that each one had to deal with me one-to-one and I with each of them. I did the same thing with my extended family. Little by little they were able to talk about my illness openly and with some equanimity.

A year after I went into remission, my husband and I arranged to spend our twenty-fifth wedding anniversary in Florida. I asked my mother, father, and brother to fly down for the weekend so that I might spend an individual day with each of them. As we walked the beaches each day in peaceful quietude, I was able to elicit a kind of "life review" with each of them, wherein feelings and remembrances that had never been expressed or discussed before began to emerge. My father told me all about his devastating experience of going bankrupt during the Depression and how he had considered suicide. He had never shared this with anyone. My brother talked about what it felt like growing up when Dad was so economically and personally insecure. My mother continued to focus mainly on facts related to our family history rather than feelings. Nevertheless, our relationship moved from a kind of superficial relating to a much more intensely felt experience. I set up the same kind of visitation schedule and one-to-one sharing with individual members of my mother's extended family in Maryland. This helped stop a great deal of the triangulation that had been occurring previously, particularly in regard to several members of my mother's family who tried to cut me off from my middle uncle, of whom they disapproved.

During this first year of my illness, with its gradual opening and expanding of feelings, particularly around separation and loss, an interesting phenomenon happened. My father suddenly emerged from his home/cocoon and started participating in a daily athletic program at the "Y" for the first time in his life; and my mother's depression finally dissipated. It was as if confronting the finiteness of my life enabled each of these family members to accept more responsibility for their own lives and their own time limits. To confront death is to take action, for there may be no tomorrow in which to carry out one's plans. This was happening in the context of my interactions with all these family members in which I focused verbally on my own needs to rearrange priorities by shifting my "gotta's" to my "wanta's"; and shared my need to take time just to "be" and not have to "do" continually in order to prove my worth, and openly discussed my realization that my real fears of dying were merely disguises for my fears of living.

I discovered during this period that one of my main fears of dying was the fear of loss of control that would necessitate my becoming increasingly dependent on my medical environment. Yet, I found that the more able I was to say "yes" to friends' offers of help, the more this fear abated. In addition, the more I was able to *relinquish* control on my own time schedule, paradoxically, the more *in* control I felt. This recognition came as I gave up many teaching duties in order to have more time for myself, my family, and friends. I also ended my student trainer's role at the clinic where I worked to have more time for consultation and education related to my current life situation.

After a year-and-a-half of maintenance chemotherapy, my doctors decided to initiate a more severe type of treatment as a preventitive measure in the hope of prolonging my first remission. It was quite risky in that my white blood count would be cut back as drastically as the leukemia cells, making me quite vulnerable to hemorrhaging and infection. When I was forewarned of this, I called my mother and asked if she and my father would come to visit and spend Yom Kippur, the traditional Jewish Day of Atonement, which marked the high point of the Jewish New Year. I explained I might need to be hospitalized for infection during this time, and I felt the need of their presence. At first my mother said they did not want to leave home, since they always spent the High Holidays there. But shortly thereafter she called to say that they would surely come if they could be of help.

This was the first time since my illness that I had asked for my parents' direct help and support. During the first seven weeks of hospitalization, I had not encouraged their coming. I had felt that their emotions might be too much for me as I was garnering all my energy to fight for life. I had also feared that their presence would be additional stress for my husband, who had all he could handle at home with the children, as well as his own business pressures. Consequently, I was protecting all of us—a pattern I had developed in my "healthier" days.

At this time I determined to take responsibility for my own feelings
and encourage my parents to take responsibility for theirs.

On the night my parents came, I spent some time alone with my
mother, telling her how much she had meant to me over the years. We
were able to cry together for the first time. The following day, I came
down with pneumonia and had to be rushed to the hospital immediately, where the medical team had to battle with infection. Although I
was critically ill, my parents could not bring themselves to visit me in
hospital until the third day. They said they felt they could be of more
help praying for me in the synagogue on Yom Kippur. This was the
first time they had confronted my malaise in the hospital, where they
saw me in my "second home" environment. Fortunately, I recovered
quickly and returned home before they left. Interestingly enough, my
brother reported that my parents returned to their home more relaxed
than he had seen them in a very long time.

My next thrust in this desensitizing process came when my parents
visited for several days that spring. This time the impetus came from
one of my children. Our children, one by one, had come to deal with
my impending death in their own individualized ways. Our oldest
daughter, who was twenty-three at the time I first became ill, was attending a university in Pittsburgh and visited me almost daily during
those first seven-and-a-half weeks. She was able to get out a lot of anger about the disruption in her life my illness had caused. When she
subsequently transferred to a school in Philadelphia, where her fiancé
was obtaining his M.F.A., she asked that I come there for several joint
sessions with her therapist. Her anger, anticipatory grief, and fears of
separation and loss were, in part, standing in the way of her moving
into marriage. Expressing anger had become a dangerous risk, since
she feared it might hasten my death. Yet an accumulation of angers
bottled up over her lifetime were acting as a barrier and protection
against the deep feelings of love that were equally painful to confront
at this time of impending loss. With the aid of a neutral and sensitive
therapist to dilute the intensity, we were both enabled to express our
resentment as well as our appreciation. Both must be said before a
loved one dies so as not to be plagued by these deep unexpressed feelings after death, when it is too late. Over a two-year period she was
able to resolve many of these feelings, and finally married.

Our oldest son, now twenty-four, has resolved his own sense of
commitment to the future in great measure by dealing directly with my
husband and myself regarding what tomorrow may bring for us all.
After dropping out of college for two and a half years, he determined to

reenter and pursue a law career. He transferred from the University of Louisville to the University of Pittsburgh so, as he put it, he could be of more help during this critical period.

Our youngest daughter, who is now nineteen, was the only child at home during these past four years until she entered college last fall. At the beginning of my illness, she found it difficult to visit me in the hospital and would always bring a friend along to dilute the intensity. Little by little, she has been able to talk about my illness and death openly. She even invited me to her high school psychology classes to discuss death and dying, as well as to address a regional Jewish youth conference on the same subject. She thus built in peer support while providing herself with a "defused" situation to confront her concerns. In addition, she took on more of the homemaking responsibilities to prepare herself for the new role she might have to assume.

My younger son, age twenty-two, attended Penn State University, where he majored in human development. Some months after my illness, he asked if he might come home to do an interview with me as part of a communication course assignment. He had always assumed the role of the family comedian and up to this point I had found it very difficult to talk to him about our feelings, because he would always turn me off with a flip comment. But when he called, I suspected he was choosing this way, on his own terms, where he could be in control, to discuss my impending death. I guessed right, and our encounter turned out to be one of the most moving and meaningful exchanges I have ever had with anyone near and dear to me. He wanted to know how it felt to be in my position, and in turn, shared his own feelings. More importantly, he wanted to know how I felt about the way he had turned out and expressed his feelings about how I stacked up as a mother. Spurred on by a new sense of confidence and freeing of self, he next interviewed my husband about his plans after I die. Did he plan to sell the house? Would he remarry? He did a magnificent job of dealing with anticipatory grief—my husband's as well as his own. He wrote a narrative for his class, describing the process of what had occurred and his own reactions. In it he noted how good it felt to help me, when I was usually the "professional helper," and how meaningful it was for him to be able to ask his father about his future plans, when it is usually his father who asks *him*, "Well, what are your plans for the future?" In short, all the children have found ways to become "the parent" when they feel we may need their support. My son's interview with my husband reflected two trends that I had recognized in all of our children over this four-year period.

1. They tended to turn more toward their father for guidance and emotional support—a role I had more frequently assumed in the past.

2. Instead of the "breaking-away-from-family" phenomenon that we had noted when all of our children had entered adolescence and early adulthood, there was now a tendency in all of them to turn back to the family for emotional sustenance and support. The possibility of family diminution threatened their own identity and even existence. When I relapsed a year ago and was not expected to live, this threat was exacerbated. After going into a second remission two months after relapse, the anxiety aspect of this "togetherness" gradually diminished and a positive caring and family cohesiveness emerged. The threat of death initially pushed them into an uneasy "huddled togetherness," but the ensuing open discussions and action toward discovering new role and identity potentials has enabled them to emerge more securely as four separate, discrete individuals. Each has a genuine sense of demonstrated concern for the family as a unit that did not exist before.

This is a long digression from my original point of departure, which was to relate the next pattern of change when my parents came for a visit two years after my illness. For the first time in two years, my parents asked me about what I was doing professionally. They had heard that I was teaching a seminar on death and dying at the university and that I had made several local television appearances in relation to my terminal status. They were also aware that I had begun to publish articles on the subject and had participated in starting several self-help groups for people and their families in life-threatening situations; but their information was all second-hand, since they had never questioned me directly. I told them I'd be happy to share the articles I had written describing these events and my thoughts and feelings from various stages of my illness. After telling them about my son's tape and narrative describing his reactions, I asked if they would like to hear the interview and read his account. They nervously acquiesced. I proceeded to give them the material in chronological, as well as emotionally detoxifying, order—going from the more cerebral and didactic to the most emotionally stirring, ending with all three of us listening together to my son's tape.

At the end of the tape, my parents broke down and wept openly for the first time. My mother's first remarks were, "I'm so scared . . . I feel like a coward when I listen to Joe and see how he's able to confront this and I can't face it." My father sobbed openly for the first time also and said he couldn't bring himself to believe that I could actually die of leukemia. I looked, and seemed to be doing, so well that he had convinced

himself a miracle would happen and it would just go away. I held both
of them as I too wept, and said it was far better for all of us to be able to
cry and confront our sadness than to pretend it would go away, only to
fall apart when I did go out of remission. This was an emotional high
point of expression of feeling for all of us. We had never sat down together as a family and openly shared our deepest feelings and vulnerabilities. My father told me before he left that he had never had such a
meaningful and rich visit.

Another pattern change occurred during this visit. For some time,
my brother had been dating a woman about whom my parents had
misgivings. Rather than confront my brother, they usually dumped
their anxiety or negative feelings about this situation on me. My
brother, sensing their negative "vibes," would avoid any discussion
about his friend with them. My father would then become irate at his
avoidance but keep it to himself, which would only reinforce my brother's avoidances. After a particularly upsetting episode, my father—in
his usual pattern—did not confront my brother, but instead dumped
his anger on me the first ten minutes of his visit. My pattern in the past
had always been to defend my brother and jump into the breach to dilute any intensities in order to protect them all. This time I turned to my
father and told him I did not appreciate his venting his rage at me. If he
was angry at my brother, please tell him, not me. And this is precisely
what my father did when he returned home. This marked my first real
thrust at detriangulation.

For the first time, I really began to get negative vibes from my family system. My brother reverted to his old pattern. He talked on the telephone to my husband rather than me, and told him he thought I had
gone too far with the "death bit" and had upset Mother and Dad by
confronting them with my writings and my son's tape. The message
was clear: my outspokenness had stirred this all up and my husband
should do something to shut me up.

Just as my husband was repeating this to me, my parents called,
complaining about my brother's situation. Suddenly, I forgot all of
Murray Bowen's admonitions about "don't withdraw, attack or defend" when one begins to twitch. I reverted to my former reactive pattern and angrily proclaimed, "If what other people think is more important than our love and concern for each other, then our family is
really screwed up somewhere." Dad immediately took over the telephone and said he and Mom were going out to visit my brother and his
girl friend that afternoon.

A few weeks later, my husband and I flew to Florida for a week and invited my brother and his friend to visit us. When we met together, my brother's friend conveyed to me the dismay they both felt over my talking so openly about death and dying. I replied that I felt this was an expression of their own anxiety over separation and loss and that I could handle my anxiety if they could learn to handle theirs. After this, their focus changed from concern about me to decisions about ending their own relationship.

Right after this visit, I appeared on NBC's televised "Today" show and my brother called to say how moved he was by the way I handled myself and the discussion of my terminality. He said he could see for the first time how helpful this kind of openness could be to a great number of people.

In this instance I felt I had put the conflict back into the system where it belonged. Since that time, I have not gotten messages from any of my family to "stop talking so openly."

One of the main problems of having to live with a fatal disease is the permanent uncertainty of remissions and relapses. Once the patient and family become psychologically prepared to accept an expected death, which then does not occur, members often experience great emotional discomfort and dislocation. I think this is particularly true of parents who must confront the unnatural process of losing a child who is predicted to die (at age forty-nine, in my case) when they are still alive and healthy (now seventy-eight, in their case).

As my predicted year-and-a-half "stay of execution" began to near its end, I found my parents would make excuses not to go on trips or leave their home unless necessary. They would tell friends confidentially that they were afraid to leave for fear they would miss the telephone ring, bringing news of my relapse and imminent death. When I got word of this regression, I decided the best thing to do was to intervene through my mother's extended family in Maryland. By this time, my uncles were over their depressions and we were all communicating quite regularly with one another—although some members were still estranged from others.

About this time, I was asked to give a workshop on death and dying for a community volunteer project in a small town near my mother's relatives. I planned to fly there the night before and fly back home the following night. I called all my aunts and my one retired uncle, told them I would like very much to see them for the day if they were interested in coming to the open workshop, after which we could have dinner together before I flew home. They all got in touch with one another, in spite of their estrangement, and showed up en masse.

In speaking to the lay volunteer group, I addressed myself to some of the unspoken concerns of my extended family, i.e., the catalytic effect of separation and loss on depression; how drugs and depression affect sexual activity; the need for family support systems. At dinner afterwards, they began to talk obliquely about these concerns. They asked how my mother and father were feeling, and I told them about their dread of leaving home. My retired uncle said he would call and ask them to visit him and his wife in Maryland—and he did. When my parents heard my formerly depressed uncle invite them, they decided that warranted their going on a trip. Their visit, in turn, brought about continued family interaction and buoyed their spirits. When they returned home, they determined to move from their rather isolated duplex into an apartment complex where many of their friends lived. This change brought about a new investment in life around them, including redecorating, increased socialization, and renewed interest in people and travel.

After three full, rich years of living with this permanent uncertainty, the inevitable happened. My leukemia cells returned. I relapsed the third summer of my illness and had to undergo radical chemotherapy. As the chemotherapy began to eliminate the leukemia cells from my bone marrow, my normal white blood cells were also destroyed, leaving me highly vulnerable to infection. During a two-week period, I battled double pneumonia with lung infection, kidney failure, a body rash resulting from an allergic drug reaction, esophageal and intestinal fungus infections, gastrointestinal bleeding, heart enlargement, and numbness in my feet and legs. This eight-week relapse was far more distressing physically and emotionally than my battle for life when I first came down with leukemia in April 1973. For a two-week period, I hovered between life and death. Three of my sisters-in-law, several close friends, plus my husband and children, constituted a round-the-clock team to supplement nursing care and assuage my fears of abandonment. Each family member worked in tandem with a friend for eight hours at a stretch during those critical days and nights. Knowledge that my family had support at all times reduced my fear that they would "burn out."

The role of my family was pivotal in my ability to cling to life. During the three-year period of my first remission, I had talked openly, at each of the children's own pace, about my impending death. Although I did not deter them from coming to the hospital during that time, I also did not encourage them to visit until my nausea had subsided. I feared that the children would "burn out" under the constant threat of my dying if they were exposed to the stress of my monthly hospitalizations over a prolonged period. In such a case, they might not then be available to me when I would most need them.

Part of my behavior was due to the fact that when I felt so sick, I did not want to have to exert the effort to respond to company, even my children; and part was due to my wish not to expose them unnecessarily to my own distress. Nor did they particularly want to come when I was so uncomfortable. As a consequence, the children rarely saw me when I was not looking and feeling well. For all our talk about my illness, I believe they came to doubt my terminality and to believe secretly that I had "licked" it. Even I, who believed my terminality "in my head," began to feel in my gut that the first remission would continue much longer. So did my husband. So did others around us who were convinced that I would continue to beat the statistics.

My relapse came as a shock to all of us. This time, I wanted the children with me, and they wanted to provide whatever care they could. My married daughter left graduate school to fill in as part of "the team." For the first time, our roles were reversed. She did the mothering with all the tenderness and sensitivity I ever could have desired. My older son, whose blood platelets were totally compatible with mine, came into Pittsburgh daily from our home during the two-week period. For three hours he would be hooked up to a machine to extract and separate the platelets and the white cells, with which I was then transfused. He underwent this procedure despite his own traumatic experience at the same hospital several years ago, when he had suffered temporary paralysis. It was his white cells that may have saved my life. My younger son, who was finishing school at Penn State, came whenever he was able to provide platelets and to offer a respite for his brother. My younger daughter became the expert "foot massager," and would sit at the foot of the bed for long periods. One afternoon when death seemed imminent, she clung to my legs as I cried out repetitively: "Jane, I'll stay with you. I won't leave you."

During those critical days we cried together, and expressed our feelings of love and fears of loss. We even found time to laugh, such as when I couldn't remember names, and called Dr. Chervenick "Dr. Zhivago"—all the while insisting that at least my mistakes were complimentary. My husband, the children, my sister-in-law, and my brother all felt that their being with me through my pain was a rehearsal for the time when we will all have to let go. The constant care they had provided for me gave them a sense of their own strength and potential, as well as assuaging their helplessness.

I am not certain now whether I acted rightly or wrongly in not encouraging the children to be on hand earlier in my illness. My sense is that they moved in when they were ready, and when I was ready for them. Like myself, they need their own emotional space, pace, and options.

The children's presence had another consequence. It indicated they were as important to me as my husband. During these four years of my illness, my husband and I have tended to turn more toward each other than toward the children, as if to squeeze in the flavor of our "retirement years" together that we will be denied. In so doing, I believe we may have neglected the children's needs for intimacy with each of us. During this last hospitalization, all of my husband's energies were focused on keeping me alive. For two weeks he remained in Pittsburgh, returning home, forty miles from Pittsburgh, only once. I am certain that the children felt some neglect and lack of communication. However, when they were all involved in my care at the hospital, we were a family once again.

Again, my parents called daily and wanted to fly up, but my husband and I discouraged them, feeling their presence would be an emotional overload for all us all. Since my brother flew up from Georgia several times, he assured them all was being done that could be done—they should remain home until the end was imminent. Their ability to "stay put" was both a testimony to their own ability to respond to our needs, as well as proof that older people have a way of enduring by protecting themselves from too painful stimuli. However, when my next relapse comes, they should be given the option of being on hand or staying home. Everyone involved needs options—not just the patient.

Since my recovery, which was considered a medical miracle, I have often been asked: "What enabled you to hold onto life against all odds?" I remember thinking that my will to live was contingent upon three factors: (1) my doctor's belief that I could make it into a second remission and my trust in him because he had never lied to me; (2) the constant care and demonstrated love and support of my entire family, close friends, and caregivers, which was partially engendered by my insistence on "terminal candor" in making my needs known, and (3) my own self-image as a fighter, which my environment reinforced.

My second remission has continued for well over a year. My terminality is something the children rarely discuss, but rather, have come to treat as a "given." They are all embarked upon their various life goals, although they tend to keep in touch and visit home frequently. My reunions with my extended family no longer focus on saying goodbye, but rather on exchanging words of love and concern in the present.

A recent wedding in Georgia marked the first big reunion of my mother's family in eight years. I spent three days talking with each family member about remembrances and told them I planned to write a family history for distribution to everybody to comment on, add to, and exchange with one another. Our older daughter, who is the "second generation" taking Paulina McCullough's seminar on working on one's extended family, accompanied me with our oldest son to this reunion and has offered to help with follow-through on family history compilation and distribution.

Through this undertaking, I have come to have a real sense of both integration and extension, of weaving the various threads of my life and my family's into a kind of unfinished tapestry that trails toward tomorrow. Having moved from the family's nucleus to the periphery of the extended family back to its nucleus, the system has not only opened up to new possibilities but is connected in ways not experienced before.

Once death has been accepted, people tend to focus on living rather than dying. My family and I are no exceptions.

REFLECTIONS

During the past four years of confronting death issues openly while living with a terminal illness, I have explored a range of principles that have helped change various systems of which I am an integral part. These principles were first applied in my own immediate and extended family in regard to opening up communication about death. They have also been applicable in changing dysfunctional aspects of my hospital system, as well as other medical systems dealing with the terminally ill and their families. To some extent, these same tenets have effected changes in my work and community systems around death issues.

I now utilize the content and process of these principles in a variety of consultation efforts involving a range of divergent systems. These include child welfare, Veterans Administration hospitals, nursing home care, and work with church, public school, and mental health groups.

Upon analyzing these transactions, the following principles appear to undergird the various system changes of which I have been a part:

1. In any system change, it is often more productive to *start from the periphery*, where emotional issues are less intense, than at the nucleus, so as to dilute intensity. Change will be facilitated if resistances are worked around, not forced. In regard to confronting death, it is helpful to cope with problems of separation and differentiation of self in one's own family before dealing effectively with the reality of death itself.

2. One of the most effective automatic mechanisms for reducing the overall level of anxiety in a system is a relatively open relationship network at the "outer edges" of the system to be changed.

3. Change can be facilitated if *cognitive areas* are confronted first. After successful working through of pragmatic or factual problems, emotional issues can be approached more effectively.

4. Change is facilitated by starting with an area that promises success. One small, accomplished change becomes reinforcing when one is attempting larger changes.

5. Distressful behavior is often the consequence of *deprivation of information* in a person, family, organization, community, or government. Without access to information, we tend to fill in the gaps with our fantasies, our projections, our past experiences — all of which can lead to dysfunctional behavior.

6. However, open access to information in and of itself is not sufficient for change. As Fred and Bunny Duhl (1975) point out, other ingredients in the process include:
   a. *Awareness of options*
   b. *Familial or peer support* (hence the efficacy of self-help groups)
   c. *Knowledge of process* (how to put options into action in a constructive way), and
   d. *Context* (a place in which to pull it all together).

7. Having open access to information with process can still create anxiety. The problem then becomes how to use anxiety to accomplish change. Learning to control one's own reactivity to negative "vibes" is crucial in implementing a change in the status quo. Control of self is a precursor to any control of reactivity in other systems. The control comes from *not responding in the automatic way the system expects*, but in *remaining neutral* or in *exaggerating the reaction that is totally unexpected*. This can be brought about by making what is covert

overt, often by owning up to one's own vulnerability, which often turns out to be the vulnerability of the person who is generating the negative vibrations. This kind of "reversal" when under attack might be: "You know how desperately I want to be perfect and you just won't let me be perfect."

8. In order to maintain this neutral stance, one must be able to *stand back as an observer* and gain cognitive mastery over what is often an engulfing emotional process. When one cannot manage this thinking–feeling–doing synthesis, it is helpful to *consult* with peers with the idea of finding out "what the hell am I reacting to?" rather than "what the hell is the system doing to me?" Help comes from *anticipating what will get one twitching* and then developing a repertoire of possible nonreactive responses. Being "rehearsed" is often enough inoculation to enable the allergy to subside.

9. Even with control over one's reactivity, any system gets uptight with change. Members of the system will try to dissuade one from doing "something different." If an individual persists, system members will accuse this person of disloyalty and threaten withdrawal of support, and isolation. The person trying to effect change can either (1) be reactive, become dissuaded, and "get back in line," or (2) decide to continue and learn better to control his/her reactivity. If the latter occurs, the system will eventually quiet down and accept change.

In conclusion, I have tried to show how my insistence on open communication about death has created reactiveness in my family and other systems of which I am a part. No one is immune to death anxiety. By confronting these anxieties, taking a differentiated position, and learning to control my own reactivity, there has been, I believe, a vital release of energy, creativity, thoughts, and feelings for myself, my family, and others who ultimately face death, separation, loss, and change.

REFERENCES

Bowen, M. (1972). Family Reaction to Death (videotape). Washington, D.C.: The Family Center, Department of Psychiatry, Georgetown University Medical Center.

Bowen, M. (1974). Toward the differentation of self in one's family of origin. In *Georgetown Family Symposia* (Vol. I, 1971–1972), ed. F. D. Andres and

J. P. Lorio. Washington, D.C.: Family Center, Department of Psychiatry, Georgetown University Press.

Carey, R. G. (1975). Living until death: a program of service and research for the terminally ill. In *Death The Final Stage of Growth*, ed. E. Kubler-Ross. Englewood Cliffs, NJ: Prentice-Hall.

Duhl, B.S. (1975). Implications of changing sex roles for family therapy and family therapists. Part I: Information without process. Dual paper presented with F. J. Duhl at the Annual Meeting of the N.Y. School of Social Work, May.

Chapter 16

A SON'S JOURNEY: REFLECTIONS AFTER MY FATHER'S DEATH

John J. Haverlick, C.S.W., A.C.S.W.

"We'll get together then, Dad . . ."
Harry Chapin*

A FATHER'S DEATH

The first winter snow covers the countryside with just a light powdery white, giving the appearance of a Currier and Ives scene. The early evening sky streaked with deep hues of orange and purple casts a softness over the landscape. The evening sun has just descended below the horizon. It is early November, and there is a chill in the air that sharpens rather than numbs the senses.

My mother, in her sixties, and I stand together in a cemetery at the foot of a no longer freshly dug gravesite. Grass has not yet grown back to cover the outline of the hole made to accommodate a burial vault and casket. The cemetery sits on the top of gently rolling hill—a scene not uncommon in this part of upstate New York. Below it and to the other side of the valley is a small college town, now dotted by lights. A church bell strikes the hour, or perhaps the half hour, off in the distance.

The gravestone as yet does not have the date of death of the man who lies at its foot. It is a gravestone that has the names and birthdates of both a man and a woman—a husband and wife—and only from the outline of the dark earth would one know that it is the husband who has died. Years before, in preparation for his death, my father had

---

*From the song, "Cat's in the Cradle." © 1974 Story Songs, Ltd.

come here with my mother to make burial arrangements. At home there is a photograph of him standing next to the purchased gravestone, a picture that once seemed both ludicrous and bizarre.

I stand clasping my arm around my mother, who is very slightly bent, and beginning to cry softly. We are otherwise motionless. My thoughts are of that day back in May when my father was brought to this site to be buried.

My mother abruptly breaks the silence. "I still can't believe that he is really down there." Once again I feel as if my insides have been torn apart anew, and the cruel reality of my father's death, his body in a casket buried before me, is forced on my senses. But it is still something I cannot, do not, will not, fully accept. I can only mutter in response, "yeah." My mother, crying a little harder now, moves away to wander among the other gravestones.

A deep chill rises through my body, shaking me. Was it the chill of the evening, or the fact that I had not slept well these past several months? Was it caused by the concern I felt for my mother's tears and pain, or the rekindling of the depth of my loss, or the stark, unrelenting reality of death?

The day my father died, I felt as though my world had been shattered. The pain that engulfed me that morning in the hospital where I had raced to see him was like no other pain I had ever experienced. Six months later, I could easily recall the intensity of that moment, although the pain was no longer really sharp.

My mother wound her way back to me, and we exchanged comments about planting some flowers and shrubs in the spring to add both a personal touch to the site and to demonstrate respect and gratitude to the man who had been so significant in both our lives.

FAMILY HISTORY

My family had accepted my father's death and gone through the funeral experience in an unremarkable fashion, leaving one to wonder whether the intense feelings of love, loss, anger, fear, and guilt stirred up by this event were, in fact, being buried inside. This was possible, since previously many other less toxic issues had been minimally opened up for discussion. On the other hand, it could be that my family's emotional reactions were genuine. Time would surely impose its sanctions if the latter were not the case.

To get a clearer perspective on what was real in this situation, I need only go back to the years preceding this model event in the life cycle of my family. In undertaking this task, it would be possible not only to obtain a clearer reading of how well my family was dealing with what is generally considered the most toxic event in everyone's life—death—but it would also give at least some beginning understanding of the potential emotional shock waves that might spread across and down the generations in the months and years ahead.

Let us consider my family before my father's death, focusing particularly on the father–son relationship. First, though, I should introduce the other family member, my older sister (see Fig. 16–1, the family diagram). She had been more emotionally tied to my parents and also lived physically closer to them. Although the emotional tie between them was close, it was also conflictual. In contrast, my relationship with my parents was calmer and more amicable, but concurrently more distant.

Growing up as a youngest son in an intact family in upstate New York was in many ways an idyllic life. The now idealized and rapidly vanishing ideal family of four—with a father as the breadwinner, mother as the homemaker, and a daughter and a son—was the family structure that formed the key boundaries of my sense of family; they provided me with a sense of belonging, being secure, protected, and cared for. I experienced these forces primarily through the relationship I had with my mother. She had taken on the expected role of "mother" with great dedication and interest.

She hovered around my older sister and me like a mother hen. Living in the country without many close neighbors reinforced the importance of my mother's family as the social hub of our lives. As I reflect back now to comments made by my professors of social work in graduate school, I see how true were their observations that I grew up in a protected environment.

My father spent a great deal of his time in his work in a local factory or in puttering around the house with what seemed to be almost an obsession, to the exclusion of spending much leisure time with us. His family were all on the West Coast, and in contrast, my mother's siblings and their families lived within approximately a twenty-mile radius of my maternal grandmother's home.

With his twenty-four years in the Navy, the World Wars were significant to my father. They also proved to be influential in uprooting all of his siblings and his mother, who ended up moving to California. Ex-

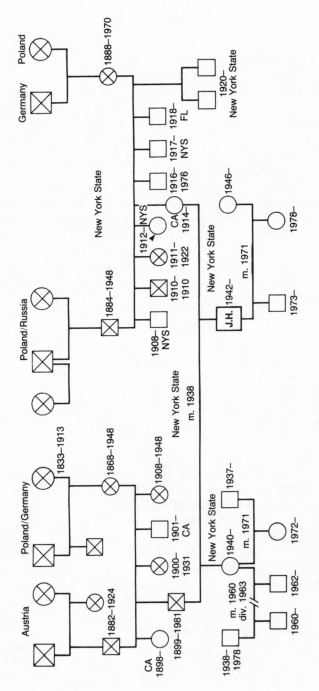

Figure 16–1. Family diagram.

cept for infrequent visits by his younger brother, they all became just names, people I knew from their frequent letters and the stories my father would relate about them.

With only what they carried with them, both sets of grandparents had migrated from Eastern Europe in the late 1890s and had eventually settled in upstate New York. My mother's family lived on a dairy farm which became the site of all family gatherings. Although I often recall the wonderful, large holiday gatherings, I see more clearly now that conflicts existed, but were then always kept under wraps. Upon my grandmother's death, in 1970, a great deal of distance between family members developed, as one might expect, and the conflict became more open. Both family systems seemed to be essentially closed. The immigration from Europe created a permanent cut-off from all extended family. This was especially true on my father's side of the family, and even though there was periodic talk about relatives of my maternal grandmother in Poland, there was never any significant contact.

To work hard, to "make a go of it," to have one's own house, to live simply, to be committed to one's family, and to avoid open conflict were, along with a fairly high tolerance for alcoholism, major themes in my family. Although my father would espouse most of these beliefs, he was always viewed by himself, my mother, and me as not quite fitting into my mother's family.

As is typical of many families, I was in an emotionally overclose relationship with my mother—one that was also overpositive—and in a more distant, intermittently conflictual, relationship with my father. There were many factors that contributed to the development and perpetuation of this pattern, including the large age gap between my father and me, the difference in levels of education, the recurring periods of competitiveness, my father's early periods of heavy drinking, and the lack of shared social or political philosophies. But it also had to do as much, if not more, with patterns existing in the extended family: the generational patterns of mothers who are overpositive with respect to their sons while being more critical of their husbands; of fathers who never really experienced fathering themselves and who were led to believe that to be hard, tough, and strong was to be manly. For almost thirty-five years of my life, these patterns had been repeated time and time again, creating distance, distrust, anger, resentment, and blame.

There are many other factors that influenced my emotionally closer relationship with my mother in contrast to that with my father. It was not until I was in my mid-thirties, when he was confronted with the life-threatening experiences of malignant tumors, that this long-term "natural order" of things was questioned and eventually altered.

The scenario thus far would not instill much confidence in anyone observing my family's efforts to deal with the death of my father; and it would lead us to believe that my family's seemingly moderate reaction to his death had as its basis emotions repressed from years of lack of insight into the family's emotional process. It would also be the type of situation in which the emotional aftershocks would be significant for the remaining family members. This had, after all, been true for my father, who not just coincidentally became more vulnerable to heavy drinking after *his* father died, who became himself a relatively distant father even though he had longed for closeness from his own father, and who maintained very emotionally and physically distant relationships with his brother and sisters.

Overall, our father–son relationship was very reminiscent of that described in Robert Anderson's play, "I Never Sang for My Father" (Guerin 1976). The film depicts a relationship that is outwardly cordial but emotionally shallow. Opportunities for connecting are avoided, missed, or never recognized. It shakes me still to watch this film and see how similarly my father and I played our "roles."

Through a series of steps—some well planned and methodical, others spontaneous and almost accidental—I set out on a journey to get to know and understand a father who, beyond the relatively one-dimensional, superficial aspects of his personality, was very little known. It was a journey uneven in its progress; frightening yet often exhilarating; painful yet growth-inducing; at times confusing but ultimately enlightening—and resulted in the development of a close personal relationship.

RECONNECTING

There are a number of articles that address the issues of reconnecting and the meaningfulness of this to the individual (Carter and Orfanidis 1976). I shall focus mainly on how reconnecting prior to a major loss can aid in minimizing the emotional aftershocks.

Throughout most of our years together, I experienced a general, underlying feeling of uneasiness, fear, and intimidation when I was with my father. In spite of his advanced age when I was born—he was over forty—he was physically very powerful. Although spankings were more common in my sister's case, the threat of the punishment was more frightening than the reality. It seemed as though we were two strangers forced to live together because of our blood ties. Otherwise, there was such a difference in interests, values, and priorities that there was little common ground for building a relationship. I tended to be judgmental—although of course my view of things was the right one—without quite realizing it, and was implicitly supported by other family members, especially my mother and maternal grandmother. Watching his efforts to fit into my mother's family, and not his own, also skewed my perception of him. I later learned that he was naturally more valued, and seen in more positive terms, by his siblings, nieces, and nephews, of whom I knew little.

Our interactions were generally brief, tense, competitive, and at times conflictual. He seemed hard, coarse, and rigid. My general sense of him was negative; I minimized or undervalued most of his accomplishments, saw him as being old-fashioned, out-of-step with more modern thinking, and wanted to be more the opposite of him than like him. He would reciprocate by being impatient at best, but more often disapproving, of my way of life.

My father's heavy drinking and smoking finally "caught up" with him when I was a junior in college. A persistent hoarseness in his throat was diagnosed as being caused by a malignant tumor. I was just twenty and was feeling less intensely embroiled in my struggles with him and had by then a better sense of my own abilities to be successful in college. We had developed a peaceful coexistence which intermittently erupted into brief skirmishes.

The threat of cancer initiated a shifting in the emotional patterns, and at that time none of us knew where it would end. Roles and responsibilities temporarily shifted in my family. I used to drive my father to the train station before dawn so he could travel to Buffalo for radiation treatments for the tumor on his larynx. I took over more of his day-to-day responsibilities while he was away. In an attempt not to disturb his routine, his way of doing things, I tried to replicate his style.

More important, for the first time in my life, I saw my father as being more vulnerable, and somewhat dependent. While he continued to bark at me about how to take care of things in his absence, there was less hardness to his orders. The car rides to and from the train station afforded us the opportunity to begin to approach one another on a more personal level. Whether it was his strength to face the illness, my deep desire to attempt to get to know him by asking detailed questions about his tumor, or a combination of both, we began to connect with one another around his illness.

The telling of the familiar "war stories" took on added meaning and gradually I reacted less negatively and experienced some compassion for him on account of his hard life and his accomplishments. I became important to his side of the family as a source of information about his condition. I began to gain a greater sense of them as people and heard about my father from a perspective that was caring, concerned, and positive. My change of roles within my family, while fueled largely by concern for my father's welfare, was influenced also by my desire to take care of my mother, which also underscored my underlying competitiveness with my father and my tendency to become an overfunctioner in times of stress.

One of the main issues around which the degree of intimacy and openness revolved was our ability to sit and talk about the prospect of his eventual death. It seemed that my taking a position about talking about death made it easier for other family members to do so as well. In some respects, as I became increasingly comfortable with the thought of losing him, I became increasingly close to him. The differences that for most of our lives had been great obstacles to closeness (with but rare exceptions) gradually began to disappear. It was especially important to me, having now become more emotionally connected to my father, that he not die emotionally alone or isolated. [Bowen (1978) and others have given special attention to this concept and demonstrated how we inadvertently end up sustaining a dying family member's pain by not attempting to open the issue of it to the extent feasible.] Because of my father's degree of comfort in talking directly about his possible death and my belief that his doing so would be better for the survivors, we were able to minimize the "conspiracy of silence" (Herz 1980) families are prone to join when the death of a loved one is imminent.

My father recovered completely and we settled into our typical patterns, which were, however, not quite the same. Subsequent malignant tumors of his colon and lung provided similar situations for reconnecting. However, of equal if not greater importance was work I took on as part of my training to become a family therapist at the Center for Family Learning in New Rochelle, New York. It was there that I ultimately learned in a more organized and thorough manner how the triangle I was in with my parents operated, and the part that I played.

I recall understanding quite readily the configuration of our particular relationship patterns. At first I went through the motions of connecting, but without giving up the expectation that my father would change. In putting together a family diagram, I suddenly realized how little I knew about him and his family of origin. Initial efforts to gather more family history opened doors between us that at one time seemed impenetrable. Probably to him, for the first time, I appeared genuinely interested and accepting of learning more about him as a man, a father, a son, and a husband.

It was not easy to let go of wanting him to be the kind of father I would have wished for (in some respects, vestiges of that will never entirely disappear). Becoming a father myself, a homeowner, and most important, emotionally accepting the responsibility for not being the kind of son he perhaps had wanted, freed us both to be more expressive of our caring and love for one another.

It was primarily through planned visits to spend time with him alone that I created a different environment between us. The subtleties and nuances of change were many. Those which were less significant seemed to be the most powerful. Having an agenda when on the telephone or in person with him, no matter how brief, was freeing. A bonding was created by looking for the common ground rather than at the differences. Monitoring my own emotional reactivity and not blaming him were all pieces of the mosaic of change.

EMOTIONAL SHOCK WAVES

The lack of openness in the family system and the degree of emotional dependence denied by the family are two major factors that influence future after shocks in the family.

Murray Bowen (1978) has described this phenomenon of shock waves in the article, "Family Reaction to Death," which was first published in 1976. Briefly, it refers to the " . . . network of underground 'after-shocks' of serious life events that can occur anywhere in the extended family system in the months or years following serious emotional events in a family" (p. 325). This concept applies more to the degree of emotional dependence, which often is denied by family members, and less to the normal grief reaction immediately following a loss.

As families pass through the family life cycle, they experience many disasters or crises, such as chronic illness, separation or divorce, aging, and death, besides other major role changes. Carter and McGoldrick (1980) have described how the way a family negotiates the various life stages affects various family members in their resolving the emotional upheaval that accompanies these events.

Because of the tendency in my family to minimize crises, I grew up seemingly unaffected by the major disturbances (divorce, alcoholism, death) that occurred. My earliest recollection of any significant event revolves around the death of my maternal grandfather, who died in 1948, when I was not yet six years old. My memories of the funeral service, which was held in his home, remain even now enveloped in an aura of unreality and naivté. I recall being more puzzled and frightened by the intense crying and sadness of my grandmother than by the peaceful stillness of my grandfather. The overriding theme was apparently to be open and expressive of one's emotions—but to a limit. Death was to be accepted, but not dwelt upon.

Life for my family and me seemed to go on without much change. I have few and very vague memories of my grandfather. I know more about my relationship with him from what my mother and other family members have described over the years. I am told there were moments in which he took special delight in me as an infant, but I do not remember his being of emotional importance to me. While it seems obvious that he was not as emotionally significant in my family as my grandmother was, a question remains as to how well we resolved the emotional upheaval caused by his death. Was there, then, an ability among the family members to absorb the anxiety set off by his death, which was, however, more overwhelming at the time my grandmother died in 1970? Or was the degree of denied emotional dependence and the ability of the family to maintain a symptomatic behavior not disrupted, as seemed to be the case with my grandmother's death?

The death of my grandmother resulted in obvious shock waves, the most notable being the physical and emotional distance that emerged among my mother and her siblings; this has filtered down to subsequent generations as well. Cut-offs on all generational levels have developed, with other family members becoming involved by taking sides. The closeness that had been exemplified by our traditional family gatherings at major holidays suddenly vanished, as if it had been a mirage.

This confirms the experience of most families, in which the number of kinship ties decreases noticeably with the loss of one's parents. How many relatives would we recognize if they passed us on the street (not including in-laws and nuclear family)? This question was asked in a study conducted by Bert Adams (1968). The average number named was 28—a figure that is not surprising. However, when this question was asked only of those who had already lost a parent, the number recognized dropped to 20 (the average derived from questioning only subjects whose parents were living was 31) (Reiss 1971).

These statistics have several implications, but of present importance is how a decrease in the relationship options increases the potential for developing symptomatology in a family system. I believe (and it is the most widely accepted view today) that the fewer the viable relationship options, the greater the risk that dysfunctional patterns will develop and replicate themselves over the generations. This would then foster the occurrence of after shocks, whether they be unexpected marriages or divorces, the increased importance of children born within two years of the death of a significant family member, more somatic illnesses, or children becoming more dysfunctional, to name a few.

With this background, further reinforced by the experience my father had in attempting to resolve the deaths of his parents (his father's death triggered his becoming a heavy drinker, and he was so physically and emotionally distant from his mother that he did not attend her funeral), the predisposition for the pattern to continue at my generational level seemed practically a foregone conclusion. However, in reconnecting with my father, I gained a more personal relationship with him, and furthermore, began acquiring a whole new extended family that I had previously known but little. In essence—at least up to this point—I have been able to reverse the usual process of losing a kinship system after a death of a parent. On the contrary, I have increased my support network.

I may have so far given the impression that adjusting to my father's death has been an easily managed experience, but that is not the case. In the aftermath of his death, I have been confronted with one of the most difficult adjustments of all. I share my experiences and thoughts in an attempt to promote a fuller appreciation of the impact one can make, personally and professionally, to minimize the fallout resulting from one's family's disasters or nodal events.

PERSONAL AND PROFESSIONAL IMPACT

The emotional processes that basically steer our lives will influence us, whether we identify them or not. If we have only 20-20 hindsight or tunnel vision, which can only give us an understanding of what is happening in the present, we will replicate the same processes in the future. During the past several years, I think I have come to see better the emotional processes in which I am now participating, and have at least begun to speculate on what they will be in the future. My father has been my greatest teacher in this up to now—understandably so, since my relationship with him was the area in which I could learn the most. However, many others have aided me in developing a more expanded understanding of myself as well.

Setting out on this journey, which many other therapists have taken (Anonymous 1978a,b; Kaplan 1980), back into my family of origin has been enriching and rewarding, not only in my personal life but also in my work as a therapist. I believe I have minimized the feelings that haunt so many of us in relation to a parent's dying. There is often a sense of relief that it is all over, but for too many it is "a relief wrapped in confusion, guilt, and a pervasive feeling of something left incomplete," as E. H. Friedman (1980) has written in connection with his own father's death. Instead of being caught up in such troubled feelings, I believe the reconnecting I accomplished before my father's death has had a substantial influence in several areas of my life.

The most immediate difference was my ability to remain available to both my mother and my sister on an emotional level to deal with the aftermath of my father's death. Specifically, I was able to share actively with my sister the emotional responsibility of my mother's need for time, support, and caring. Instead of acting on my tendency to distance from intense emotional situations or choosing to be available out of guilt or other people's expectations, my involvement was rooted in an inner desire to be connected. Since my father's death, a more personal relationship has evolved between my mother and me. Because I am aware of the tendency for increased distance or cut-offs to develop after significant deaths, I have become more sensitive about maintaining a relationship with my sister that is not contingent on my mother's involvement. I do this out of my caring for her and wanting to share important emotional experiences that tie us together because we are brother and sister.

When I first became a father, I typically defined my role in contrast to how I viewed my father: I was going to avoid all the mistakes I felt he had made with me and give to my son all I felt I had missed. As my father and I came to a better understanding and emotional acceptance of one another, my role as a father became shaped more by the relationship I began to develop with my son. I experienced less worry about replicating the old ways.

With my daughter's birth, there seemed to be more of a "natural" affinity for one another than had existed between my son and me, but I did not feel that the difference was as great as it might have been. There are, of course, constant shifts amongst all of us, but I relate to each of them more as separate individuals and less as an extension of some unresolved past pattern with other significant family members.

As the years pass, there is an increasing incidence of major illness and death within my extended family. Aunts and uncles whom I had taken for granted, as I did my father, seem mortal. I find increasingly that I want to get to know them on a more personal level before they too are gone. In return, I will perhaps learn more about myself as well. This sense of extended family has become important for me to pass on to my children, so that they will have a broader view than I did of belonging, being secure, protected, and cared for.

Unfortunately, the attempt to stay as connected as possible in one's family can bring about negative fallout as well. The act of remaining in contact with some family members who are involved in conflicts or cutoffs with other family members can be judged by one side or both as being unsupportive and disloyal. It can be difficult and isolating not to be influenced by this reaction of disappointment or hurt. It is, nonetheless, important to remain true to one's own beliefs and values and to attempt to minimize those of one's reactions based on seeking the approval or acceptance of others. This can be an endless endeavor.

My functioning on both personal and professional levels has been affected in two substantial areas: relationships with men, and how I deal with the issue of death.

I have found that as my level of comfort in being with my father increased, so too have my relationships with men become more relaxed and intimate. Concerns about being "manly," or measuring up to other men, on the one hand, or, on the other, fear of having homosexual tendencies, if I felt affection or an attraction for another man, essentially ceased to exist. Issues such as these, with which many men are struggling, have become an area of special interest to me.

Death and its effects pervade our lives. Because of my father's courage and strength to face his own impending death and his ability to discuss it in an open manner, the intense dread and avoidance of this issue has been greatly reduced. In my family, I am better able to monitor my own emotional reactivity when listening to an older relative talk about a life-threatening illness. This invariably results in a greater openness between the two of us than is possible to other family members. The dividends of this to me as a practicing therapist have been immeasurable; it has permitted me to be emotionally available to families in which the threat of death, whether in the form of suicide or serious illness or old age, is present.

Additionally, my ability to deal with other intense emotional issues has increased significantly. This is confirmed by other students of family systems theory who have worked in their own family's emotional field to develop more personal, one-to-one relationships. This is work that is done not only around a particular issue or event but a life-long -pursuit.

It may be too soon to know what the long-range impact will be of the shock waves unleashed by my father's death. The emotional fallout is there, although, as J. S. Kuhn (1978, p. 182) has written, it "is no more visible as an entity than the wind. But, like the wind, it can be identified by its effects." The more this becomes apparent, the more I will know the answer to the question, how well did my father and I really get to know one another?

Perhaps this question will someday begin to be answered by my son and me. Songwriter Harry Chapin, who tragically died in an automobile accident the same year as my father, sings in "Cat's in the Cradle": "And as he hung up the phone it occurred to me, my boy was just like me, my boy was just like me" (Chapin 1976).

REFERENCES

Adams, B. N. (1968). Kinship in urban setting. Chicago: Markham.

Anonymous (1978a). Taking a giant step—first moves back into my family. In *The Best of the Family 1973–78*, pp. 209–215. New Rochelle, NY: The Center for Family Learning.

Anonymous (1978b). The management of loss in the therapist's own family. In *The Best of the Family 1973–78*, pp. 249–254. New Rochelle, NY: The Center for Family Learning.

Bowen, M. (1976). Family reaction to death. In *Family Therapy: Theory and Practice*, ed. P. Guerin, pp. 335–348. New York: Gardner Press.

Bowen, M. (1978). *Family Therapy in Clinical Practice*. New York: Jason Aronson.

Carter, E., and McGoldrick, M. (1980). The family life cycle and family therapy: an overview. In *The Family Life Cycle*, ed. E. Carter and M. McGoldrick, pp. 3–20. New York: Gardner Press.

Carter, E., and Orfanidis, M. (1976). Family therapy with one person and the family therapist's own family. *Family Therapy: Theory and Practice*, ed. P. Guerin, pp. 193–219. New York: Gardner Press.

Chapin, H. (1976). "Cat's in the Cradle," from the recording *Greater Stories—Live*. Los Angeles: Elektra Records. Copyright 1974 Story Songs, Ltd.

Friedman, E. H. (1980). Systems and ceremonies: A family view of rites of passage. In *The Family Life Cycle,* ed. E. Carter and M. McGoldrick, pp. 429–460. New York: Gardner Press.

Guerin, P. J., Jr. (1976). The use of the arts in family therapy: 'I never sang for my father.' In *Family Therapy: Theory and Practice,* ed. P. Guerin, pp. 480–500. New York: Gardner Press.

Herz, F. (1980). The impact of death and serious illness on the family life cycle. In *The Family Life Cycle,* ed. E. Carter and M. McGoldrick, pp. 223–240. New York: Gardner Press.

Kaplan, B. E. (1980). Close encounter of the extended family kind. In *The Family* 8(1).

Kuhn, J. S. (1978). Realignment of emotional forces following the loss. In *The Best of the Family, 1973–78,* New Rochelle, NY: Center for Family Learning.

Reiss, L. (1971). *The Family System in America.* New York: Holt, Rinehart and Winston.

Chapter 17

REACTION TO DEATH IN A FAMILY

Peter Titelman, Ph.D.

My initial contact with Bowen family systems theory occurred in 1971, when I entered the family therapy training seminar at Western Psychiatric Institute and Clinic in Pittsburgh, led by Paulina McCullough, M.S.W., and Murray Charlson, M.D. During my two years in the training program, I became very interested in Bowen's theory, and I began utilizing it in my clinical work with families.

My extended family work began on an informal basis in the fall of 1973, when I returned from the Georgetown University symposium on Family Psychotherapy and began gathering material for my own family diagram. In the spring of 1974 I joined an extended family group led by the late Lois Jaffe, M.S.W., at the Irene Stacy Community Mental Health Center, Butler, Pennsylvania, where I was a staff member. The group met on a weekly basis, for eighteen months.

In what follows, I shall describe how I came to understand, and began to modify, my position in the primary triangle of father, mother, and son. I shall discuss the impact of the nodal events of my maternal grandfather's suicide and the death of my mother on myself and my family. The focus will be on the initial efforts to understand my position in the family and to differentiate a self in it during the period 1974–1977; however, the effort to become a more clearly defined self is a life-long process.

FAMILY HISTORY

Family of Origin

Figure 17-1 is a five-generation family diagram. My family of origin is a middle-class, nonpracticing Jewish one. It consisted of my parents, my older sister, and myself. I was born in Los Angeles and lived there until I was eleven. At that time, my father, who was a political activist union organizer, was out of work. We moved to a small town in Pennsylvania, where my father went to work for my uncle in a sportswear company founded by my paternal grandfather. When I was fourteen, our family moved to New York City. I attended high school there, and became infatuated with basketball and jazz. My sister went off to a liberal arts college in Vermont. In her junior year she went to study in London for a year and ended up staying there and marrying an Englishman. My father spent eight years as a sales manager of the family-owned business. During those eight years my mother went back to finish her last year of undergraduate school and then joined the faculty of a prestigious teachers college, based on her considerable ability and experience in the field of early education.

After graduation from a small liberal arts college in Indiana, I went to Pittsburgh for graduate study in psychology. The same year I started graduate school, 1966, my parents took a leave of absence from their jobs and spent a year in Europe. The following year they returned to New York briefly and then retired and moved permanently to the south of France.

My wife and I were married in Pennsylvania in 1968. Pittsburgh became my home, and my wife's, until the fall of 1978, when I became director of a family therapy unit in a community mental health clinic in western Massachusetts. My wife is one year younger than I. We have a son, who was born in 1978. He was born in Massachusetts, following our move from Pennsylvania.

Somehow, I, a nonpracticing Jew, and my wife, a nonpracticing Catholic, managed to get ourselves married by a Catholic priest—albeit a friend of mine—in a university chapel. We denied the importance of choosing an appropriate ritual to mark our marriage. My family, notably my parents, who were living in France, did not attend the wedding, which was predictable in that rituals regarding important nodal events have been downplayed in my family. My parents had eloped with the consent of their mothers, and they suggested that it would be much more practical for them to give us a gift of a good deal

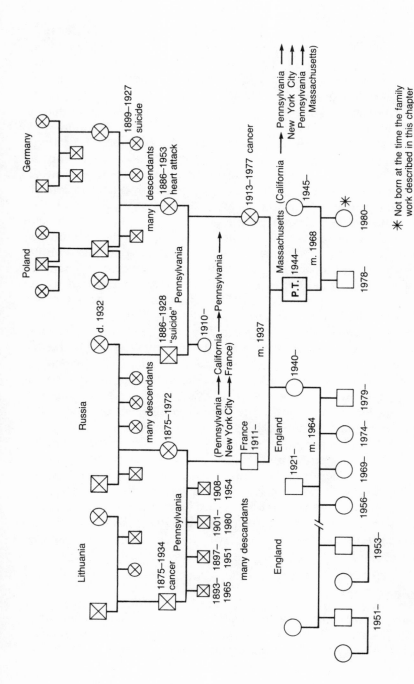

Figure 17-1. Family diagram.

* Not born at the time the family
work described in this chapter
was undertaken.

319

of money rather than spend all of it to come to our wedding. Following an argument between my wife and her mother regarding wedding plans, my mother-in-law wrote letters to my paternal aunt and uncle and maternal aunt indicating to them that the wedding would not be taking place. As a result, they did not attend.

In many ways I fit the description of a youngest brother of an oldest sister. I was always spoiled and overprotected by my mother, and was accustomed to being taken care of by women. My position in the family was characterized as the "slow, but deep and sensitive one." In contrast, my sister was the "quick, but superficial and materialistic one." These designated roles were part of the projection process from both of my parents, and also their parents. My sister was very quick in school. She was able to write term papers in one night and to grasp concepts quickly. However, my mother always pointed out to me, when I expressed envy of my sister's easy success in school, that while my sister was bright and quick, she did not really dig into things as "sensitively and deeply" as I did. As far back as I can remember, when I was growing up, I was perceived as being a slow learner, needing extra help educationally and emotionally. I very much played out this role. For example, I did not learn to read until I was eight years old. This was an interesting phenomenon, particularly since my mother was the director of a private, progressive elementary school that I attended. It was her notion that children learn at their own pace, and that some children—and I was a prime example of this—develop more slowly and should not be pushed to learn or achieve until they are ready. My mother spent many hours teaching me and coaxing me to read, using all the imaginative techniques she could muster. She even had me cut out pictures of my favorite automobiles as one way of capturing my interest, and in the hope that I would learn to read the names of the cars. I was the "tortoise" and my sister was the "hare." Later, when my sister quit college before she graduated and I continued for my doctoral degree, I believe my mother perceived these outcomes as confirmation of the positions my sister and I played, and her beliefs about child development.

Extended Family

My mother and father were married in 1937. They had known each other all their lives. They were first cousins, and they had grown up in the same city. My paternal grandmother was the sister of my maternal grandfather. She was the second oldest child and the oldest daughter, and he was the youngest child of the six siblings.

My father was the youngest of five boys, with the oldest being fifteen years his senior. When my father was born, I am told, my grandmother so much wanted a daughter that the doctor told her she had had one. It was not until the next day that my grandmother was told she had had another son rather than the daughter for which she had hoped. My father's role in his family of origin is that of "charming baby."

My mother was the youngest of two daughters. My aunt was seen as the intelligent, studious one. She did well all through school and was groomed to go to college; she went to an Ivy League school. My mother, on the other hand, was seen, and lived out the role early in her life, as being the attractive, cute one who the family felt should become an actress because she was not too bright. She was not considered college material. After being involved in theater in high school, my mother realized she could not make acting a career and then decided to go into teaching, something the family felt she could master. Rather than go to college, she went to a teacher-training school.

The most significant nodal event in my mother's family of origin, and possibly in the whole family system, was the death of my maternal grandfather, in 1928. My mother told me in 1974 that her father had committed suicide. Before that my aunt had told me that his death was caused by a heart attack. This nodal event became the central issue in my efforts towards the differentiation of self (more about this later).

Both my father and my mother were named after the same person, an aunt from the common side of their family. (It is a tradition of Ashkenazic Jews to name a child after a family member who has recently died. My parents, and a mutual cousin, received names that began with the same letter as, but were not identical to, the name of the aunt.) Their aunt was the sister of my maternal grandfather and my paternal grandmother. She was the fifth child out of six. Her position was directly above my grandfather, who was the youngest child in their family. My grandmother was the second oldest child.

Pattern of Marital Fusion in Family of Origin

My parents were quite fused in their marital relationship. They were first cousins; they had had a relationship (although at times not very close) throughout their entire lives. My mother reported that she was the pursuer in the relationship with my father. She saw him as dashingly handsome, and always had had a crush on her two-year-older cousin. As they were growing up, she felt he really had not shown much interest in her.

Once my parents were married, my mother's role as the overfunctioning member in the overfunctioning–underfunctioning reciprocity began. This adaptation involved my mother's giving up some of her own direction, and therefore self, in order to take care of my father. My mother willingly followed my father to California when my father decided to give up being a lawyer and get involved in political union work. While my parents lived in California, my mother founded a private, progressively oriented elementary school, of which she was the first director. However, after five years of being involved in that project, she reluctantly gave it up to move with my father to Pennsylvania, where he began working in the family-owned business. This move followed his having been out of work for nearly a year.

My mother made great adaptations in her life style to take care of and protect my father's sense of self; however, she did this out of her need to take care of him. Her role of being overresponsible and overconcerned with my father's functioning seems to have been preordained by her father's having committed "suicide." My mother has indicated that during the period that my father changed jobs several times in California and was then unemployed, she was concerned that he might have been depressed. This concern may have been related to her experience with her father and her fear that my father, too, would become dysfunctional, depressed, and possibly suicidal.

Prior to beginning family work, my feeling was that my parents were very similar, as if they were one person. After I began doing some family work I further understood the emotional oneness that characterized the parental relationship. One of the expressions of their fused relationship was their inability to deal with anger openly. In this regard, each was adaptive to the other and was afraid of hurting the other's feelings by asserting individual differentness.

Patterns of Fusion in the Family of Origin

Of the two diagrams in Figure 17–2, one diagram illustrates the marital fusion mentioned above. The other indicates the characteristic form that the nuclear family emotional system took in my family. It shows a "globbing" together of my mother, father, and myself, with my sister being in a position of more distant fusion, hooked into the ego mass

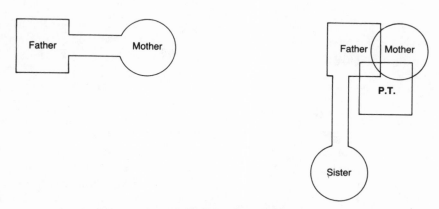

Figure 17–2. Patterns of fusion in the family of origin.

through her relationship with my father. This diagram indicates the characteristic ego mass, under stress, that was common during my years of growing up. Over the last few years I have become more aware of the considerable presence of tension and distance that exists, along with the fusion, in the family of origin.

Symptom Patterns that Control Fusion in the Family of Origin

The diagram shown in Figure 17–3 indicates the presence of two major symptom patterns, i.e., means of controlling fusion within my family of origin. The first is the pattern that I have already described—dysfunction in my father and overfunctioning in my mother. This dysfunction took the form of father's depression and mother's overconcern and worry about his emotional state, even when he was not dysfunctional. My father experienced periods of depression before the family's moving back to Pennsylvania; these were apparently related to his being unemployed and not knowing what direction he wanted to take occupationally. Another period came on with his growing dislike of his job as a sales manager during the time that we lived in New York.

Finally, following my paternal grandmother's death in 1972, my father became depressed, and he has continued having "ups" and "downs" since that time. My father had visited my grandmother several months before her death. However, when she died, in September 1972, he decided not to come to the United States for her funeral.

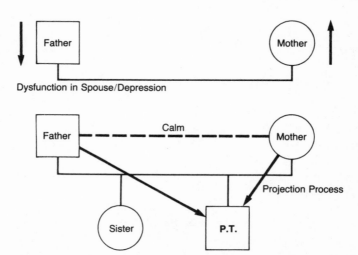

Figure 17–3. Symptom patterns that control fusion within the family of origin.

Overtly he was saying that funerals as rituals were meaningless to him and that he had seen her when she was alive, and that was all that was important to him. She was ninety-seven years old when she died. However, I believe his avoiding her funeral could have been a way of not dealing with losing her. My mother supported him in not coming to the funeral, since she also looked upon the ritual as barbaric. This feeling, I believe, was rooted in her experience of her father's funeral, in which his body had lain in an open casket for three days in her home prior to burial. Furthermore, the death of her father when she was thirteen was understood by my mother as having been a suicide and therefore evoked extreme distress. Just as my parents did not put stock in weddings, they also did not believe in funerals.

Another pattern for controlling fusion that was present in my family of origin was projection of anxiety to a child. My parents, particularly my mother, were always keen observers when looking out for potential problems that I might be developing. They were always quick to intervene to seek outside confirmation that I was having a particular problem, and finally they would seek to treat it.

Significant Triangles in My Family of Origin

Figure 17–4 illustrates three significant triangles in my family of origin. The first one (a) is a triangle of my father and my sister in the close position and myself in the outside position, with conflict existing between my sister and me. The relationship between my father and me was less intense than the one he had with my sister. The following is an example of the special closeness between them: During a vacation from college, I returned home for a week, looking forward to spending some time with both of my parents. Within a day of my return home, my sister called from England, very upset regarding her relationship with her future husband, who at that time was in the process of getting a divorce from his first wife. My sister asked my father to fly over and see her, and my father agreed to do so. Before I knew what was happening, my father took off for London, where he spent a week with my sister. I had no chance to see him during my vacation. I remember thinking that the situation was typical, that somehow my father and I had difficulties getting together and that often my father and my sister would be close, and I would be the outsider. I felt that she got more of his attention, and I resented it.

In (b), the triangle of mother, sister, and me, the pattern was versed: fusion between mother and me with my sister as the outsider,

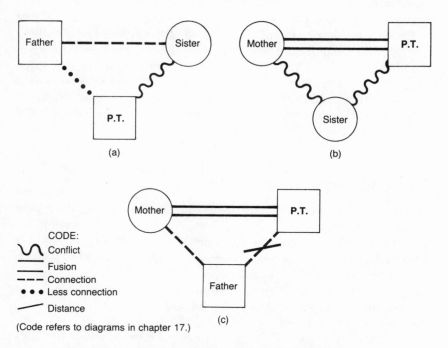

(Code refers to diagrams in chapter 17.)

Figure 17-4. Significant triangles in family of origin.

in conflict with both my mother and myself. The conflict between my sister and myself and between my sister and my mother was related to my sister's fairly accurate perception that I was being favored by my mother and spoiled, and that expectations of my sister were greater than those of me. My sister resented my mother's "babying" me and being overly close with me.

The third significant triangle (c) within my family of origin involved my mother, my father, and me. In this parental triangle I was in the overly close position with my mother, and my father was in a less close relationship to both my mother and myself. For example, my choice of profession as a psychologist seems in some way to be an extension of my mother's interest in early childhood education and psychology, as well as her special interest in mental health. My mother was a primary force in establishing the first mental health center in the small town in Pennsylvania where we lived for three years. I attribute her desire that our family produce a therapist to her unresolved feelings regarding the "suicide" of her father, my maternal grandfather. As I went further along in school, beginning particularly in college, we would seek each other out to discuss various intellectual issues of common interest; they would generally exclude my father. I remember an incident that occurred several years after I was married. My wife and I were visiting my parents in France, and after dinner my mother and I got into one of our characteristically intellectualized discussions regarding some theoretical issue in the mental health field. I remember the negative reactions of both my father and my wife. For the first time I was able to see how my mother and I got together and fused around intellectual issues and excluded them.

Comparison between Parallel Triangles in the Paternal Extended Family and the Family of Origin

Figure 17–5 illustrates the significant triangle in my father's family of origin. It is similar to the one described for me and my parents. However, there was also conflict in the marriage. My father was in conflict with his father until the latter had terminal illness, when my father was twenty-two years old. At that time, my father and his father came to some reconciliation. However, my father was left with a great deal of guilt about the negative relationship he had with his father. I believe that my father promised his father that he would become a lawyer, chiefly out of the guilt he felt for not having a better relationship with him. It was that promise that set my father off on the road toward a ca-

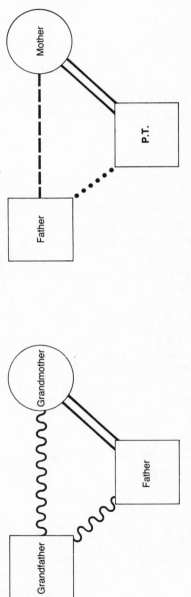

Figure 17–5. Parallel triangles in the paternal extended family and the family of origin.

reer that he would not have chosen for himself. I believe his position in that significant triangle—being overly close with his mother and in conflict with his father—played an important role in his permanent inability to settle on an occupation that would satisfy him.

My father gave me a great deal of information about how the triangle between him and his mother and father worked. He recalls being in the middle of a fight between his mother and father when he was thirteen. He got very angry at his father for having a girl friend and was reproving his father for treating his mother as he did. My father describes his father as being a "man about town." He made his own wine, enjoyed playing pool, and enjoyed going out on the town. My grandmother, in contrast, was a homebody and did not like to socialize or drink.

There are parallels in both my father's and my position in regard to parents. In both triangles, the mothers were the stable, overfunctioning parent and the fathers were the charming but irresponsible parent. It should be predictable that in my current nuclear family my wife and son would be in the close position and I would be in the outside position. This, in fact, is the way that triangle is functioning—to some extent. It is interesting to note that our son is named after his paternal great-grandfather and his paternal grandfather. If I had not begun to work on altering my position in the primary triangle of my mother, my father, and me, I think it would be probable that my son, as a current youngest male in our family, would be less responsible, and underfunctioning in relation to the women in the family. (Following the birth of my daughter in 1980 there was an altering of the triangle—my son and I becoming closer.)

Multigenerational Transmission Process

In this section, I shall indicate how I see my position in regard to a three-generation family projection process. Figure 17–6 illustrates two major factors in this process; the basic theme is this three-generation projection process involves first, men being conceived as weak or fragile and, second, the "suicide" of my maternal grandfather.

My mother was thirteen years old, and my aunt seventeen years old at the time of my grandfather's death. During the period just after his death, my grandmother functioned very capably, even running a small bookstore. My aunt, who had discovered my grandfather's body at the time of his death, proceeded to go to college. Her choice of occu-

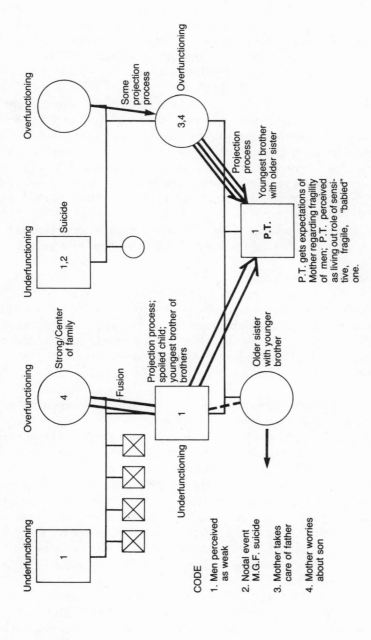

Figure 17-6. Three-generation family projection process.

Underfunctioning

Overfunctioning

Strong/Center of family

Underfunctioning

Suicide

Overfunctioning

Overfunctioning

Some projection process

3,4

Projection process

Youngest brother with older sister

P.T. gets expectations of Mother regarding fragility of men; P.T. perceived as living out role of sensitive, fragile, "babied" one.

Fusion

Projection process; spoiled child; youngest brother of brothers

Underfunctioning

Older sister with younger brother

1
P.T.

CODE

1. Men perceived as weak

2. Nodal event M.G.F. suicide

3. Mother takes care of father

4. Mother worries about son

329

pation may well have been affected by her reaction to her father's death. My aunt worked for the Red Cross for many years, and she was involved in many rescue missions to help people who had suffered in natural disasters, such as tornadoes and floods. I think it possible that my aunt's occupation of rescuing people, through her work in the Red Cross, was related to finding her father dead and not being able to rescue or help him.

In my mother's family of origin, my aunt played a stronger, more overfunctioning role and my mother played a more dependent, underfunctioning role. My mother was seen as the slower, but more sensitive, child in comparison with my aunt, who was designated as brighter and more competent. In many ways, my mother's position in relation to my aunt is parallel to my position in relation to my sister. We are both the younger sibling with an older sister, and both played the role of the slower and more sensitive child.

The projection process moving down from my mother's relation to her family of origin and then to me involves the following sequence:

1. Men perceived as weak;
2. Nodal event: maternal grandfather commits "suicide";
3. My mother takes care of my father and worries that if she does not do so, he will become depressed, or more depressed, dysfunctional, and potentially suicidal. This would account for my mother's constant watchfulness and overprotectiveness of my father, and
4. Mother worries about son.

On the paternal side of the family, the projection process involves my father as the spoiled child, the youngest brother of five brothers. My only living paternal uncle describes my father as always being the sensitive, emotional one in the family, the brother who needed to be protected. The projection process between my father and myself involved my father's feeling more capable and less a "baby" by projecting his concern about being in that position toward me. Through the projection process, whereby I lived out my father's concerns regarding being the babied one, my father managed somewhat to extricate himself—or pretended to—from that position. My position of being fused with my mother was similar to my father's position of being fused with his mother.

It is interesting that my paternal grandmother, who was the strong center of my father's family of origin, was the older sister of my maternal grandfather. My maternal grandfather is described as having been a very sensitive individual, whereas my paternal grandmother was, from my own experiences, a very stoic and strong individual. Thus, in both of my parents' families, the fathers were peripheral figures, weaker than the mothers. It is my hunch that the need to take care of men on my father's side and the need to be taken care of by women on my mother's side has a common root in the common family of my paternal grandmother and my maternal grandfather.

Significantly, the issue of suicide has been a multigenerational theme. In gathering family history, I was told that my maternal grandmother's youngest sister committed suicide in reaction to an unhappy love affair. She died at the age of twenty-eight. There was the "suicide" of my maternal grandfather; and finally there was my mother's concern that my father was suicidal. Indeed, when depressed he mentioned feeling that at times life was not worth living. Following my mother's death, my father definitely talked of suicide, and it seemed to me a serious possibility.

In such a family it should be no surprise that I was programmed to become a therapist—particularly a family therapist, which, in the context of my family of origin and extended family, would fill the position of therapist for the family.

Not only did I serve to syphon off anxiety for my parents, through the projection process, by being a child that needed to be helped, but also I grew up being a mediator and "therapist" for my family. Being closer to my mother in the primary triangle in the years while I was growing up constituted an important factor in my becoming a "therapist" within the family and in my choice of profession.

MODIFYING SIGNIFICANT TRIANGLES AROUND THE ISSUE OF DEATH

At Thanksgiving in 1973 I spent many hours gathering data about my extended family from my maternal aunt. She informed me that my maternal grandfather had died, in 1928, of a heart attack.

Summer Visit with My Parents

In the summer of 1974, my wife and I took one of our trips to France to visit my parents. (These visits were emotionally intense, particularly because there was often more than a year between visits, and then when we did spend time together, it usually involved two to four weeks of close contact.) During this visit my father was feeling and acting depressed. At times, he was argumentative, particularly with my mother, and at other times, seemingly sad and irritated with himself. My father had suffered a previous period of depression following the death of his mother, in 1972. As I mentioned before, my father decided not to attend his mother's funeral. For me, attending my grandmother's funeral—the first one I had ever been a part of—was an extremely signficant event. My grandmother had lived a long life, and the emotional climate among the many family members at her funeral was one of sadness and closeness, but not of terrible grief. Rather, the relatives who were present, my uncle and aunts and many, many cousins, were able to share an array of significant stories and experiences regarding our family. At the luncheon following the funeral, my patriarchal uncle showed pictures of my grandmother with five generations of family members. My experience of the funeral was one of solidarity and family connectedness. I wrote my father a long letter telling him about the event; later, he thanked me for sharing it with him.

During that same 1974 visit, my mother expressed more openly than she ever had previously her concern regarding my father's depression. She indicated that she was unhappy over having to worry about my father; that his being depressed kept her from socializing as much as she liked, and that she was becoming restless in retirement. She also expressed concern that my father might be suicidal, and that that prevented her from going on a trip alone to England to visit my sister and to do some things on her own. In short, she was afraid to leave my father alone, and had not done so for a long time. My mother expressed her concern with much emotion.

Then she went on to tell me about how she believed that her father had committed suicide. She spoke of how she and her mother had been away for the weekend, in the country, and were expecting my aunt and my grandfather to join them; but they received the message from a relative, that my grandfather had died. My mother said that my grandfather had been depressed regarding business failures. He had the habit of lighting his cigarettes on the stove burner; but when he was found dead by my aunt, he was in the kitchen, with the kitchen door closed—something he usually did not do—and the gas from the stove was on. My mother always believed that her father had killed himself because of depression in relation to business problems. This idea was solidified for her while being driven to her father's burial. She was riding in the back seat, and two of her first cousins, i.e., two of my father's brothers, were sitting in the front. She overheard them saying that because my grandfather had killed himself, the family would probably not get his life insurance. Understandably, my mother was terribly upset.

Past behavior on her part was now seen in a new light, e.g., her assertions that life insurance was something she did not believe in, or the difficulty she experienced when any member of our family was separated from her. Now I saw these phenonema in the light of my mother's unresolved feelings about her father's "suicide." (My reason for putting quotation marks around *suicide* will become clear later.)

Finding out how my mother perceived the circumstances of my grandfather's death was very significant for me. It helped me see my mother's overprotectiveness toward my father and me, and her over-concern and overresponsible position towards both of us from a different perspective. I found myself being less reactive toward these behaviors of hers.

In reviewing the circumstances of my grandfather's death, my mother seemed to be unburdened of a heavy responsibility. My mother tried to persuade me to talk with my father to try to help him feel less depressed. I indicated to her that I thought she was overly concerned about my father, that perhaps it was important for her to do something for herself, and that she should be able to go to England without my father if she was not in the mood to accompany her.

Within a few months of our visit, my mother was able to leave my father in France by himself and go to London to visit my sister and to initiate her search for a part-time job. My father was relieved not to tag along with my mother when he preferred to stay at home and garden. My mother succeeded in finding a part-time consultation job in her field, one that would involve her spending a month in England every few months. Her spirits picked up and her sense of being able to follow her own interests indicated, I believe, a better functional level between herself and my father.

In addition to my having been able to share my mother's experience regarding my grandfather's death, I think that the position I had taken, not to collude with my mother in perceiving and treating my father as severely impaired, was a deliberate move away from my usual position in the triangle with my mother and father. I also believe this detri-angling stance served as a stimulus for my mother to take a more differentiated position in relation to my father.

Christmas Visit with My Parents

During a visit in December 1975, I purposefully raised the issue of my
maternal grandfather's death in the presence of my aunt and my
mother. I had predicted that facilitating more openness between my
mother and aunt regarding my grandfather's death would help de-
toxify my mother's feelings about her father, and that process, in turn,
would help me gain perspective in the relationships with my mother
and my dead grandfather. My general effort was aimed at getting my
mother to deal more openly with her concerns about her father's suicide and thus not have to project those concerns onto my father and
myself.

In the discussion between my mother and my aunt, which took
place in a restaurant, I was surprised when the two women did not become too emotionally reactive upon beginning a discussion of this
topic. A frank exchange of their perceptions of how my grandfather
died ensued. My aunt maintained, without apparent defensiveness,
that he had died of a heart attack. My mother described how she had
always believed that it was a suicide, on the basis of comments that she
overheard from a discussion between her older cousins on the way to
the burial. My aunt spoke of how she was the one who discovered that
my grandfather was dead. She told of how she returned home that
day, went into the house, smelled gas coming from the kitchen, and
found the kitchen door closed. She said that she assumed that my
grandfather must be dead. At that point, she went next door to her
aunt's house and got someone else to come back to her house. My aunt
did not actually discover her father's body, nor did she see him until
the funeral was being arranged.

My mother's account of my grandfather's death involved her understanding that he had been depressed about his business, that the
family was concerned about him, and that on the day of his death he
had not been feeling well. Supposedly, he had gone to a pharmacist
and asked for some medication. However, as my aunt pointed out, the
life insurance company paid on the policy following my grandfather's
death, and that indicated to her that it was not a suicide.

During their discussion, neither of them seemed to change her position regarding my grandfather's death. However, I believe that as a
result of this open discussion, my mother felt some relief. From that
time on, until her death in January 1977, my mother began to assert
more goal-directed behavior involving her own wish to return to her
career. She made some modification in her overfunctioning position in

relation to my father, as shown by her no longer feeling that she had to stay at home with him and be responsible for him if he did not want to travel with her or be involved in an activity with her. Before her death she exhibited signs of working toward more autonomy from my father, although her concern about his depression remained.

In the course of the same visit with my parents in which I brought up the issue of my grandfather's death with my mother and aunt, I also began direct work on altering my position of being overclose with my mother and not being connected enough with my father. In advance of the trip, I carefully reviewed the characteristic traps into which I had fallen in regard to the primary triangle during past visits with my parents. I decided that the issue of my identity as a psychologist was important, and one around which my mother and I would characteristically fuse through the form of intellectualizing closeness. I decided that I would develop a strategy to try and modify that pattern. During the months leading up to the visit at Christmas, I found myself becoming increasingly more productive in my efforts to complete my doctoral dissertation. In addition to my beginning efforts to differentiate a self in relation to my family of origin, the other significant event was the conclusion of my five-year psychoanalysis. The analysis terminated just a couple of days before the Christmas visit. I see it as no mere coincidence that my work with my family of origin was being stepped up at the time of termination of my analysis.

I planned to make a strong effort to spend more time with my father on a one-to-one basis and less time with my mother. When we arrived in England for a two-week visit with my parents, part of which would be with my parents and also my sister's family, I sought out my father on several occasions. During our discussions, I shared with him my progress on my dissertation and my hopes and efforts to bring my doctoral studies to a conclusion. I even showed him some of the material I had been writing.

Predictably, my mother sensed my movement toward my father and my attempt not to engage her in intellectual discussion, and experienced a painful loss. One afternoon, while I was alone with her, near the end of the trip, she remarked how much she missed having the chance to talk with me, and that she felt I must be angry with her in that I seemed to be avoiding her. My effort was to stay in contact with her but not fuse with her, and particularly to avoid falling back into the old pattern of our intellectualizing together. However, during that trip my mother's sense of loss and frustration, in reaction to the differentiating efforts I was making, took the form of being critical of my wife's professional and educational activities. Interestingly, it was my father who came to my wife's defense when at one dinner discussion my mother's quizzing and critical questioning of my wife was escalating. My father's new position in relation to my wife, which had been changeable, and usually followed the lead of my mother, may have been related to my efforts to detriangle from the relationship with my parents, and have a better one-to-one relationship with my father. Some of my father's criticism of my wife was, at least at this time, temporarily dissipated. It resulted in a more positive and direct relationship between my father and my wife.

As we flew home from that Christmas visit, I felt quite satisfied with the efforts I had put into motion regarding my relationship with my parents. I was aware of a closer relationship with my father and a new feeling of autonomy in regard to my relationship with my mother. Furthermore, I was aware of my mother's sense of loss, and her efforts to revive the old triangle, but I felt that I was managing not to be forced back into the old position. And I was able still to feel a positive connectedness to my mother.

The period following that Christmas visit of 1975 was very productive for me. My wife supported my decision to cut back my time at work to make a real push at completing my dissertation, between February and June of 1976. During the middle of this period, while I was rushing to complete my first draft, I received a letter from my mother telling me that by the time I would be reading her letter she would be having a hysterectomy in London. She wrote, in positive terms, that her doctor had told her, based on an examination in early January after my wife and I had left England to return to the United States, that he would like her to take some medication and then have a hysterectomy in March, "because she would be better off without it." Predictably, she tried to minimize the danger of her physical condition and to reassure and protect me. Upon receiving her letter, I decided that I would call her in the hospital and try to find out exactly what her physical status was. I decided that, because my mother would probably try to hide a bad prognosis from me, I should have to find a way to get the information I was looking for. Thus, I decided to take the approach of asking how she felt, and then when she would not be expecting it, I would ask her point-blank if they had got all the cancer or not. I spoke with my father first, since he answered the telephone in my mother's hospital room; he was very optimistic that all would be well for my mother. He reported that the doctor felt that he had gotten all the cancer. I then spoke with my mother and carried out my plan. I was relieved when she responded to my directness without any seeming defensiveness.

My mother reported that the doctor said she had just a "speck" of cancer on the tip of her uterus, and that he felt that he had gotten all of it.

At this point, I felt much relieved and my concern for my mother was put on the "back burner" as I redirected my energy toward completing the first draft of my dissertation by the end of spring, which was the deadline. I now realize that all members of our family were using a great deal of denial about the seriousness of my mother's cancer. A small amount of investigation and/or discussion with people familiar with cancer would have indicated to us that the kind of uterine cancer she had is usually fatal.

Visit with My Sister and Parents

In the summer of 1976 my wife and I again visited my family in England and France. We made the trip separately, and I went to England a week before my wife to attend a family therapy conference held by the Tavistock Institute at Cambridge. Fortunately, and probably not completely coincidentally, my mother also had planned to be in England at the time I would arrive for the conference. We made arrangements to spend the day and evening together in London before my going to the conference. I remember that day as being very special. I was exhausted from my flight from the United States. We spent the afternoon walking in a beautiful park and then ate lunch at a restaurant that was my mother's favorite. I felt a sense of warmth and connectedness with my mother, but not the old sense of fusion. There was very little triangulation of other family members, including my father, in our discussion. Although we did touch upon my work and progress toward the completion of my dissertation, it was only discussed briefly. The interaction focused mainly on private, nonintellectualized contact. My mother assured me that her health was excellent and her operation had been, as far as she understood it, a total success. She appeared to be in good physical health.

Following my attendance at the family therapy conference, I was joined by my wife. We then spent several days with my sister and her family. At the same time, my parents were also visiting with my sister's family. This was a very conflictual visit. The conflict seemed to center between my parents. In looking back from this vantage point, my sense is that their conflict involved my mother's continuing interest in spending more time in England and her desire to be more active again professionally, in contrast to my father's desire to remain in France coupled with his isolated, moody, depressed behavior. Their conflict seemed to filter down to and come between my sister's family and my parents, and it was also acted out by my wife and me.

Then my wife and I spent ten days in France with my parents. However, for the first time, rather than staying with them in their small house, in which privacy was somewhat difficult, we stayed in a nearby town, in an apartment they owned. Much of my energy during this part of the visit was spent on completing my dissertation; every morning I spent several hours working on it. Although I experienced being less fused with my parents, this visit had its share of conflicts. In spite of some conflict between my parents and my wife, and between my parents and myself, the focus of the conflict seemed to be more between my parents. Some of the conflict appeared related to my father's irritability and depression and my mother's reaction to them. While she continued to be overresponsible for him, she was no longer as sympathetic to his unrealistic demands.

Although I did not know it at the time, that visit was to be the last time I saw my mother alive. It seems symbolic that I accomplished the final writing of my dissertation on the flight home from the visit with my parents and on the few days following our return. At the end of November I received my Ph.D. I felt triumphant and relieved. On the evening of the day I defended my dissertation I spoke with my mother on the phone. She was extremely happy for me. However, I detected from her voice that she was in poor physical health. She reported that her hoarseness was just due to a bad cold that she had gotten while working on her consultation job in England, and that she has not been able to shake it. My mother's pride in her "son the psychologist" came through in her next letter, in which she expressed her certainty that I would be "the best psychologist ever."

A process beginning with my mother's concern regarding her father's "suicide" may have run its course through the projection process, whereby I became first the object of concern and worry, in need of therapy as programmed by my position in the family, to my becoming a caretaker, i.e., a therapist. I hope that my functioning, at this time, is that of a consultant/coach, in my professional work, rather than the "helper" that was part of the original family programming, i.e., the projection process in which I was involved.

On Christmas Day, we spoke with my parents and found that my mother was feeling very poor and that she was in the process of going through many tests. I suspected my parents were withholding information that indicated my mother's cancer had not been arrested. I was reassured by my parents, though, that the tests were not indicating cancer; but they were perplexed as to what was ailing my mother. Again, I believe I was using some denial in avoiding the possibility of my mother's death. Late in January I received a telephone call from my father, who was very upset about my mother's condition. He described her as having no energy, looking poor, and being very concerned about herself. However, he indicated that actually there was no real need for concern and that I should not be worried. A few days later, on January 26, my mother called me and spoke of feeling very poor; she felt frustrated by not knowing what was wrong, and she had concluded that she might be depressed. She asked me if I had any thoughts about whom she might contact among therapists. I will never know how much denial was being used by my mother to avoid dealing with her approaching death.

It may have been predictable, in terms of my mother's life course, that she would have to see human tragedy, in this case her own, in psychological terms. For those were the terms in which she understood her father's death.

My Mother's Death

Early on the morning of January 28, 1977, I received a call from my sister, waking me from my sleep. She informed me that my mother had died several hours before, having only been hospitalized the previous evening. Tremendous denial, of course, had been going on on the part of my sister and my father in regard to my mother's deteriorating health. At the time of her death she had lost so much weight and looked so poor that it certainly could not have been accounted for by the depression that she herself insisted she was suffering.

The earliest my wife and I were able to get to England, where my mother had died, was twenty-four hours later. My aunt, my mother's sister, also went to England to be with the family. My father had not been with my mother at the time of her death. He had been called during the night and been told that he should go to the hospital immediately. Apparently, my mother awoke in the middle of the night, unable to breathe, and died very quickly thereafter. It was a source of severe upset and terrible guilt for my father that he was not with my mother at the time of her death. Everyone was shocked by her death. The doctors had not detected cancer with the tests; however, the autopsy showed that the cancer had reached her lungs and put pressure on her heart.

I had known while I was growing up that my parents did not believe in funerals and that it was their wish to be cremated. Both my parents perceived funerals as barbaric, unnecessary rituals. From my work as a family therapist dealing with families who were grieving over deaths in their family, and specifically because of the influence of Murray Bowen, I knew that for myself it would be necessary and beneficial that there be some ritual process to help me deal with my mother's death. To this end, my sister was very supportive. She and my father—he for many hours after my mother's death—stayed in the hospital room with my mother's body. I believe that this was important and something that my father had to do.

My sister indicated that she, my father, and my aunt did not desire that there be a viewing of my mother's body, or even a funeral. My sister said that was my mother's wish. She said that the possibility of seeing my mother's body before cremation was an option that had been left open for me, and thus I arranged to have a viewing of my mother's body on the day prior to her cremation. Only my wife and I went to the viewing. My father, my sister, and my aunt decided that they wanted to remember her as she was when she was alive. I believe the function of my family's aversion to a ritual—a funeral or some equivalent—in relation to death had more to do with being unable to face death fully than with being nonreligious.

It was a terribly sad experience to see my mother in the state of death. My wife and I spent some time in the presence of her lifeless body. Although I knew this was no longer fully my mother, it was necessary for me to see her in death to begin the process of saying goodbye. My wife left me alone for a few minutes in the presence of my mother's body. Those few minutes were both bleak and lonely, but necessary. Before I left I kissed my mother's cold forehead and said my goodbye.

I decided to take my mother's ashes back to France. One week after her death, I flew, with my father, to his home in the south of France. I carried the ashes in a container in my suitcase, without consulting him. My decision not to seek his opinion was based on his emotional state and his being anti-ritual. During the week I spent with my father I immersed myself in my mother's books, photographs, and journals. I helped my father sift through my mother's personal belongings. He and I talked at length, cried, and consumed considerable wine. One afternoon and evening we drank two bottles of champagne. Each day I thought about my mother's ashes, but felt unable to talk with my father about my wish to bury them in their garden. Finally, the last day before I was to return to the United States arrived. Late in the afternoon I told my father what I had done, hoping that he would not be offended. After I told him about the ashes and asked if he wanted to help me bury them, he declined to participate. By now the sun was setting. Quickly, with little light left, and uncertain about the emotional reactions my actions were triggering in my father, I hastened to put the ashes on the surface of a flower bed. There was no time for the ritual I had hoped to undertake. The next morning I left France. When my father and I parted it was emotionally intense for both of us. I felt a close bond, and much sorrow at knowing he would be alone with the grieving process.

In August, I returned to France to spend two weeks with my father. When I arrived at his house, I immediately went to see if my mother's ashes were still visible in the garden, or whether they had been dissolved by nature. They were still there, untouched and undissolved. I had decided that if they were still there, I would try to bury them under one of two cherry trees that had a special meaning for my parents. With some trepidation I again approached my father to see if he would participate in this effort to create a burial/memorial ceremony. I was pleased that he agreed immediately. Under a burning sun and clear blue sky, dressed in shorts, shirtless and barefoot, we scooped up the ashes and transported my mother's remains to the base of the cherry tree, where we carefully buried them. The day I was to go back home I had my father take a photograph of me in front of the cherry tree. That picture resides with another that shows my mother picking cherries. They depict for me the connective process of life and death as a part of nature.

My experience in dealing with my mother's death confirmed what I had learned from Murray Bowen's writings on dealing with the death of a member of one's own family (Bowen 1978). I felt strengthened in the face of my mother's death by my having been able to take an I-position with respect to the steps necessary for me in dealing with her death. The need for ritual in facing death, distinct from the family of origin's denial of ritual, was another step toward the never-ending process of differentiating a self in my family of origin.

IMPLICATIONS

In this chapter I have presented an explication of my family history and my position in relation to my family of origin. This was followed by an exploration of my initial efforts to differentiate a self in my family of origin, attempting to explicate a multigenerational projection process and my efforts to modify my position in the triangle with my parents, during the period 1974–1977. The focal points of my work were determined by the impact of the nodal events of my maternal grandfather's suicide and the death of my mother.

I would like to draw a few conclusions from the extended family work in which I have been engaged. Three major issues warrant comment: the role and importance of uncovering a key nodal event in relation to the multigenerational projection process in the family; the significance of dealing with death in doing extended family work, and the role of and relation between ritual and nodal events in the family system.

The discovery of a central nodal event, in my case the "suicide" of my maternal grandfather, can be a key to understanding the multigenerational transmission process. In history gathering, assessment, and planning interventions in one's family, the uncovering or fortuitous discovery of a key nodal event in the extended family can transform one's perspective on the family system. Such a discovery, with ensuing reflection and work, may be a key to understanding the integrated relatedness that exists between the processes of nuclear and extended family systems.

There is no objective truth about one's own, or any, family. It is not sufficient to do an archeological investigation and uncover and trace all the facts regarding the *who, what, where, when,* and *how* of the family systems, over three-plus generations. Naturally, the more relevant historical data one gets about the family and how it operates, the better equipped one is for conceptualizing one's part in it and how to change one's position. However, understanding a nodal event within the entire nuclear and extended family systems also involves understanding its meaning for the individual members within the family. What is central is how the interpretation of the meaning of nodal events is or was utilized as the basis of individual action and joint interaction within the family. The multigenerational themes, transmission process, and interlocking triangles are not the residue of an objective, factual process. Rather, the "truth" of nodal events, or any historical processes within the family, is the nexus of the multiple personal perspectives of the individual members. Truth and meaning are multiperspective, they are not univocal. Over time, nodal events are recorded publicly and interpreted privately in a variety of ways. Family myths and family secrets then emerge as means through which anxiety is controlled and family homeostasis is maintained. It does not matter that my maternal grandfather may, in fact, not have committed suicide, in the sense that my mother and some members of the family perceived and experienced it that way. My mother's experience and interpretation of my grandfather's death as suicide played an important role in how she perceived and treated men, particularly my father and me. (Since this chapter was originally published in 1979 several more members of my extended family have indicated that it was their understanding that my grandfather committed suicide.) In understanding a family system it is not enough to understand the factual veracity of events—it is valuable, in addition, to understand its personal meanings and the reciprocally determining interaction with its alteration of meanings.

It is widely believed among systems therapists that the addition or subtraction of a family member represents the most significant type of nodal event in the family. In my experience, the death of a significant family member is the most important nodal event in a family system. At such times, the family is subject to the greatest stress and the greatest potential for change, positive or negative. Death in the family is the nodal event with most power for evoking the extreme potentialities for taking *I-positions* or *We-positions*. Further, I should like to suggest that death(s), particularly those caused by suicide, illness, or accident, create both the maximum opportunity for the development of undifferentiation and the maximum opportunity for an individual doing extended family work to define a self in relation to his or her family of origin.

My extended family work has highlighted the importance of family rituals as ways of dealing with anxiety, loss, and change in the family. The absence or denial of ritual, religious or secular, appears to indicate the presence of fusion and the denial of dealing with painful issues, such as death, as illustrated in my family. Without rituals that carry a shared significance for the family, the hazards and difficulties in dealing with loss and other emotional shock waves from significant nodal events and/or changes in the stages of family development are much more problematic.

Finally, I want to pose a question that was asked of me when I presented the foregoing material at the Third Pittsburgh Family Systems Symposium: Bowen says that it takes at least three to ten generations for schizophrenia to develop through the family projection process.

How many generations through the multigenerational projection does it take to develop a family therapist? My family history suggests that it is also at least a three-generation-plus process whereby the family creates a therapist to "cure" its problems. My hope is that I will not fulfill that mission.

REFLECTIONS

Continued efforts to understand and modify my functioning position in my family have confirmed and broadened my thinking since 1979, when this material was first written. The following are a few further reflections, from the perspective of 1986.

The theme of suicide in the family continued as my father became overtly suicidal during the first year following my mother's death. What was the relationship between my mother's anxiety about my father's suicidal potential and his subsequent suicidal threats? The answer is complex and, I would suggest, not to be answered by cause-and-effect thinking. The reciprocity and intertwining of new and old players with complex multigenerational patterns is exquisite.

Bowen (1984) speaks about how a detailed knowledge of one's immediate family of origin can provide a fairly good base from which to predict, backwards, the multigenerational patterns and functioning in the family. In 1979, I had only an inkling that the anti-ritual pattern within my immediate family of origin was solidly rooted over many generations. In 1980, my extended family work shifted focus to moving further back in the generations. I increased my contact with close and distant cousins, mostly on the paternal side. Contact with a cousin in her late seventies, in October 1980 — an individual with access to a great deal of family history — led me to the discovery of eight great-aunts and uncles from whom my paternal grandfather was cut off. My father did not even know of their existence, although most of them lived within a few miles of where my father grew up. I discovered that my paternal grandfather and one great-uncle had changed the spelling of their name from Teitelman to Titelman, another possible indication of emotional cut-off in the paternal extended family. Additional indicators of cut-off include a considerable number of divorces within the parent, grandparent, and great-grandparent generations, and a wide geographical spread. When I began my extended family work in 1974, I understood something about the fusion that was manifest in my family of origin. By the time I wrote the paper in 1979, I perceived my family as fused, but less cohesive and containing more covert conflict than was indicated by the myth of family harmony. However, it was not until the last few years that I was able to see, based on a better understanding of Bowen family systems theory and increased acquisition of multigenerational data, that my fused family of origin was, in fact, a small splinter branch of an explosive family that was characterized by major emotional cut-off within the paternal extended family. Figure 17-7 is an updated version of the paternal family diagram based on new material I received about the family. This information was unknown to my father and my paternal uncles and aunts. The material regarding the emotional cut-off helps me understand further the roots of the anti-ritual theme in my family. And it highlights the important notion that to the degree there is cut-off in one branch or subgroup of a family, there will be reciprocal fusion in another branch or subgroup in the next generation. In this case I link the cut-offs within my paternal extended family to the cohesive, emotionally fused character of my immediate family of origin.

On January 1, 1981, I videotaped a discussion with my father, in which we talked about the family. At the end of almost two hours of my father's reminiscing about his family, I asked him how he felt about the process of burying my mother's ashes, and its meaning for him. There was no hesitation—he confirmed its value; creating and undertaking a burial ritual was important for both of us. My father's positive response was confirmatory evidence for me of the value of my effort to find a way to deal with death in my family.

Subsequent contacts with my extended family led to the discovery that, in addition to myself, there are at least five psychotherapists, three psychiatrists, and one psychologist (four on the paternal side and one on the maternal side) in the current generation. One of the psychiatrists is a family therapist. I discovered his existence when we were both listed to give presentations at a national meeting of the American Association of Marriage and Family. Consonant with the dynamics of our family system, he did not respond directly to a letter I sent him. We have yet to make contact with each other. The persistence of cut-offs is powerful. Therefore, I would expand my final comment—that it took at least three generations in my family to produce a family therapist—to say it took more than three generations for the extended family to create several therapists to "cure" its problems. I wonder how many therapists will emerge in future generations.

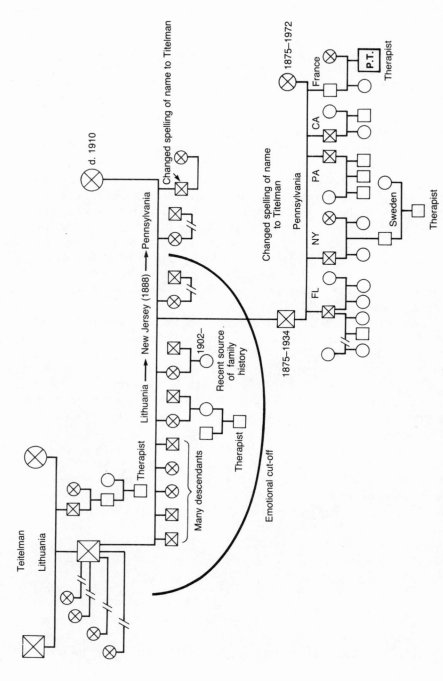

Figure 17-7. Paternal family diagram.

REFERENCES

Bowen, M. (1978). The family reaction to death. In *Family Therapy in Clinical Practice*. New York: Jason Aronson.

Bowen, M. (1984). The therapist's family of origin. Workshop for Family Living Consultants of the Pioneer Valley, Northampton, Mass., March.

INDEX